Approaches to Teaching
Sand's *Indiana*

Approaches to Teaching World Literature

For a complete listing of titles,
see the last pages of this book.

Approaches to Teaching Sand's *Indiana*

Edited by

David A. Powell
and
Pratima Prasad

The Modern Language Association of America
New York   2016

© 2016 by The Modern Language Association of America
All rights reserved
Printed in the United States of America

MLA and the MODERN LANGUAGE ASSOCIATION are trademarks
owned by the Modern Language Association of America.
For information about obtaining permission to reprint material from
MLA book publications, send your request by mail (see address below)
or e-mail (permissions@mla.org).

Library of Congress Cataloging-in-Publication Data

Approaches to teaching Sand's Indiana / edited by
David A. Powell and Pratima Prasad.
pages cm — (Approaches to teaching world literature ; 137)
Includes bibliographical references and index.
ISBN 978-1-60329-209-2 (cloth : alk. paper) —
ISBN 978-1-60329-210-8 (pbk. : alk. paper) —
ISBN 978-1-60329-211-5 (EPUB) —
ISBN 978-1-60329-212-2 (Kindle)

1. Sand, George, 1804–1876. Indiana.   2. Sand, George,
1804–1876—Study and teaching.   I. Powell, David A.,
editor.   II. Prasad, Pratima, 1969– editor.
PQ2404.A76 2015
843′.8—dc23   2015030336

Approaches to Teaching World Literature 137
ISSN 1059-1133

Cover illustration of the paperback and electronic editions: *Portrait d'Hortense
Baller, future Mme Jacob-Desmalter*, by Hortense Haudebourt-Lescot (1784–1845).
Musée du Louvre. © 2015 RMN–Grand Palais / Art Resource, New York

Published by The Modern Language Association of America
85 Broad Street, suite 500, New York, New York 10004-2434
www.mla.org

CONTENTS

PREFACE

Published in 1832, *Indiana* was George Sand's breakaway novel after several collaborative publications with Jules Sandeau. It is often seen as her "venue à l'écriture" 'coming to writing' and a precursor to the rest of her fictional work, as it contains many of the themes of her novels that followed: the constraints placed on married women by the Napoleonic Code, class inequities, the parallels between marriage and slavery, and the political circumstances of the Bourbon restoration and the July Monarchy.

Over the past three decades, the status of *Indiana* has changed both in Sand's corpus and in the nineteenth-century literary canon. Before, her pastoral novels of the 1840s (*La mare au diable*, *La petite Fadette*, and *François le champi*) were said to exemplify her work as a novelist, but today it is *Indiana* that is written about most frequently in critical articles and scholarly books. It is only natural, then, that this shift should also translate into the realm of teaching. The responses to the MLA survey in preparation for this volume revealed that humanities courses in the United States and abroad include *Indiana* in their curriculum more consistently than any other novel by Sand. When taught in French, *Indiana* is part of surveys of French literature as well as of specialized courses on nineteenth-century French culture, French women writers, and French colonial literature. In courses on nineteenth-century French narrative, *Indiana* is taught alongside other well-known novels of the century: François-René de Chateaubriand's *René*, Madame de Duras's *Ourika*, Stendhal's *Le rouge et le noir*, Honoré de Balzac's *Père Goriot*, and Gustave Flaubert's *Madame Bovary*. In broader French courses, *Indiana* is also frequently paired with French literary texts as diverse as Madame de Lafayette's *La Princesse de Clèves*, Jean-Jacques Rousseau's *Émile*, Bernardin de Saint-Pierre's *Paul et Virginie*, and Simone de Beauvoir's *La femme rompue*. Outside French departments, *Indiana* makes a regular appearance in women's studies and gender studies curricula as well as in comparative literature courses, where it is teamed up with novels such as Harriet Beecher Stowe's *Uncle Tom's Cabin* and Charlotte Brontë's *Jane Eyre*.

Although the body of scholarly criticism on *Indiana* is rich, covering a wide range of topics, there is no comprehensive teaching resource for the novel. In this volume, our goal is to provide resources, ideas, and perspectives for the variety of disciplinary contexts in which *Indiana* is taught. The pedagogical tools contained in the volume will benefit instructors teaching the novel for the first time as well as those who have been teaching it for years. In part 1, "Materials," we offer an analysis of primary and secondary sources: editions and translations of *Indiana*, critical studies of the novel, historical studies that pertain to the novel, and biographies of Sand, including electronic resources. These introductory materials are intended to help instructors sift through the dense literary and sociohistorical background of *Indiana*. In part 2 of the volume, "Approaches," our contributors' essays display an array of critical methodologies through which the novel can be approached in the classroom: feminist, narratological, historical, cartographic, and postcolonial, to name a few. The essays place literary questions, such as the divide between Romanticism and realism, in the broader historical and legal frameworks of the novel. Finally, the essays provide suggestions for integrating *Indiana* into courses both in and outside French literature programs.

We wish to convey here our gratitude to those who have participated in what has been an enriching and rewarding experience of scholarly and pedagogical collaboration. Many thanks also to those staff members at the MLA who have helped guide us through this process.

Part One

MATERIALS

Editions and Translations of *Indiana*

French Editions

Sand composed *Indiana* in early 1832; it was published in May of that year in Paris by Roret and Dupuy. Thereafter, it went through many printings (three between May and September). Several additional editions included emendations to the original version of the novel: Gosselin (1833), Perrotin (1842), Hetzel (illustrated works; 1852–56), and Michel-Lévy frères (1861). Brigitte Diaz provides an up-to-date overview of the various reprintings and revisions, as well as an insightful summary of the themes and structures in her presentation of *Indiana* in the new collected works of George Sand (Sand, *Œuvres complètes* 9–65). In his 2004 survey of texts and contexts of the novel, Éric Bordas offers a cogent analysis of its nineteenth-century editions, pointing out that the cuts and changes, both stylistic and substantive, made by Sand between the first edition and the last make for very different texts. Thus the critical evaluations of *Indiana* by Sand's contemporaries may puzzle today's readers, since all the modern editions of *Indiana* are based on the 1861 version. Professors should take this fact into consideration, especially if they are relying on, or referring to, reviews of critics during Sand's time (Bordas, *Éric Bordas* 11–20).

In modern times, Béatrice Didier's 1984 edition seems to be the preferred text for instruction, at least in the United States. Almost all the respondents to the MLA questionnaire who teach Sand's novel in French stated that they used this edition. Because in the United States college bookstores are constrained to order foreign-published books through an American distributor, it may be more convenient to deal with an American publisher. David Powell's edition of *Indiana* is published by the University of Delaware Press. It does not include Sand's prefaces, however, in keeping with the policy of the series editors. We reference both the Didier and the Powell editions throughout this volume.

English Translations

Indiana was first translated into English in 1845. Between the nineteenth and the twenty-first centuries, the novel has been translated numerous times into English. George Burnham Ives's early-twentieth-century translation has seen many iterations, including one as recent as 2011. Today, the most commonly used translation is by Sylvia Raphael. Although it is the most modern and the most available, instructors teaching the novel in English may wish to also consult other translations, particularly if their pedagogy includes frequent close readings. Françoise Massardier-Kenney's essay in this volume reviews *Indiana*'s English translations and discusses the challenges involved in teaching the novel in translation.

Note on Bibliographic Notations in the Volume

Quotations from or references to the two French texts used in this volume, Didier's and Powell's, are accompanied by page numbers in the format (x [y]; z), x being the Didier edition, y the Powell edition, and z the Raphael translation. Quotations from Sand's prefaces to the novel are only from the Didier edition and the Raphael translation. For the essays in this volume that describe teaching *Indiana* in English translation, only Raphael is used; any modification of that translation has been indicated.

All references to Sand's autobiography, *Histoire de ma vie*, use the Georges Lubin edition, the two-volume *Œuvres autobiographiques* ("Autobiographical Works"). Translations of *Histoire de ma vie* are from *Story of My Life*, edited by Thelma Jurgrau. All French quotations from Sand's correspondence refer to the twenty-five volume *Correspondance de George Sand*; translations of the correspondence are by our contributors.

Background Readings

French History

Among the many informative studies of nineteenth-century French history, some are especially helpful to instructors in contextualizing *Indiana*. Guillaume de Bertier de Sauvigny's *La restauration* ("The Restoration") is a comprehensive reference. Sauvigny paints a complete picture of the time in which the novel is set, paying attention to politics and economics as well as to social, religious, and intellectual life. Jean Tulard's magisterial *Les révolutions de 1789 à 1851* ("The Revolutions from 1789 to 1851"; the fourth volume of Jean Favier's *Histoire de France* ["History of France"]) situates the novel in the tumultuous revolutions of the eighteenth and nineteenth centuries and illuminates France's long march toward a parliamentary form of government. A focused study, David Pinkney's *The French Revolution of 1830* tackles such topics as the motives of the revolutionaries of 1830, the nature of the rebel crowds, and the effect of that revolution on the composition of France's ruling elite.

It is productive for both instructors and students to read *Indiana*, a socially engaged novel, in the framework of social histories of this period. Two studies that address the configurations of family and patriarchy are Roddey Reid's *Families in Jeopardy: Regulating the Social Body in France, 1750–1910* and Lynn Hunt's *The Family Romance of the French Revolution*. Both these works are of particular interest to teachers of nineteenth-century French literature, as their analyses rely heavily on imaginative fiction (often popular fiction) of the eighteenth and nineteenth centuries. Alain Corbin's numerous investigations of the history of *mentalités* in the nineteenth century and James Smith Allen's insights into the reading culture of the period in his *Popular French Romanticism: Authors, Readers, and Books in the Nineteenth Century* also serve as useful accompaniments to *Indiana*. Although Philip Nord's *The Republican Moment: Struggles for Democracy in Nineteenth-Century France* attends primarily to the second half of the nineteenth century, it resonates with *Indiana*, as it is concerned with France's turn from authoritarianism to republicanism and with the kind of civic activism that Sand practiced during her lifetime. Feminist and socialist debates of nineteenth-century France are illuminated in Claire Moses and Leslie Rabine's *Feminism, Socialism, and French Romanticism* and Moses's *French Feminism in the Nineteenth Century*. Instructors and students of *Indiana* may read these broader cultural and political histories of feminism in nineteenth-century France alongside the substantial body of critical scholarship on the representation of women, gender, and power in Sand's novel.

Literary History

Sand's oeuvre has had a checkered career in accounts of literary history. Gustave Lanson's *Histoire de la littérature française* (1895; "History of French Literature") gives little attention to Sand's works. Lanson classifies Sand as a lyrical Romantic in the vein of François-René de Chateaubriand and George Gordon Byron but also identifies different moments in her evolution as a novelist, such as her socialist and rustic periods. Henry James devotes three chapters to Sand in his literary history of the nineteenth and early twentieth centuries ("George Sand" [1914]). Discussing her work with that of Gustave Flaubert, Honoré de Balzac, and Émile Zola, James often speaks of her style in laudatory terms. It is largely thanks to him that she is well known in the English-speaking world.

Regrettably, through most of the twentieth century up until the 1980s, studies of Sand tended toward the biographical, paying more attention to her extraordinary life than to her works. A number of late-twentieth- and early-twenty-first-century studies have reevaluated and rehabilitated her literary practice and thus her place in nineteenth-century literary history, alongside other women authors. They include Isabelle Naginski's *George Sand: Writing for Her Life* (translated into French as *George Sand: L'écriture ou la vie*), Naomi Schor's *George Sand and Idealism*, Christine Planté's *La petite sœur de Balzac* ("Balzac's Little Sister"), Margaret Waller's *The Male Malady: Fictions of Impotence in the French Romantic Novel*, and Margaret Cohen's *The Sentimental Education of the Novel*. Collectively, these works provide a new perspective on the place of Sand's fiction in three major literary modes of the nineteenth century: Romanticism, realism, and idealism. From a different literary standpoint, Léon-François Hoffmann's *Le nègre romantique: Personnage littéraire et obsession collective* ("The Romantic Negro: The Literary Character and the

Collective Obsession") and Christopher Miller's *The French Atlantic Triangle: Literature and Culture of the Slave Trade* help place *Indiana* in the context of other works of the time that are set in France's slave colonies.

Colonial History

Twenty-first-century students are particularly intrigued by the themes of slavery and colonization in *Indiana*. Understandably it is the Caribbean and not the Indian Ocean, where part of *Indiana* takes place, that dominates colonial histories of the early nineteenth century. The colonization of Haiti and the Haitian revolution are the subjects of C. L. R James's *The Black Jacobins* and Laurent Dubois's *The Avengers of the New World: The Story of the Haitian Revolution*, which are also useful for understanding slavery and colonization in the Indian Ocean. To fully grasp the history of French slavery, particularly Atlantic slavery, one may read Lawrence Jennings's *French Anti-slavery: The Movement for the Abolition of Slavery in France, 1802–1848*, David Brion Davis's *The Problem of Slavery in the Age of Revolution, 1770–1823*, and Sue Peabody's *"There Are No Slaves in France": The Political Culture of Race and Slavery in the Ancien Régime*. *Francophone Slavery*, the Web site created by Doris Kadish, of the University of Georgia, contains a great deal of information on slavery in nineteenth-century francophone literature.

With respect to the Indian Ocean, Edmond Maestri's edited volume *Esclavage et abolitions dans l'océan Indien, 1723–1860* ("Slavery and Abolitions in the Indian Ocean") features essays by some of the foremost historians of slavery and colonialism. It is a comprehensive resource, as it covers the period from the introduction of the Code Noir ("Black Code") to the time that immediately followed nineteenth-century abolition of slavery. Megan Vaughan's *Creating the Creole Island: Slavery in Eighteenth-Century Mauritius* and Françoise Vergès's *Monsters and Revolutionaries: Colonial Family Romance and Métissage* delineate the complex histories of race, slavery, and creolization in Mauritius and Reunion Island. Jean-Michel Racault's *Mémoires du Grand Océan: Des relations de voyage aux littératures francophones de l'océan Indien* ("Memoirs of the Great Ocean: On the Connections between Traveling and Francophone Literatures from the Indian Ocean"), a literary genealogy that extends from the seventeenth to the twentieth century, helps place *Indiana* in French writings about the Indian Ocean.[1] These studies of the Caribbean and the Indian Ocean can be supplemented with readings selected from the growing body of scholarship on race and colonialism in *Indiana*.

Biographies

Biographies of George Sand began to appear at the end of the nineteenth century in France, England, and the United States. Most of these texts dwell on her private life, especially her romantic dalliances, though they claim to deal with her work as well.[2] After this first wave, the next major biography to be published, in 1952, was André Maurois's *Lélia ou la vie de George Sand* (*Lélia: The Life of George Sand*). As the title suggests, Maurois sees Sand's life directly reflected in her works; in particular, he reads her *Lélia* as an admission of her own sexual frigidity. The following year, Pierre Salomon published his *Née romancière: Biographie de George Sand*, a valuable biography that nonetheless, like Maurois's text, has a patronizing undertone.

From the 1970s on, various feminist biographies were published: by Noel Bertram Gerson, Curtis Cate, Ruth Jordan, Joseph Barry, Tamara Hovey, Renee Winegarten, and Donna Dickenson. Of these, the books by Cate, Barry, Dickenson, and Winegarten stand out, relaying information on Sand's works and providing nuanced analyses of events in her life. They pave the way for twenty-first-century contributions, including those of Belinda Jack, Elizabeth Harlan, and Benita Eisler. Although they each have their merits, Jack's is the most influential. Powell's entries in *Dictionary of Literary Biography: Nineteenth-Century French Fiction Writers* ("George Sand") and *Encyclopedia of Lifewriting* ("George Sand") give concise biographical information, and his volume *George Sand* in the Twayne World Authors series provides an overview of her life and works. Because Sand led an extraordinary life, her presence on the Internet tends to emphasize biographical detail at the expense of her writing. But a Web site maintained by the French Ministry of Culture, *George Sand, 1804–1876*, pays balanced attention to her life, travels, writings, and engagement with theater. Finally it should be noted that her life has inspired a number of filmic productions: a BBC miniseries titled *Notorious Woman* (currently accessible only at the Museum of the Moving Image in New York City) and the five films *Au pays de George Sand* (1926; "George Sand's Homeland"), *A Song to Remember* (1945), *Jutrzenka* (1969), *Impromptu* (1991), and *Les enfants du siècle* (1999; "The Children of the Century"). Several of Sand's novels have also been adapted to the screen or television: *Fanchon, the Cricket* (1912, 1915), *Leoni Leo* (1917), *La mare au diable* (1923; "The Devil's Pool"), *Mauprat* (1926, 1972), *Indiana* (1966), *François le champi* (1976; "The Country Waif"), *Ces beaux messieurs de Bois-Doré* (1976 [a miniseries]; "The Gallant Lords of Bois-Doré"), *Les maîtres-sonneurs* (1980; "The Bagpipers"), *La ville noire* (1981; "The Black City"), *Les amours romantiques: Laure et Adriani* (1984; "Romantic Loves: Laure and Adriani"), and *Little Fadette* (2004).

Studies of *Indiana*

Today, *Indiana* stands irrefutably as one of the canonical French novels of the early nineteenth century, alongside works such as Victor Hugo's *Notre-Dame de Paris*, Stendhal's *Le rouge et le noir* ("The Red and the Black"), and Balzac's *Le père Goriot*. The modernity of the text, its complex narration, and its intricate treatment of race and gender have inspired innumerable critical studies since the last decades of the twentieth century. Colloquiums on Sand, many of which have resulted in proceedings, have been held in locations as varied as the United States, Canada, France, Japan, Tunisia, Hungary, and Germany. Because it is impossible to discuss the full range of topics covered in essays, articles, and books on *Indiana*, we merely indicate here the major trends in critical work on the novel.

Over the years, there has been increasing interest in how Sand's first novel is narrated. Some critics have been intrigued by its novelistic structure, in particular by its enigmatic conclusion (Béteille; Hirsch; Harkness, "Writing"; Ippolito). The novel's acute awareness of the power of language, the ambiguity of its narrative authority, and its genre have been debated at length (Dayan; Diaz, "'Ni romantique'"; Didier, "Fiction exotique"; Naginski, "George Sand"; Schor, Introduction). *Indiana*'s intertextual associations with the works of Jacques-Henri Bernardin de Saint-Pierre, Balzac, Flaubert, and Stendhal have been explored (Buchet-Rogers; Booker; Hecquet; Ippolito; Prasad, "Espace"). Questions of gender and feminism together form a sustained critical thread in late-twentieth-century studies of the novel, one that endures today. These studies discuss the novel's representation of women (Petrey, "George" and "Men"; Rabine, "George Sand"; Schor, "Portrait" and "This Essentialism"; Frappier-Mazur; N. K. Miller, "Writing" and *Subject* 206–28), its treatment of the dynamics of gender and power (Boutin; Harkness, *Men*; Massardier-Kenney, *Gender* and "*Indiana*"), and the poetics that sets the novel apart from the works of Sand's male contemporaries (Naginski, *George Sand*; Schor, Introduction; Planté; Zanone; Didier, Introduction; Nesci; Laforgue; Poli). While astute critics had detected the theme of slavery in *Indiana* very early on (Rogers), it was not until the 1990s that scholarship began to mine the novel's rich colonial subtext. Since then, a substantial body of research investigating the representation of race, *créolité*, *métissage*, and colonial history in the novel has emerged (C. Berman; Bernard-Griffiths; Kadish, "George Sand" and "Representing"; Little; Machelidon, "George Sand's Praise"; Prasad, "Espace" and "Intimate Strangers"). *Indiana*'s colonial subtext also contributes to the novel's popularity in the classroom.

Beyond these trends in criticism, studies of *Indiana* have explored subjects as varied as revolution, social and political history, and sexuality. For further bibliographic information about studies on George Sand—both *Indiana* and other works—one may consult the Web site of the George Sand Association (http://gsa.hofstradrc.org) and of Les Amis de George Sand (www.amisde georgesand.info/).

NOTES

[1] For instructors who wish to provide their students with a visual awareness of the distance between metropolitan France and Île Bourbon (Réunion), some online maps may prove useful: http://www.davidrumsey.com/maps1000051-25237.html (Rumsey); https://maps.google.com/maps?hl=en&q=indian+ocean&ie=UTF-8.

[2] Biographies that exploit Sand's love life are not limited to the nineteenth century; several mid-twentieth-century studies also show more interest in her romantic affairs than in her writing career.

Part Two

APPROACHES

Introduction

Having published several titles in collaboration with Jules Sandeau under the signature J. Sand—"La prima donna," "La fille d'Albano," and more famously *Rose et Blanche* (all in 1831)—Sand's first solo novel, *Indiana*, was indeed a success during her lifetime. She composed *Indiana* in early 1832 and published it in May of the same year. When the novel first appeared, reviews in periodicals commented favorably on Sand's penetrating psychological analyses, on the accuracy of her observations, and on the faithful and candid representation of contemporary France.[1] Although most of Sand's contemporaries were skeptical in their evaluation of the novel's conclusion—which did not appear in the first printing of the novel—the advent of Sand on the literary scene was, in large measure, met with enthusiasm. After reading the novel in one night, Sand's mentor, Henri de Latouche, likened Sand's writing to that of Alphonse de Lamartine, Honoré de Balzac, and Prosper Mérimée—that is, to authors who represented both the Romantic and realist movements dominating the early-nineteenth-century literary scene (Sand, *Correspondance* 2: 88n1). Indeed, published on the heels of Victor Hugo's *Notre-Dame de Paris*, Stendhal's *Le rouge et le noir*, and Balzac's *La peau de chagrin*, Sand's first novel brought together several of the literary tendencies of the era. Whereas its characters display the full-blown *mal du siècle* of the Romantic generation, its 1832 preface exalts social realism. Sand's novel inherits François-René de Chateaubriand's Romantic aesthetic of untrammeled spontaneity, but its trenchant social commentary and descriptive precision look ahead to the high realism of Gustave Flaubert's *Madame Bovary*—in fact, Flaubert's titular heroine has been described by many critics as a descendant of Indiana. To these two modes, Sand affixes a third—namely, the idealism that would mark her work throughout the nineteenth century: in the novel's much-debated conclusion, the heroine is seen in an idyllic and utopian retreat with her companion Ralph.

Indiana also reflects the significant historical and political juncture at which it was published. The novel appeared two years after the bloody 1830 revolution and during the July Monarchy, a regime that came under attack from both liberal and conservative political circles in the country. The uprising of republicans against the monarchy in June 1832 reflected deep-seated dissatisfaction with the regime, even if it did not in any way rival the 1830 revolution. Between March and September 1832, a cholera epidemic took the lives of approximately 20,000 Parisians (out of an urban population that then numbered 785,000) and 100,000 French overall. It was at the beginning of the breakout of this epidemic that Sand composed *Indiana*. Social and economic conditions demanded improvement in the rights and the living conditions of various sections of the population. Less than a year before the novel's publication, the country had seen civil unrest in the first of the *canut* revolts, an uprising of Lyon's silk workers that would characterize the labor concerns of the Industrial Revolution. Living under the dictates of the 1804 Napoleonic civil code and with divorce abolished in 1816, women in the early nineteenth century had limited rights over property and diminished power within the institution of marriage.[2] In France's overseas colonies, revolution and change were afoot. The news of Haiti's slave revolt and its subsequent declaration of independence from France in 1804 did not go unnoticed in France's other slave colonies, such as Île Bourbon (now Reunion Island) in the Indian Ocean, where part of *Indiana* is set. By the time of *Indiana*'s composition, the slave trade had been abolished by European powers, but slavery persisted in France's colonies, and momentum in the French abolitionist movement to eradicate slavery was growing.

Although *Indiana* does not describe in intricate detail the historical and political events of its time, it confirms the famous assertion by Sand's contemporary Alfred de Musset that the Romantic generation was a product of the uncertainties created by two historical cataclysms: the death of the monarchy in 1793 and Napoléon Bonaparte's capitulation in 1814 (ch. 2). *Indiana* bears witness to the trauma produced by revolution and repeated regime change, as well as to the sharply divided ideological variances that historical turbulence created in the French body politic. The July revolution of 1830 serves as a backdrop for the heroine's personal drama; political debates on republicanism, monarchy, and Bonapartism rage among the men in Indiana's household. A large part of the novel is set during the very end of the Bourbon restoration (1815–30), whose superficiality and cut-throat opportunism the novel captures accurately. Moreover, European happenings are bound up with colonial fortunes in *Indiana*, as the characters go back and forth between France and Reunion Island. The text alludes to colonial slave society and to the creolized identities they engendered. The heroine's malaise is due in part to her in-between identity as a Creole; she belongs fully neither to metropolitan France nor to the colonies where she grew up with her brutal slaveholding father. Perhaps most significant, Sand's novel takes up the cause of remedying women's unequal status within the institution of marriage in the early nineteenth century. As Sand states emphatically in her 1842 preface to the novel, "j'ai écrit *Indiana* avec le sentiment non raisonné, il est vrai, mais profond et légitime, de l'injustice et de la barbarie qui régissent encore l'existence de la femme dans le mariage, dans la famille et la société" 'I wrote *Indiana* influenced by a feeling, unreasoned, it is true, but deep and legitimate, of the injustice and barbarity of the laws which still govern the existence of women in marriage, in the family, and in society' (46–47; 13).

The essays in the second part of this volume, "Approaches," make sense of these literary, historical, social, and political issues in diverse ways, taking up what we identify as four key themes in the body of scholarly criticism on the novel: modes of literary narration, gender and feminism, slavery and colonialism, historical and political upheaval. The articles in the first section, "History and Geography," address the complex temporal and spatial questions raised by the novel. Because historical themes are often less accessible to students than the narratives of love and marriage, we open the volume with Lauren Pinzka's article about pedagogical techniques that allow students to recognize how Sand transcribes and mythologizes history—especially the violence of history—in the novel. Pinzka's contribution may be read alongside that of James Smith Allen, who approaches the novel as a cultural artifact. He contends that studying literature is key to understanding history and makes a compelling argument for the inclusion of *Indiana* in the curriculum of a history course. Peter Dayan and Carolyn Berman focus their historicized readings on human property, a concept that may strike twenty-first-century students as archaic but one that was considered natural in many restoration circles. Dayan pays attention to the ways in which Indiana contests the hierarchies established by Napoleonic principles in restoration society, according to which husbands own their wives. Human ownership of a different kind informs Berman's teaching of *Indiana*: the history of French colonial slavery and the emancipation of French colonial subjects serve as helpful didactic analogies that illuminate the condition of metropolitan French women. These essays on history are complemented by Patrick Bray and Margaret McColley's classroom explorations of the rich geographic landscape of the novel. Bray's essay shows us that a spatial approach to teaching *Indiana* is productive not only for understanding how nineteenth-century protagonists negotiated the laws and constraints of space and movement but also for clarifying students' experiences of mobility, place, and space. McColley's dissection of colonial space in the novel will prove useful to those instructors who wish to explore the geography of the Indian Ocean and the French presence there.

The interrelated themes of race and gender have fascinated late-twentieth- and early-twenty-first-century scholars of *Indiana*, and according to responses we received to the MLA survey, these themes also happen to generate the most impassioned classroom discussions on the novel. In the next section of the volume, "Race, Femininity, and Masculinity," the essays by Doris Kadish and Véronique Machelidon explore critical scholarship on race in the novel and nineteenth-century writings on abolitionism, slavery, and racial classification. Charles Stivale and Nigel Harkness take on the novel's unique treatment of masculinity, essential for complicating any straightforward expectations that uninitiated readers may have about the role of the masculine or of male characters in the work of a female author. Stivale details the intricate development of masculine characters in *Indiana*, especially Ralph; Harkness scrutinizes the ambiguous authority of the novel's male narrator. Isabelle Naginski and Aimée Boutin describe the ways in which their teaching of the novel guides students in detecting and parsing out gender hierarchies, whether through close reading of discrete chapters or through feminist theoretical texts. Boutin's essay also pairs well with Harkness's, since both contain tips on using narratology effectively in the analysis of the novel. Engaging with race and gender, Molly Krueger

Enz introduces students to Sand's variation on the tragic mulatta stereotype in nineteenth-century American literature. Enz's essay, like those by Berman and Françoise Massardier-Kenney in other sections of the volume, will be beneficial to instructors teaching *Indiana* in English translation and alongside American and British fiction.

Although *Indiana* is now part and parcel of the nineteenth-century French canon, its pedagogical reach and possibilities go well beyond the nineteenth-century literature curriculum. The essays in the section "Comparative Perspectives" feature approaches to *Indiana* outside the context of French Romanticism and realism. Kathrine Bonin makes her students take a comparative leap by examining *Indiana*'s relation to the eighteenth-century idea of the literary island, thereby elucidating Sand's ties to the Enlightenment intellectual tradition. Focusing on the legal context of *Indiana*, Lynn Penrod introduces the novel to students of two seemingly unrelated disciplines: law and literature. Her account of *Indiana*'s interdisciplinary potential—one that exposes law students to literature and North American literature students to codified French law—may be compared with Allen's ideas about teaching *Indiana* in a history classroom. Massardier-Kenney's evaluation of the various English translations of *Indiana* offers practical resources and perspectives to anyone teaching the novel in a comparative literature or world literature course.

The last section, "Literary Contexts," contains essays that explore the novel's engagement with literary techniques, tropes, and myths of the early nineteenth century. John T. Booker and Shira Malkin throw a spotlight on the genre of the melodrama and its peculiar storytelling techniques. Malkin demonstrates how to exploit the full dramatic potential of the genre by leading her students through in-class theatrical performances of key scenes in the novel. Christopher Bains offers pedagogical ideas on the mechanics of literary portraiture, Allan Pasco on the tension in the novel between Romanticism and realism. Our volume closes, fittingly, with Margaret Waller's essay on the benefits of ending a course on Romanticism with *Indiana*. Waller argues that teaching *Indiana* as a final text energizes classroom debate, because the novel is a variation on the sentimental and Romantic tradition as well as an impassioned, critical, and realist rewriting of it.

A quick perusal of our contributors' chapters will reveal that even the most strictly pedagogical essay offers a fresh new reading and analysis of the text. Full of unique ideas and original perspectives, the essays in this volume cover a vast range of subjects pertaining to *Indiana*. Instructors of Sand's novel, whether teaching in French or in English, whether veteran or novice, will find here a variety of approaches and materials that will enhance their teaching of *Indiana* and contribute to students' understanding and appreciation of the novel.

NOTES

[1] We are referring specifically to reviews of the novel that appeared in three journals of 1832: *L'artiste* (Pyatt), *Journal des débats* (Charlie), and *Le national* (Sainte-Beuve).

[2] Title 5, chapter 6, of the civil code, which deals with laws relevant to married persons, can be read in French at http://www.easydroit.fr/codes-et-lois/Chapitre-VI-Des-devoirs -et-des-droits-respectifs-des-epoux-du-Code-civil/S52116/ and in English at http://www .napoleon-series.org/research/government/code/book1/c_title05.html#chapter6.

Teaching Historical Myth and Memory in *Indiana*

Lauren Pinzka

One of the delights of teaching *Indiana* lies in introducing students to a twist on a familiar nineteenth-century story with a decidedly different take on marriage and male dominance. Add to that the fascinating narrative voice and the even more intriguing literary persona behind that voice, and it is no surprise that students find themselves fully engaged in Sand's debut solo work of fiction. Less accessible are the historical ramifications of the novel. Literature is indeed one of the most illuminating windows into our past, and, given the general unfamiliarity of American students with France's complicated series of revolutions, *Indiana* can not only provide them with some needed insight but also teach them to be more sophisticated textual readers. We read fiction, however, not to discover the empirical truth of the past but to learn how that past is interpreted and transformed by the author. The concept of myth provides a useful tool for examining how the inscription of the past into history filters the past anachronistically, adding important psychological, heroicizing, and ideological dimensions to human events. The depiction of historical events may differ according to gender, social class, and experience. Reading *Indiana* is witnessing how one privileged female author memorialized her culture's violent past.

I always open with a discussion of the surface or manifest level of the text, in this case, a love story taking place just before and during the July revolution of 1830. I then lead the students to more sophisticated readings of the novel by unearthing the hidden subtext of the work through examination of rhetorical features such as repetitions, ellipses, and contradictory word choices. Although it is my personal interpretation that Sand reveals far more sympathy for violent

revolution than her public image of social pacifist would suggest, I resist imposing a particular reading on the work and instead lead the students to form their
own conclusions about Sand's attitudes toward revolution.

It is critical to approach the novel by teasing out the difference between
historical and cultural myths and empirical historical events. Because of its
prevalence, students readily grasp the process of mythifying. The last section of
Roland Barthes's *Mythologies*, albeit difficult, provides a fascinating foundation
for the function and manipulation of myths. Simply put, the word (or image)
becomes myth as it takes on the meanings of past associations. For example, the
term *French Revolution* is nourished by the richness of its past but is emptied
of much of its value through use over time. The word (or image) is transformed
from its basis in knowledge of specific events to an essentialized concept. Pa-
triotism, for instance, is associated with a flag, and bloodshed, with the French
Revolution. A sometimes (for Barthes, always) deliberate impoverishment of
history in the service of ideology helps create our view of the world. In another
era, Freud spoke of the manifest and latent meanings of a word to describe the
apparent meaning and the subtle associations that we are no longer capable of
consciously identifying. Another excellent introduction to the topic of history
and myth is Pierre Nora's "Entre mémoire et histoire," in *Les lieux de mémoire*,
where he explains history as the problematic and incomplete reconstruction
of what has ceased to exist. Like Barthes, Nora sees the use of history as an
inevitable emptying of history transformed and deformed, appropriated for the
needs of the writer or speaker, and so on (29). Frank Bowman's notion of "de-
symbolization" in his work on philosophy and religion in French Romanticism is
another useful resource. To engage students, I always ask the class to consider
the cultural and historical myths prevalent in the United States as well as in
France. They can readily identify John F. Kennedy for the baby boomer generation, September 11th for their age group; May '68 and the 1998 World Cup live
on in the memories of the last two generations in France. One of the largest
hurdles in teaching *Indiana* is its distant and foreign context. In a course organized around myth or representation of history, I assign a relevant history book
in English (to save time). (I recommend Peter McPhee's *The French Revolution, 1789–1799*.)

Before we enter into the specifics of historical mythmaking, I always situate
the author's perspective on the events depicted. Writing her novel well after
many of the turbulent events to which the novel alludes, Sand had experienced
most of them vicariously through the eyes of her aristocratic grandmother, with
whom Sand spent her childhood. Furthermore, it is significant to the political
ramifications of the novel that it was written just after the upheaval of 1830. The
surprisingly understated treatment of this revolution confirms the conventional
wisdom that the dust must settle before history can integrate itself into fictional
form (Peyre 89). The trauma of emigration, the Terror, compulsory military
service under Napoléon, and the territorial invasion in 1814 and 1815 hindered
any immediate examination of events. It was the children of the victims of the

Revolution who studied its effects and made it into a fictional subject, and only once Charles X's oppressive policies had awakened popular dissatisfaction and sufficient freedom had been achieved (89; Mozet 14). One of my goals in the classroom is to show that although the Revolution and the Terror are far from central topics in Sand's novel, they hover over the novel like a bad dream and are mythified—that is, appropriated in the service of ideology. It is the students' task to identify the references and to determine the political agenda at work. I also stress that myth is a form of repressing and concealing history; as important as her writing about the traumatic era are the historical forces Sand represses. The reader is constantly confronted with references to things either hidden or buried: "cachée" 'hidden' (144 [105]; 96), "à la dérobée" 'secretly' (173 [130]; 123), "enveloppée" 'wrapped' (185, 190 [141, 145]; 134, 139), "un voile" 'a veil' (325 [260]; 257); the impossible desire of penetrating another's thoughts and secrets; and, the most striking, the oddly double-veiled portrait of Ralph in Indiana's bedroom. It is for the students to determine what is beneath the mask of the finished text.

As an initial assignment, I ask the students to uncover examples that may bolster Barthes's claim of myth as an impoverishment of history. I frequently have students prepare such questions orally and assign a different student to write a short paper, to be posted online, for each class period. Two students are then in charge of discussing the student's paper in class. I try to elicit as an example the description of Raymon's mother as one of those women "qui ont échappé aux échafauds de 93, aux vices du Directoire, aux vanités de l'Empire, aux rancunes de la Restauration" 'who have escaped the scaffolds of '93, the vices of the Directory, the vanities of the Empire, and the grudges of the Restoration' (78 [45]; 41). The student will note not only the reductionist portrayal of history but also the use of enumeration, which has the effect of equalizing the significance of the events in question, each with its assigned defect. In typical myth-making fashion, Sand reveals more of a desire to perpetuate symbols of political events than to analyze them. Reinforcing the use of "les échafauds" 'scaffolds' as a haunting and reductionist symbol of the Revolution, Sand's narrator explains that Raymon fears their reinstitution and the flow of "le sang innocent" 'innocent blood' (167 [124]; 117). The clichéd final expression obscures the political implications that the enemies of the Revolution, frequently aristocrats, were blameless. It is the perfect example of Barthes's theory of myth in the service of ideology and is an excellent starting point for a discussion of historical myth.

The revolution of 1830 is also dramatically presented in the context of its symbol: "Mais quels furent sa surprise et son effroi en débarquant, de voir le drapeau tricolore flotter sur les murs de Bordeaux!" 'But how surprised and alarmed she was when on disembarking, she saw the tricolour flag flying on the walls of Bordeaux!' (290 [232]; 226). Instantly the political struggle is linked to the symbolic tricolor, followed by an even more familiar association with revolution, bloodshed: "Une violente agitation bouleversait la ville: le préfet avait été presque massacré la veille; le peuple se soulevait de toutes parts; la garnison semblait s'apprêter à une lutte sanglante . . ." 'A violent disturbance was disrupting the town; the prefect had been almost murdered the night before; on all sides the people were rising; the garrison seemed to be preparing for a bloody struggle . . .' (290 [232]; 226; trans. modified). Not only does "sang" 'blood' semantically unite both revolutions, but Sand also reduces the participants in the struggle to the ideologically charged term "le peuple" 'the people.'

Although the most obvious application of the concept of myth is in Sand's treatment of historical events, a different form of mythifying takes shape through character development. As Naomi Schor points out, not only do the characters embody political ideals, but "each protagonist incarnates an abstraction; the ideal toward which the idealist novel tends is always a form of allegory" (Introd. xiv). The students must pay careful attention to the ideological positions that each character allegorizes, what myths about those positions are being perpetuated or undercut, and what the narrator is telling us about them. Isabelle Naginski's work can also point the student to how Sand gives each character, in keeping with his or her political position, a "specific mode of speech" (*George Sand: Writing* 61): Delmare's, fossilized and archaic; Raymon's, eloquent and triumphant; Ralph's, inarticulate (until the end); Noun's, practically inexistent; Laure de Nangy's, a pastiche of the language of her class; and Indiana's, a language of resistance (61–62, 72). After the initial discussion of mythmaking, I point out that Delmare's character construct personifies, as Schor explains, an "instantiation of an idea, the Law, which reduces women to the status of objects of exchange, to the abjection of virtual slaves" (Introd. xiii). The hackneyed character of Delmare is described as "un homme de fer" 'a man of iron' (86 [53]; 48; trans. modified), brutal, imperious, and combative, corresponding to the myth of Napoléon as an impulsive and brutish warrior who embodies many of the characteristics of the myth surrounding the emperor: ambition, military prowess, a self-made man. Despite Sand's abhorrence of the Napoleonic legal code and of the emperor's hypocritical embrace of the Catholic Church, she viewed Napoléon as an honorable man betrayed by his entourage (Sand, *Œuvres autobiographiques* 1: 691). Is it a coincidence that Delmare is forced to retreat from France only to discover his betrayal by Indiana and Raymon?

Sand uses one of the occasional political interludes in the novel to critique aristocratic self-interest through the character of Raymon, who was modeled on a noted pamphleteer of his era. Raymon is infuriated when the king, Charles X, imprudently permits the rise of the absolutist Polignac ministry, threatening to bring the pamphleteer and his whole class down with him. His only concern is for the plight of his own social group. Raymon opposes the king's absolutism and contemplates being enrolled "sous ses bannières belliqueuses qui flottaient de toutes parts, appelant au grand combat les plus obscurs et les plus inhabiles" 'under the warlike banners which were waving on all sides to summon the most obscure and incapable to the great fight' (262 [206]; 200). Sand illustrates here the complexity of the position of many aristocrats who often had liberal leanings but, unsurprisingly, their own class interests at heart, as demonstrated by the volte-face of the nobility after 1789 when it realized that it was not going to be the head of the new regime. It is important for the student to note the critical voice of the narrator: "Raymon fut en toute occasion le champion de la société existante. . . . Cela était simple: Raymon était heureux et parfaitement traité" 'On every occasion Raymon was the champion of the existing social order. . . . That is easily explained: Raymon was happy and very well treated' (166 [124]; 117). Confirming the belief that insightful historical commentary requires the passage of time, the students will note that Sand's only explanation for the cause of the 1830 July revolution is Polignac's repressive policies (260–62 [205–06]; 199–200), leaving the reader with only Raymon's point of view and perhaps betraying Sand's class prejudices as well.

Ralph, provocatively presented as an egotist and a dullard despite his eventual hero status, is obviously linked to the republic and its positive ideals of equality and pacifism: "il voulait exclure tous les abus, tous les préjugés, toutes les injustices; projet fondé tout entier sur l'espoir d'une nouvelle race d'hommes" 'he wanted to banish all abuses, all prejudices, all injustices, a plan based in its entirety on the hope of a new race of men' (167 [124]; 117); we note the choice of "hommes" 'men' foreshadowing perhaps Indiana's exclusion from her own story in the novel's conclusion.

Finally, Indiana has no clear political position, having been prevented from intellectual development by her mentor, Ralph, but she exemplifies a position of resistance to authority that, in the context of ongoing social strife, suggests a legitimate political position in its own right. Given her ostensibly apolitical nature, it is jolting when she attacks the concept of divine monarchy and the influence of the Catholic Church, predicting that God will sweep both away (249 [195]; 190). Sand suggests obliquely that Indiana's political indifference masks the heart of a revolutionary.

Once the three preponderant political positions in *Indiana* have been located—the royalist, the Bonapartist, and the republican—I invite my students to proceed to a different style of reading, a pursuit of the latent, hidden level of the work. Which political positions are absent from the text? One answer is the position of the revolutionary. It is not surprising that a woman of Sand's social class and political beliefs would eschew violence, although women like Olympe de Gouges and Charlotte Corday were active participants in the French Revolution. In fact, women participated heavily in all of France's revolutions. A careful and methodical reading of the novel will reveal, among other things, that a revolutionary stance appears systematically in subtextual forms.[1] I note especially the abundance of references to heads (166, 184, 198, 215, 224 [116, 140, 152, 166–67, 174]; 123, 133, 146, 161, 170), with multiple and provocative variants on the expression "perdre la tête" 'losing one's head': "la tête s'égare," "un étrange vertige s'emparait alors de sa tête," "un vertige . . . s'empara de ma tête" (221, 224, 240, 254, 339 [171, 173, 187, 199, 272]; 167, 169, 183, 194, 268). Similar traces of revolutionary violence can be found in the following terms and expressions:

"sang" 'blood' (60, 62, 82, 104, 106 [29, 31, 50, 70, 72]; 25, 27, 45, 64, 66)

"sanglant" 'bloody' or 'bloodstained' (209, 269, 303 [161, 212, 242]; 155, 207, 237)

"sang-froid" 'calm,' 'coolness,' 'cold,' 'phlegm' (113, 116, 150, 152, 163 [78, 81, 110, 112, 121]; 71, 74, 102, 105, 114)

"[re]trancher" 'cutting' (156, 205 [115, 158]; 108, 152)

"enfoncer le couteau" 'plunged the knife in' (184 [139]; 132)

inflected forms of the word "exécution" 'execution' (184, 208 [140, 161]; 133, 155)

"victime" 'victim' (197, 207, 237 [151, 160, 185]; 145, 154, 182)

"bourreau" 'executioner' (184 [140]; 133)

inflected forms of the word "torture" (193, 222, 240, 269, 278 [147, 172, 187, 213, 220]; 141, 167, 184, 208, 215)

the overwhelmingly repeated "terreur" 'terror' (161, 172, 186, 187, 193 [120, 129, 142, 142, 147]; 113, 122, 135, 135, 141)

Furthermore, the terse fashion in which Sand dismisses the outbreak of the July revolution and recounts it from the point of view of her most apolitical character can be seen as support for the theory that she is suppressing a dominant force of her era. The repetition of references to many things being hidden suggests a layer beneath the surface of the text; likewise the Bourbon restoration is repeatedly referred to as a masquerade with aristocrats metamorphosing into "cette foule de masques" 'that masked crowd' (77 [44]; 40; trans. modified), and political moderation "servit de masque aux antipathies" 'served to mask hostile groups' (129 [91]; 84). Political sentiment serves as a "masque" 'mask' for expressing "sa haine et sa vengeance" 'hatred and vengeance' (171 [129]; 121). The last two examples establish that the mask conceals aggression, a further textual hint that violence has been occulted from the text.

The careful reader cannot fail to note the suppression of the violence of Sand's era in the use of the term "les illusions de trois jours" 'the illusions of three days' (126 [89]; 82), the brief initial period during which Indiana believed that Raymon was capable of authentic feelings for her. The reprisal of the historical allusion ("Elle se disait avec terreur qu'elle était pour lui le caprice de trois jours" 'Terrified, she told herself that for him she was a three-day whim' [150 (110); 102]), this time accompanied by the provocative word "terreur" 'terror,' suggests that Indiana's blind passion for Raymon is an erotic analog to *les trois glorieuses* (the July revolution, referred to in French as the "three glorious days") that occurred just before *Indiana* was written and is referenced in the novel, albeit obliquely, when Indiana lands in Bordeaux. The theme of the mask and the metaphor of the theater are both fertile ground for invoking the French Revolution's preoccupation with transparency, masks, and conspiracy as a metaphor to discuss the Revolution (Hunt, *Politics* 44). Revolution is also repeatedly compared to acts of nature ("les orages politiques" 'political storms' [295 (236); 230; trans. modified], "le tourbillon des révolutions" 'the whirlwind of revolutions' [235 (184); 180]) typical of proponents of revolutions like Maximilien Robespierre ("la tempête révolutionnaire" 'the revolutionary storm') and Camille Desmoulins, who qualified the events unfolding around him as the "torrent révolutionnaire" 'revolutionary torrent' (qtd. in Ungvari 10; my trans.).

As a homework assignment or short paper topic, I may ask the class to consider if Ralph and Indiana possess traits or use the language of a violent revolutionary, a political figure that otherwise seems absent from the text. This question could lead to a discussion of the forms of near sexual bondage in the text with Indiana as victim: "Dispose de moi, de mon sang, de ma vie. . . . [P]rends-moi, je suis ton bien, tu es mon maître" 'Do what you like with me, with my blood, with my life. . . . Take me, I am your property, you are my master,' declares the desperate Indiana to Raymon, who suddenly entertained an "infernale idée. . . . [I]l tira son visage de ses mains contractées, et regarda Indiana avec un sang-froid diabolique; puis un sourire terrible erra sur ses lèvres et fit étinceler ses yeux, car Indiana était encore belle" 'infernal idea. . . . He lifted his head from his clenched hands and looked at Indiana with diabolical calm; then a terrible smile hovered on his lips and made his eyes gleam for Indiana was still beautiful.' Indiana clings to him with "la terreur d'un enfant" 'the terror of a child' (297 [237]; 232). This disturbing scene is heightened by the use of the words "sang" 'blood' and "terreur" 'terror.' Yet Indiana is also associated with a passion for the hunt, which she shares with Ralph, and is qualified as "cruelle par vertu" 'cruel out of virtue' (210 [162]; 156). It is through what may be considered a quasi-sadistic activity that Indiana reveals a seemingly paradoxical side of her character, a side we also witness in the shocking near seduction scene when she dons Noun's hair. It is Ralph who is more commonly associated with the perpetration of violence despite his bland personality and progressive politics. It is his task to bleed Raymon when he is wounded by Delmare (64 [32]; 28), an act that symbolically suggests the necessity of bloodshed to achieve political utopia. Having informed Indiana of Noun's suicide, "Ralph venait d'enfoncer le couteau et d'entamer une affreuse blessure" 'Ralph had just plunged the knife in and had made a ghastly wound.' More shocking still is that "le sang-froid extérieur avec lequel il consomma cette opération cruelle lui donna l'air d'un bourreau aux yeux d'Indiana" '[t]he external coldness with which he carried out this cruel operation made him seem like an executioner in the eyes of Indiana.' She labels his act "votre vengeance" 'your vengeance,' whereas the narrator terms it "la maladresse d'exécution" 'a clumsy execution,' insisting on its "violence." To complete this metaphorical tableau of the Terror and its executioners, the action then turns to Raymon, who, on entering the grounds of the château, "sentit sa tête se refroidir" 'felt his head go cold' (184 [139–40]; 132–33; trans. modified). Countless examples can be found in the text of Ralph's attraction to violence, including his denial of that attraction.

One of the most compelling topics in any discussion of the novel is that of Ralph and Indiana's androgynous characteristics. An analysis of gender myths (covered elsewhere in this volume) makes for a fruitful addition to the class discussions on historical mythmaking. Although on its surface the novel deals with the conflicting but well-worn masculinist ideologies of monarchism, republicanism, and empire, the subtext hints at other, more obscure, and sometimes taboo subjects. The feminine coded ideal in the conclusion of the novel—an escape from warlike, revolutionary Europe to an idealized, Rousseauistic return to nature—is marked nonetheless with the stigma of incest and crime. The narrator feels repentant as he questions Ralph, who, twice on one page alone, refers to "nos crimes" 'our crimes' and "notre crime" 'our crime' (342 [274]; 270). Yet "cet homme n'avait pas un crime dans la mémoire" 'he had not a crime in his memory,' affirms the narrator, who is "confus comme un voleur pris sur le fait. . . . Il me semblait que j'étais coupable envers lui" '[e]mbarrassed like a thief caught in the act. . . . It seemed to me that I had wronged him' (336 [269]; 265). Most ostensibly, the guilt may stem from the incestuous nature of Ralph and Indiana's relationship. As a psychoanalytic critic, I push my students further and ask if this guilt refers in fact to Sand's discomfort with her characters' attraction to violence. We know from her *Correspondance* that although Sand was a proponent of democracy, she also excused Robespierre's excesses, writing in 1837 that the Terror was a necessary means of self-defense (qtd. in Vermeylan 164). In 1852 she repeated that the Terror was excusable because, at the time, there was no universal suffrage (*Correspondance* 11: 14). In her autobiography, Sand wrote that she would have been a Jacobin had she been alive in the 1790s (*Œuvres autobiographiques* 1: 116).

I prompt students to tease out their own interpretations of the novel's ostensible and hidden political agenda. As an example of a different direction of inquiry, I note a constant repetition of the word *empire* throughout the novel to refer to love. It would be fascinating to explore the use of this word and Sand's sentiments toward the emperor. I encourage the students to read between the lines, discovering among other things a text haunted by but suppressing violent revolution and an author who may repress or otherwise conceal her attraction to that violence that, as her *Correspondance* reveals, is at odds with her later public persona of "la bonne dame de Nohant" 'the good lady of Nohant' (Naginski, *George Sand: L'écriture* 2; my trans.). It is a joy to present to the students a nuanced and complex view of an author for too long sidelined and primarily read for her "romans champêtres" 'rustic novels.' *Indiana* brilliantly commands a more compelling image of George Sand. It is ultimately a testimony to the legacy of violent revolution that hangs over the entire nineteenth century.

NOTE

[1] In the interest of space, I only provide a maximum of five examples per word; the English is generally not provided because the French subtext is often lost in translation.

Creole Emancipation: *Indiana* and French Colonial Slavery

Carolyn Vellenga Berman

George Sand wrote her breakthrough novel *Indiana* (1832) out of a "horror" at female "enslavement" (*Story* 924). Although France was one of the major slave-trading and slave-owning nations at the time, what Sand had in mind was not literal slavery but the metaphorical slavery of French wives. Yet the historical context of French colonial slavery can be illuminating for students encountering the novel for the first time. What follows is my strategy for teaching *Indiana* in English translation to upper-level undergraduates in a self-designed liberal arts degree program. Since there are generally no prerequisites where I teach and undergraduates with diverse educational backgrounds mix with highly educated auditors in each class, the challenge is to bring students together in a meaning-ful collective project. In my course Dreaming of Freedom: Popular Novels in the Anti-slavery Era, for example, students read novels like *Robinson Crusoe*, *Mansfield Park*, *Indiana*, and *Jane Eyre* alongside slave narratives. In the light of the historian Robin Blackburn's overview of colonial slavery, we ask, What is freedom, and why does it matter? How does slavery differ from other forms of structural inequality—for example, the status of undocumented workers in the United States today?

The first class discussion of *Indiana* aims at discovering traces of national colonial history in the text. Students are quick to notice the key word "Creole" (*créole*) and its various uses in the novel.[1] As they note, it describes Indiana Delmare, a "lovely girl from the Indies" (44).[2] This "beautiful exotic flower" is the child of a refugee from Napoleonic Spain, raised in Île Bourbon and "stu-pidly married" to a Napoleonic colonel turned industrialist (44). The novel also describes her "foster sister" and chambermaid, Noun, as "the young Creole with big black eyes who had aroused the admiration of the whole county at the Rubelles fête" (25, 36).

Instead of offering an authoritative account of the term *Creole* at this point, I ask students to make their own hypotheses about its meaning. Although the connotations of the Creole in the text are highly charged, they are not coherent. As we discuss, Raymon de Ramière, an aristocrat participating in governance during the Bourbon restoration, initially falls in love with Noun before becom-ing smitten with her mistress. Nunlike with her "Creole voice, a little veiled and so gentle that it seemed made to pray or bless," Indiana offers her would-be seducer Raymon the guilty thrill of desecration when he sleeps with Noun in Indiana's bed (45; trans. modified). His subsequent confession (addressed to the bed) indicates the profanity of his regard for Indiana's own prospectively burn-ing Creole flanks: "Oh Indiana! . . . Have I not opened the door of your alcove to the devil of lust? . . . And the mad ardour which consumes the limbs of that sensual Creole, will it not come, like Deianeira's tunic, to attach itself to yours and gnaw at them?" (65–66; trans. modified).

Students accustomed to Anglo-American depictions of slavery often wonder whether Indiana and Noun are "passing" as white. I ask them to suspend their notions of racial difference and attend to the differences that appear significant in the text—for example, Creole versus French or Creole versus Parisian. Later in the novel, the narrator announces, "Women of France, you do not know what a Creole is like," and Raymon de Ramière concludes that "the troubles those two Creoles have caused me will serve as a warning, and I want no longer to deal with any but frivolous, light-hearted Parisian women" (103, 183; trans. modified).

This opposition makes students wonder about the author herself. Was she a Creole or a Parisian? And if she was a French author who had never been to the Indian Ocean, why did she choose to write a novel about two Creoles from Île Bourbon? To answer the last question, we briefly examine Sand's description of her project. In her autobiography, Sand commented that she wrote her first novel "all in one spurt, without any outline. . . . The only thing I had in me was a very clear and ardent feeling of horror at brutal and beastly enslavement" (*Story* 924). The bondage she had in mind was not the forced servitude of colonial subjects, but the restricted legal status of French wives, as she explained in the preface to the 1842 edition: "I wrote *Indiana* influenced by a feeling, unreasoned, it is true, but deep and legitimate, of the injustice and barbarity of the laws which still govern the existence of women in marriage, in the family, and in society"; "the cause I was defending is that of half the human race; it is that of the whole human race; for the woe of women entails that of men, as the woe of the slave entails that of the master" (13). The trope of *l'esclavage de la femme* looms large in Sand's descriptions of her project; we note the slippage from *femme* as "woman" to *femme* as "wife" in this metaphor.

It is easy to imagine a better poster child for the rights of women in marriage than Sand's adulterous and suicidal heroine, Indiana. Yet Indiana's origins in Île Bourbon make sympathetic transactions between *femme* and *esclave* possible. "Brought up in the wilds," as the narrator explains, "living surrounded by slaves whom she could help and console only with her pity and her tears, she had become used to saying, 'A day will come when my life will be completely changed, when I shall do good to others; a day when I shall be loved'" (51; trans. modified). Freeing slaves appears to be a natural extension of Indiana's emancipation from the slavery of her marriage to Colonel Delmare (Schor, *George Sand*; Kadish, "Representing"). Indiana denounces this kind of slavery in strong terms after she has spent the night at her lover's home: "I know I'm the slave and you're the lord. The law of the land has made you my master. You can tie up my body, bind my hands, control my actions. You have the right of the stronger one, and society confirms you in it. But . . . I went to breathe the air of liberty, to show you that morally you're not my master" (176–77).

Students prepare for the second part of our discussion of *Indiana* by reading a now notorious letter drafted in 1848, which shows how Sand continued to link the rights of women (or rather, wives) to the changing contours of French colonial slavery. In her letter "Aux membres du comité central," Sand rejects efforts to nominate her for political office on the grounds that a married woman could not guarantee her "political independence" under current laws (401).[3] "As for you, women," she writes in a plea to put female suffrage on hold,

> What bizarre caprice is driving you to parliamentary struggles, you who cannot even bring to them the assumption of your personal independence? What, your husband will sit on this bench, your lover perhaps on that other one, and you will claim to represent something, when you cannot even offer representation for yourselves? A bad law makes you the *half* of one man, mores worse than the law make you very often the half of another man, and you believe that you can afford some responsibility to still other men?   (407)[4]

Addressing herself to women positioned much like Indiana—with a husband in one party and a lover in another—Sand's letter rejects the attempt to gain voting rights for women before rights in marriage as premature, making a mockery of "this famous enfranchisement of women that we have heard so much about." Far more "easy and immediately attainable," in Sand's view, would be an effort to "return to [married] women the civil rights of which marriage alone deprives them and which spinsterhood alone conserves for them; a detestable error of our legislation that effectively places women in a grasping dependency on men and makes marriage a condition of eternal status as a minor" (402).

The reform of family law that Sand desired would correspond with the reform of national governance and colonial slavery in the second French republic: "When it is asked how a conjugal partnership could survive, in which the husband is not the absolute head, litigant, and judge, without appeal, this is like asking how the free man could do without a *master* and the republic without a king" (403). Writing in 1848, the year in which republican France (once more) emancipated its colonial slaves, Sand thus declares that "[married] women are in principle slaves, and . . . the moment has come to recognize in principle, their rights to civil equality" (404–05). Until family laws are changed, however, "[married] women will always have the vices of the oppressed, that is to say, the ruses of the slave" (404). As Sand explains, "The slave man can revolt against his master and regain frankly and openly his liberty and dignity," but "the slave [married] woman can only deceive her master and regain slyly and treacherously a liberty and dignity that are false and deflected from their true aim. What then is the freedom that [married] women can seize by fraud? That of adultery" (405).[5] By exploring the "ruses of the slave" and the "liberty" of adultery in the novel, we begin to consider how *Indiana* broaches questions of civil rights through (extra)marital relations.

Next, the class prepares for a close reading of the novel by reading an overview of colonial history in Blackburn's comparative study *The Overthrow of Colonial Slavery*. We focus on two moments in the decades before the publication of Sand's novel.[6] First, we read about the French transition from monarchy to elected government in the early 1790s, when a debate over the voting rights of free people of color set the stage for slave revolution and colonial secession. The French National Assembly initially took care to declare that by "put[ting] colonists and their property under the special safeguard of the nation and declar[ing] guilty of treason whoever seeks to foment risings against them" it would not challenge the institution of colonial slavery (qtd. in Blackburn 179). Yet this provision did not address the voting rights of free people of color. The assembly instructed the colonies that "[a]ll persons aged twenty-five years and upwards, possessing real estate or, in default of such property, domiciled for two years in the parish and paying taxes, shall meet" to vote on the colonial assemblies (180). But efforts to hold elections on this basis, including qualified free people of color, were crushed in Saint-Domingue, where the General Assembly chose instead to grant voting rights to all white males, whether or not they were taxpayers. This defiance prompted the French legislators to consider the question of race and voting rights more explicitly by voting to extend political rights to free people of color whose parents had been free-born. Although this decree affected only about four hundred people, the governor of Saint-Domingue warned that its introduction would "provoke civil war, secession or even an invitation of the British fleet" (189). In the midst of this crisis, the slaves in Saint-Domingue broke into open revolt. By 1793, France found that it had to adopt a radical stance of national inclusion. The National Convention abolished slavery in all the colonies in 1793 with an emphatic guarantee of political rights, declaring that "all men, without distinction of colour, domiciled in the colonies, are French citizens and enjoy all the rights assured under the Constitution" (225).

The second moment occurred in the decade before *Indiana* appeared, after Napoléon had turned many of these French citizens (back) into slaves and then lost French possessions ranging from the newly proclaimed "black republic" of Haiti (formerly Saint-Domingue) to colonies taken over by the British. As foreign powers, particularly Britain, worked to restore a limited monarchy in France, "those blacks and mulattoes whose freedom had been recognised by the Bonapartist or British authorities in principle retained their status; this included some slaves who had been manumitted at government expense to serve in the militia in the years 1801–10," but "those who could not prove their title to freedom were vulnerable to re-enslavement or were impressed by the colonial authorities for service in special battalions" (Blackburn 477). When those subjected to slavery revolted in Martinique in 1822, the subsequent security measures affected free people of color as well as slaves. In a case which became a cause célèbre in France, three free men of color, including Cyrille Bissette, were branded in 1824 and transported to prison in France for reading to their friends a pamphlet entitled *De la situation des gens de couleur libres aux Antilles françaises* (477–78). The high level of interest in the ensuing legal battles in France, where a final verdict in 1827 exculpated all but Bissette, indicates how the terms of emancipation and the status of emancipated peoples remained a crucial problem for the French, even as slavery (like monarchy) remained officially intact during this decade.

These historical incidents reverberate through our reading of *Indiana*. Our discussion focuses on the themes of creole recognition ("reconnaissance") and misrecognition ("méconnaissance"). We begin with Raymon's refusal to recognize his creole mistress, Noun—or to acknowledge his paternal responsibilities for her child. Raymon meets Noun at the Delmare estate, intending to offer her money but no acknowledgment for the unborn child, whom she describes as "a being who will be even more unfortunate than me" (63). Grateful for Noun's willingness to forgive him, he ends up making love to the pregnant Noun in her mistress's bed and clothes. But Raymon's gratitude and recognition for Noun's generous love quickly degenerates into misrecognition, as he sees only the part of her that is Indiana's dress—an accessory testifying to the virginal purity of its absent part. Drunkenly enjoying the "double reverberation" of a set of mirrors, "all that Raymon saw of [Noun] was Indiana's dress. If he kissed her black hair, he believed he was kissing Indiana's black hair. It was Indiana . . . he dreamed of on that modest, immaculate bed when, succumbing to love and wine, he led his disheveled Creole there" (64–65; trans. modified). The violence of this misrecognition becomes clear on the following morning, when Indiana discovers Noun's corpse.[7]

Now we proceed with a close reading of one of *Indiana*'s most crucial scenes. When Raymon has convinced Indiana to let him visit her alone at night, he returns with mixed feelings to "this room which he had not entered since the most sinister night of his life, fully furnished with his remorse" (139; trans. modified). The furniture of guilt, however, allows Raymon to enjoy another double reverberation. Finding Indiana in "a scarf from the Indies, casually tied in the Creole manner," Raymon "stayed on the threshold," fearing (or perhaps desiring) "that when she turned round, she would present to him the livid features of a drowned woman" (139; trans. modified).

Indiana does just that, by holding out a handful of the dead woman's hair. Testing what she has just learned from Ralph, she taunts him with the violence of his earlier misrecognition. "Do you recognize it?" she asks, allowing him to think that she has cut off her own hair (140). Delighted by this proof of her affection, Raymon takes the hair in his hands, only to discover that it belongs to her absent foster sister:

> But as he took hold of it, as he gathered up in his hands the rich bundle of hair with some locks reaching right to the ground, Raymon thought he felt something dry and rough in it that his fingers had never felt in the tresses round Indiana's brow. He experienced, too, an indefinable nervous

shudder when he felt it was cold and heavy, as if it had already been cut a long time, and when he noticed that it had lost its fragrant moisture and vital warmth. And then he examined it closely and sought in vain for the blue sheen which made it look like a crow's blue-tinted wing. This hair was completely black, like Indian hair, heavy and lifeless.   (140)

Reading the English translation, students note several things: the number of separable body parts (hands, hair, locks, fingers) and verbs for touch or feeling, as well as the key opposition between "vital" and "lifeless" and the colors (blue and black). But teaching this text in English also requires a modification of the translation of the final line, as follows: "this hair was of a Negro black, of an Indian nature, of a dead weight." For in this gothic moment of recognition, Raymon discovers that he is holding a remainder of the woman he effectively killed, by uncovering—and revealing—the subtle signs of her racial difference.[8]

Although a particularly observant reader might have inferred this racial distinction from Noun's status as foster sister ("sœur de lait") to Indiana, making her the likely daughter of "the negress who had been my wet-nurse" (109), all the overt barriers between the two Creoles until this point have been class distinctions. The revelation of racial difference in this charged scene thus gives an added "weight" to Noun's death. Negro, Indian, and dead, the hair in Raymon's hand requires recognition, and Indiana thus repeats, "Don't you recognize this hair, then?" (140). Confronted with both his guilt in the death of Noun and the very object of his fetishism—the hair that once reminded him of the virginal Indiana—Raymon faints. But then he recovers by taking refuge in a deceptively ample *reconnaissance*: "Poor Noun!" he cries, "It was her I wronged, and not you. . . . She sacrificed her life for my peace of mind. . . . Give me that hair, it's mine. . . . It's all that remains of the only woman who truly loved me" (141; trans. modified). Like a clever imperialist, Raymon recognizes his guilt by professing gratitude in the service of repossession, interpreting Noun's death as a loving self-sacrifice that trumps his own crimes toward the dead.

This reading paves the way for a discussion of the false liberties promised to French colonial subjects, as they haunt the final encounter between Indiana and Raymon. Much like the initial emancipation proclamation to the slaves, Raymon's final letter to Indiana in Île Bourbon proves to be a quickly forgotten ploy. Prompted by his letter, which "painted a somber, terrible picture of the revolution which was developing on the horizon in France, and . . . hinted to Indiana that the moment had come to put into practice the enthusiastic fidelity, the perilous devotion, of which she had boasted," Indiana abandons her husband in Île Bourbon and travels as a stowaway on a ship to France (205). Presaging her reception in France, the sailors rowing her to the ship pretend to welcome her dog, Ophelia, on board, only to break her skull: "[Indiana] begged the oarsmen to take [Ophelia] on board, and they pretended to get ready to do so, but just as the faithful animal was coming near them, they broke her skull, with loud guffaws, and Indiana saw the corpse of this being who had loved her more than

Raymon floating on the water" (219).[9] The sailors' pretense matches Raymon's invitation to Indiana, whom he describes as an "enslaved woman who was only waiting for a sign in order to break her chain, for a word in order to follow him" (52): "Three days after the letter had been sent to Bourbon Island, Raymon had completely forgotten both the letter and its purpose" (222).

When Indiana arrives on her former French estate, she is denied even the place of a mistress or slave. "Recognize me, then," she cries to Raymon. "It's me; it's your Indiana; it's your slave, whom you recalled from exile. . . . Do what you like with me, with my blood, with my life; I am yours, body and soul. I've travelled three thousand miles to belong to you, to tell you that; take me, I am your property, you are my master" (231–32). But the tongue-tied Raymon acknowledges instead his new Parisian wife, Laure. "You are in my house, Madame," declares Laure, and Raymon manages only to confirm this: "'She's my wife,' replied Raymon with a stupefied look" (232–33; trans. modified). By the late 1820s, of course, when *Indiana* is set, Napoleonic and restoration France had shown the general emancipation of French slaves to be just as hollow a promise as Raymon's to Indiana.

Examining the complex echoes of French colonial history in Sand's novel allows students to gain an appreciation for the (trans)national engagement of Sand's domestic fiction—and its complex imaginative effects. Repeated scenes of creole misrecognition in the novel link the fates not of slaves but of freed colonial subjects to those of metropolitan women in *Indiana*, exploring how both are condemned to passive citizenship and fraudulent forms of liberty. Sand was unhappily aware that the French restoration government not only condoned a clandestine slave trade but also reabolished divorce, "wishing to restore to marriage all of its dignity in the interest of religion, morals, monarchy and families" (Ronsin 238). The judicious introduction of historical context enriches class discussion of *Indiana* and sparks students to develop their own readings of the novel.

NOTES

This essay draws on chapter 3 of my book, *Creole Crossings*.

[1] For a history of the usage of the term *Creole* and its significance in nineteenth-century French, British, and American fiction, see C. Berman, ch. 1.

[2] As my course is taught in English, all quotations from Sand's novel are taken only from Raphael's English translation.

[3] All translations from this letter are mine.

[4] I provide the class with an English translation of the letter. The original French for this last phrase is "vous n'êtes pas seulement la représentation de vous-mêmes" ("Aux membres" 407). For criticism of this unsent letter, see Deutellbaum and Huff; Moses and Rabine.

[5] Sand's original French for "slave [married] woman" is "esclave femme" ("Aux membres" 405).

⁶These events are central to French national and colonial history but not specific to the Indian Ocean context referenced by *Indiana*. For local histories, see Vaughan; Vergès.

⁷The Powell edition of *Indiana* includes striking illustrations of this scene as well as the following one.

⁸The original French for this final phrase is "d'un noir nègre, d'une nature indienne, d'une pesanteur morte" (192). Larousse's 1869 *Grand Dictionnaire* proclaimed that "*Creole* women . . . are above all remarkable for the beauty of their hair, the blackness of which is incomparable," while noting that when "the Negroes born in the colonies . . . are free," "the only difference that exists between them and the white *Creoles* consists roughly in the color of their skin and the form of their hair" ("Créole"; see Miller, *Blank Darkness* 95, for thoughtful comments on this definition).

⁹This murderous reception of the dog also calls to mind the notorious French execution of the Haitian leader Toussaint Louverture.

Wandering in the Text:
Spatial Approaches to Teaching *Indiana*

Patrick M. Bray

Our experience of space is a social construction. Whether we are relaxing at home, riding in a train, walking on the street, or hiking through a forest, our perception of what surrounds us cannot be separated from the ways in which we project meaning onto our environment, and our environment is refashioned to conform to our desires. Cities, both planned and unplanned, hold countless layers of meaning. They adapt to their natural geography according to political and aesthetic values. Neighborhoods develop according to the dynamics of collective and economic forces. Monuments preserve an image of the past and serve as landmarks orienting our mental and symbolic map of a city. Storefronts, billboards, traffic signs, and passersby all compete for our attention: "La cité est un discours, et ce discours est véritablement un langage" 'The city is a discourse, and this discourse is truly a language' (Barthes, "Sémiologie" 1280; my trans.).

While real spaces are already representations, space in a novel is by definition always textual, which is to say that fictional space is conveyed by written language and participates in the novel's network of meaning. A reading of George Sand's *Indiana* that is attentive to questions of the representation of space, at the levels both of the text and of the historical and geographic context, will inevitably produce insights about the function of space in the French imagination of the 1830s. Indiana Delmare's adventures in traversing real places (Paris, Bordeaux, the Atlantic and Indian Oceans, and others) inform the reader about the particular historical moment following the disappointing revolution of July 1830 and in particular the way nineteenth-century women were policed in their movements. But these real places also carry symbolic meaning in the novel, as they suggest the various psychological states of the main character and especially the ideological lens of the male narrator.

The two main female characters in *Indiana*, Indiana and her foster sister and servant, Noun, are defined not only by their presumed races and classes, but also by geography—they are "créoles," women of European or mixed origin born in the colonies. Indiana's name calls attention to her geographic otherness. She remains an exotic beauty in France, but at the same time her European ancestry sets her apart in Île Bourbon (today's Réunion) from the majority of the island's inhabitants. She is always an outsider, always out of place, whether in high society in Paris or in the wilderness of Île Bourbon. The novel's narrator and male characters emphasize repeatedly the value society places on stability and order. Everything and everyone has a category and a place; to cross boundaries or to change places risks upsetting the moral foundation of society. The narrator succinctly characterizes the philosophy of Indiana's abusive husband, Delmare: "Chacun chez soi" 'everyone for himself' (132 [95]; 87) or perhaps "everyone is master in his own home." But since Indiana has no home, no place where she belongs, the spatial and gender politics of her time are so stifling as to endanger her very being. Her only options seem to be suicide by drowning (following Noun) or suicide by antisocial rebellion (following her eventual companion, Ralph).

In a society where everyone must know their proper place, mobility (both in the metaphorical sense of social mobility and the literal sense of moving through space) amounts to a criminal act. Within the first few pages, Indiana's melancholic condition is explicitly linked to the immobility imposed on her and everyone else at her husband's terminally boring country estate:

> On eût dit, à voir l'immobilité des deux personnages [Indiana and her cousin Sir Ralph] en relief devant le foyer, qu'ils craignaient de déranger l'immobilité de la scène; fixes et pétrifiés comme les héros d'un conte de fées, on eût dit que la moindre parole, le plus léger mouvement allait faire écrouler sur eux les murs d'une cité fantastique; et le maître [Delmare] au front rembruni, qui d'un pas égal coupait seul l'ombre et le silence, ressemblait assez à un sourcier qui les eût tenus sous le charme. (53 [22])

> On seeing the two motionless figures [Indiana and her cousin Sir Ralph] sitting prominently in front of the fireplace, you would have thought that they were afraid to disturb the stillness of the scene. They seemed fixed and turned into stone like the heroes of a fairy-tale, and you would have thought that the least word, the slightest movement, was going to make the walls of an imaginary city collapse upon them, while the gloomy master of the house [Delmare], whose regular step was the only break in the dark silence, was rather like a magician who had cast a spell over them.   (18)

Delmare has complete freedom of movement as master of the house; in the opening pages he paces around the salon in a desperate attempt to stave off boredom and only succeeds in finding a joyful diversion when an intruder is spotted trespassing on his domain. As the above passage suggests, this immobility hides a structural instability; any movement of our two "heroes" will destroy the illusion, and Delmare's authority will crumble. But the narrator's fairy tale also alerts the reader that when the walls of Delmare's fantastic city fall, they will also crush the two heroes, Indiana and Ralph. The novel's double ending satisfies the denouement foreshadowed in the fairy tale but allows for the hope of new spaces far from society's influence.

Given the immobility imposed on Indiana by her husband on one side and the suicidal inclinations of those closest to her on the other, Indiana's negotiation of the spaces around her is remarkable. Her practice of space regularly consists of remembering one place while moving through another; in a sense she experiences two places at once. As Michel de Certeau theorized, to practice space is to disrupt what he calls the "loi du propre" 'the law of the proper' of place, which is the natural law ruling that every place, by definition occupying a single location and moment, must be unique.[1] One cannot physically occupy two places at the same time, and two objects cannot occupy the same place.

Yet Indiana repeatedly calls forth images of one place while inhabiting another. When Raymon de Ramière is led into Indiana's bedroom by Noun, he is surprised to discover tastefully eclectic furnishings, ranging from a harp, romance novels, travel books, a palm branch, and engravings of Paul and Virginie and of Île Bourbon (101 [67]; 61). Everything in her room in the sober French countryside evokes an image of her island home far away. As if to render literal Indiana's mental absence from her physical presence, Raymon lulls himself into the illusion that Noun, wearing Indiana's clothing and seducing him in Indiana's room, is in fact Indiana; Noun conjures up Indiana's body, but Indiana is elsewhere.

Indiana's disruption of the law of place, of the boundaries between places, is most evident in the various episodes when she wanders by herself. Every time Indiana breaks free of her dependence on men, she wanders in spaces unfamiliar to her in what is described by the narrator as a delusional state. After Raymon leaves her the first time, she wanders Paris alone, apparently mistaking the Seine for the stream in which Noun drowned (226–28 [175–77]; 171–73). On Île Bourbon, she walks in the wilderness and sees images of Paris in the cloud forms above the mountains (253–54 [199–200]; 194–95). Upon her return to France in the wake of the July revolution, she gets lost in Bordeaux and, without identity papers, is registered at a hospital as a Jane Doe (290–92 [232–34]; 226–28). Finally she ends up alone and destitute in a hotel room in Paris, which the narrator describes as a veritable "non-lieu" devoid of memories and meaning and in stark contrast to the Paris of her dreams (299 [238]; 234–35).[2] During each of these prolonged walks, the variety of strange images encountered in these new spaces provokes a profound reverie in Indiana, who believes that she is in some other place. Out of place in a rigidly immobile society, she wanders entranced by the illusion of interpenetrated places where her seemingly incompatible desires and duties might happily coexist.

Indiana's wandering is clearly an expression of her desire for greater freedom of movement, a desire to control her own destiny; as the narrator sums up, "chez elle, tout se rapportait à une certaine faculté d'illusions, à une ardente aspiration vers un point qui n'était ni le souvenir, ni l'attente, ni l'espoir, ni le regret, mais le désir dans toute son intensité dévorante" 'everything [for her] was linked to a certain ability to create delusions, to an ardent aspiration towards something that was not memory, nor expectation, nor hope, nor regret, but desire in all its consuming intensity' (254 [200]; 194–95). Her spatial "illusions" are not based on memory, hope, or wish fulfillment; rather, they are the pure expression of desire. Her wandering is therefore very disturbing to the men of the novel: Delmare, Raymon, the narrator, and especially Sir Ralph. Analyzing any one of these passages closely (a useful in-class activity), the reader discovers not only Indiana's associations of disparate images and places but also the narrator's subtle manipulation of the scene to characterize her wandering as dangerous and insane. Her thoughts while walking in Paris are a "rêverie stupide" 'dazed reverie,' a "méditation sans idées" 'mindless meditation,' and "un état de somnambulisme" '[a state of] sleepwalking' (226 [175]; 172). According to the narrator, her evening walks in Île Bourbon, where she sees the Louvre and Notre-Dame in the clouds over the ocean and imagines herself flying away to the city of her dreams, appear to the outsider to be only the symptoms of madness: "pour qui eût observé alors ses yeux avides, son sein haletant d'impatience et l'effrayante expression de joie répandue sur ses traits, elle eût offert tous les symptômes de la folie" 'for anyone who might have seen her eager eyes, her breast panting with impatience, and the terrifying expression of joy on her face, she would have shown all the symptoms of madness' (254 [200]; 194). Her expression of joy is "terrifying," her desire for movement "madness."

The narrator's invention of a fictional observer makes explicit one of the most understated yet disturbing aspects of the novel: the almost constant surveillance of Indiana's every movement. In fact, Sir Ralph miraculously tracks Indiana down every single time she strays off, to "save" her from her dangerous illusions. He prevents her from falling into the Seine and convinces her that she really wanted to commit suicide (229 [178]; 174). The reader learns a few pages after the description of Indiana's evening walks in Île Bourbon and her apparently delirious dreams of Paris that Sir Ralph always watched over her from a distance, spying on her from behind tree branches from the rocks below (258 [203]; 197–98). After she escapes the island, arrives secretly in Bordeaux, and then finds herself destitute and unknown in an anonymous hotel in Paris, Sir Ralph of course discovers her location; as the narrator cheekily declares, "[I]l s'en présenta un [médecin] qu'on n'avait pas été cherché. . . . Je n'ai pas besoin de vous dire son nom" '[A doctor] appeared who had not been sent for. . . . I don't need to tell you his name' (301 [240]; 236). Though over the course of the narrative Ralph becomes a sympathetic Romantic hero, his love for Indiana compels him to watch over her continually. His surveillance or perhaps voyeurism does not prevent her from exploring her freedom of movement and her desire for new places, but his concern for her safety amounts to a condescending paternalism.

The novel's conclusion informs us after hundreds of pages that the narrator is not omniscient but rather a young man in search of adventure who has heard Indiana's story from the mouth of Ralph himself and from the gossip of the inhabitants of Île Bourbon. In this Russian doll of narrative voices, the innermost thoughts and dreams of Indiana turn out to be born from the imagination of Ralph and the male narrator, and these are born from Sand's imagination: thus a woman author imagines what men imagine a woman to imagine. In a final twist, the rational and misogynistic narrator repeats for himself in the wilds of Île Bourbon the same experience of delusional wandering he attributes to Indiana. While contemplating the island's volcanic rock formations, the narrator dreams that he sees architectural motifs from every civilization and, upon closer inspection, makes himself believe for a moment that he can read hieroglyphs or cabalistic signs in the graphic-seeming contours of the rock (331–32 [265–66]; 261–62). He spends so much time at these "puerile" pursuits that he fails to notice an oncoming rainstorm, gets lost in the forest, and wanders for two days in the wilderness until he happens upon Ralph and Indiana's hut, where he hears their intriguing story. The novel's fiction of its genesis therefore imitates Indiana's creative practice of space—just like Indiana's wandering, the fictional text invents new places, utopias, where the desire for a better world can exist in the space of a dream.

A spatial approach to *Indiana* enriches student understanding of the novel in a variety of ways. *Indiana* works well in a course on spatial discourse in French literature; students can draw comparisons and contrasts between Indiana and narratives of wandering in the picaresque novel (Rabelais's *Gargantua*, Diderot's *Jacques le fataliste*), in surrealism (Breton's *Nadja*), and in the works of the situationists. In a survey of nineteenth-century French literature, Indiana's alienating experience of Parisian space could be compared with that of Rastignac in Honoré de Balzac's *Le père Goriot* and with Charles Baudelaire's *Les fleurs du mal* and *Le spleen de Paris* among countless others. In a course on women and space or gender and the city, Indiana's desire for freedom of movement and a place to call her own resonates with feminist texts across the centuries, from Christine de Pizan's *La cité des dames* and Germaine de Staël's *Corinne* to Colette's *La vagabonde* and Agnès Varda's film *Sans toit ni loi*.

Indiana's many different passages detailing the eponymous character's wandering in Paris and in the wilderness lend themselves particularly well to in-class close-reading exercises. While these long, descriptive passages are often skimmed quickly by even experienced readers, they prove essential to an understanding of Indiana's distinctive practice of space. To enhance student participation in the classroom, instructors might ask students to locate on a map at home all the places mentioned in a given passage. How many of the places still exist? How far did Indiana travel? What monuments could she have seen, and which ones does the text not mention? The layer function on *Google Earth* allows students to overlay a map of Paris from 1834 (only two years after the publication of *Indiana*) onto a satellite image of the city today; the map is part of the *David Rumsey Historical Map Collection* (http://rumsey.geogarage.com/). Looking at this map, the reader unfamiliar with Paris discovers that Indiana's walk along the Seine begins at the Institut de France and continues past the Corps Législatif (today's Assemblée Nationale), across the river from the Louvre. It is of course the Louvre she sees in the clouds above Île Bourbon. To get a feeling for the strangeness of nineteenth-century Paris, students might be encouraged to read selections from an English guidebook of the city from the time. An excellent choice would be Edward Planta's *A New Picture of Paris*, published in Paris at regular intervals by Galignani; *Google Books* has dozens of scanned copies available from the 1820s and 1830s.

Finally, while it may seem quite strange to students that Indiana's movement is so constrained and policed, a very productive exercise consists of asking students to describe their own practice of space. How often do they walk and to where (to work, to class, with friends)? Do they take public transportation? Who observes where they go (friends, parents, security guards)? Do they have any obstacles to their movement (curfews, restricted-access dorms)? With the profusion of GPS technologies and handheld devices, students are able to publicize more than ever before possible their every movement to friends and relatives but also to corporations and law enforcement officials. While social networking sites such as *Google Latitude* or *Foursquare* allow people to explore playfully their environments and broadcast their location to friends and interested strangers, our every movement is tracked and commercialized. Perhaps our practice of space is no less fraught than Indiana's wandering in the 1830s.

NOTES

[1] "Est un *lieu* l'ordre (quel qu'il soit) selon lequel des éléments sont distribués dans des rapports de coexistence. S'y trouve donc exclue la possibilité, pour deux choses, d'être à la même place. La loi du 'propre' y règne: les éléments sont les uns *à côtés* des autres, chacun situé en un endroit 'propre' et distinct qu'il définit. Un lieu est donc une configuration instantanée de positions. Il implique une indication de stabilité" 'A *place* is an order (whatever it may be) according to which elements are distributed in relationships of coexistence. The possibility is therefore excluded, for two things, to occupy the same spot. The law of the "proper" rules there: elements are one *beside* the other, each situated in a spot "proper" and distinct to it that defines it. A place is therefore an instantaneous configuration of positions. It implies an indication of stability' (Certeau 172–73; my trans.).

[2] According to Marc Augé, a "non-lieu" is a place where one cannot read social relations because these places are interchangeable and the people who pass through them remain anonymous.

Teaching the Geography of Île Bourbon in Colonial Context

Margaret E. McColley

When discussing *Indiana* in two undergraduate French studies courses, Notions of the Exotic in the Age of Exploration and Empire and The Colonial Gaze, my students and I take careful notice of George Sand's representation of the geography of Bourbon Island, examining how the author conveys attitudes about the French empire through her main characters and their relationship to place, offering a critique of the misuse of power in the sphere of French influence mapped by the novel. As we embark on this path of discovery, we discuss the implications of the fact that Sand never actually traveled to Bourbon Island but learned much about its geography through her friend Jules Néraud, "Le Malgache" (Sand, "IV: A Jules Néraud"). We use this knowledge as a compass to guide our reading as we explore Sand's imaginative construction of the island, considering how the island serves a generative purpose in the novel, producing meaning within the text by shaping the perspective of Indiana and Ralph. This approach underscores the ways the island is privileged over continental France in its various roles as site of memory, homeland, and natural terrain for transformation of one's inner geography. We explore questions such as these: How is Bourbon Island represented as a site of memory? How does solitary walking in the island's natural environment alter the way Indiana and Ralph view France? How does close contact with the volcanic landscape and the island's flora and fauna lead to their personal transformation?

Visual and Narrative Mapping

I begin by guiding students through an in-class, visual exploration of the location and topography of Bourbon Island (now Réunion) and the Mascarene archipelago in the Indian Ocean; both historical and present-day maps of these are available online. Satellite maps allow us to zoom in on particular topographical features described in the novel and traversed by its characters, such as the port of Saint-Paul, the Bernica ravine, the Salazes mountains, and the lava area known as Le Brûlé de Saint-Paul. First, we compare nineteenth-century maps from the *David Rumsey Map Collection* (Rumsey) to a present-day hybrid map (a satellite image of the island with geographical markings) provided by the Nations Online Project (*Satellite View*). We then view two maps of French colonization: one that shows the various stages of empire building over time and place ("Reunion") and another that shows the nineteenth-century French colonial project on a global scale and allows students to zoom in on Île Bourbon and the Mascarenes (Lefèvre). Although the nineteenth-century maps do not reveal all the island's topographical features, the hybrid map shows that it is composed of two adjoining volcanoes, the dormant Piton des Neiges in the northern half of the island and the active Piton de la Fournaise in the southern half. The island's surface is largely dominated by three enormous calderas named Mafate, Cilaos, and Salazie and is covered in rain and cloud forests, immense gorges, ravines, and waterfalls (*Pitons*). This comparative study of historical and present-day maps provokes discussion among students about the role of hypothesis and imagination in the development of maps before the development of modern technologies.

It may at first seem as if Bourbon Island does not take on geographic prominence in the novel until the last few chapters, but by tracing the changing roles the island plays from the early chapters, one can appreciate its importance to the novel as a whole. We learn that, for example, Indiana grew up on Bourbon Island as the daughter of a slaveholding plantation owner who sought refuge there during the Napoleonic Wars, that she owns "une chétive habitation" 'a modest dwelling' there, and that when Delmare's factory fails, he flees to Bourbon Island to take refuge from financial ruin and start anew in colonial affairs (203 [156]; 150). By chapter 24 he is working daily at his warehouse at the port of Saint-Paul, conducting trade with India and France (252 [198]; 191). Indiana's cousin Ralph possesses a fortune in part from the sale of plantations that he once owned on the island (206 [159]; 153). Reading for these details allows students to chart the commercial endeavors that give structure to the novel's plot and mobilize its main characters to travel to the island.

Longing for "Home"

The upper-level undergraduate French classroom often includes students who are living away from home, have just returned from study abroad in a francophone country, or have come to the United States from international locations to study and are assimilating to life on the American college campus. For these reasons, they readily identify with concepts such as homeland as we read for a construction of Bourbon Island through memory. Sand marks Bourbon Island as Indiana's homeland early on in the novel, in chapter 2, in a scene framed by gender difference, where Ralph is growing weary of Indiana's mood. Here, in the presence of Delmare, Ralph urges Indiana to return to a state of well-being, one left behind on the island. When Indiana protests, Ralph pleads, "Donne-nous tort, ma chère cousine, en te portant bien, en reprenant ta gaîté, ta fraîcheur, ta vivacité d'autrefois; rappelle-toi l'île Bourbon et notre délicieuse retraite de Bernica" 'Prove us wrong, my dear cousin, by being well, by regaining your former bloom, cheerfulness, and vivacity. Remember Bourbon Island and our delightful retreat at Bernica' (58 [27]; 23). This first mention of Bourbon Island in the novel, then, is as a site of memory whose distance is marked temporally.

Indeed, Indiana's malaise is partly due to her sense of alienation in France, for she remains a stranger there as a Creole withering in the confines of her

French estate. Although she may appear to be welcomed into French high society as an heiress from the colonies, she remains unassimilated. Her status as
one born to colonists so far away is elucidated through a frivolous exchange of
gossip at the ball at the Spanish embassy:

> Cette jeune personne . . . c'est la fille de ce vieux fou de Carjaval qui a
> voulu trancher du Joséphin, et qui s'en est allé mourir ruiné à l'île Bour-
> bon. Cette belle fleur exotique est assez sottement mariée, je crois; mais
> sa tante est bien en cour.   (81 [49])

> That young creature . . . is the daughter of that crazy old Carjaval who
> wanted to set himself up as a partisan of Joseph Bonaparte and, a ru-
> ined man, went off to die in Bourbon Island. That beautiful, exotic flower
> has made a pretty stupid marriage, I believe, but her aunt is in favor at
> court.   (43)

The casual mention of Bourbon Island as a place where someone "went off to
die" reveals the indifference of the speaker about the island as a dwelling place
with deep meaning for the novel's main characters. In chapter 7, for example,
Sand describes Indiana's bedroom, where we see in progress on her loom a
tapestry, "si frais, oeuvre de patience et de mélancolie" 'newly worked in melancholy patience,' that depicts "les cimes de l'île Bourbon et les rivages bleus de
Saint-Paul" 'the peaks of Bourbon Island, and the blue coastline of Saint-Paul.'
As we continue to look around her bedroom, we gain a better understanding
of how the island is woven into her fabric of self. Indiana's longing for place is
exteriorized through other objects, such as a harp "dont les cordes semblaient
encore vibrer des chants d'attente et de tristesse" 'still vibrating with songs of
sad longing' and a palm branch hanging over the head of her bed (101 [67]; 61).
This latter object doubles as souvenir of Bourbon and harbinger of her return to
the island, when Ralph will confide to her, "combien de fois je vous ai regardée
dormir dans ces roseaux, ombragée sous le parasol d'une feuille de latanier!"
'how many times I have watched you sleeping among these reeds with a palm
leaf for a sunshade!' (319 [255]; 251). Looking further, we find that travel books
on Indiana's mahogany shelves are intermingled with love stories in such a way
as to suggest that travel may ultimately liberate her from the matters of the
heart paralyzing her at Lagny (101 [67]; 61). And, as the presence of *Paul et
Virginie* on these shelves introduces Jacques-Henri Bernardin de Saint-Pierre's
intertext, we are invited to consider how Indiana's fate may either copy, or differ
from, Virginie's. Bourbon Island thus appears sporadically in the early stages of
the novel as a far-off destination of commercial exchange, but soon it becomes
apparent that the island is a site of desire and longing for Indiana and a central
feature of her inner geography. After my students and I have examined how notions of home and homeland and problems of assimilation pertain specifically
to the text, I open the discussion to address these notions according to my stu-

dents' experiences of travel and displacement. I ask them, for example, whether home is a notion that one carries inside, and, if so, how it is bound to memory and to geography. Does the sense of *home* differ from that of *homeland*, and, if so, how? What is the meaning of *inner geography*?

Forgetting France

When we finally disembark on Bourbon Island in chapter 24, the geographic transition is upward soaring, for Sand emphasizes the island's most unique topographical feature—the sudden, extreme vertical rise of its volcanic mountains from the ocean:

> Bourbon n'est, à vrai dire, qu'un cône immense dont la base occupe la circonférence d'environ quarante lieues, et dont les gigantesques *pitons* s'élèvent à la hauteur de seize cents toises. De presque tous les points de cette masse imposante, l'oeil découvre au loin, derrière les roches aiguës, derrière les vallées étroites et les forêts verticales, l'horizon uni que la mer embrasse de sa ceinture bleue.   (253 [198])

> In truth, Bourbon is simply an enormous cone, with a base whose circumference measures about one hundred miles, and with gigantic peaks which rise to a height of ten thousand feet. From nearly every point of that impressive mass, the eye can discern in the distance, behind the steep rocks, behind the narrow valleys and the tall, straight trees, the unbroken horizon enclosed by the blue girdle of the sea.   (193)

What follows is a rich and complex description of the island, in which Sand calls attention to the intricacies of the island's topography, plant, and bird life.

When approaching this final section of the novel, I find it most provocative to discuss with my students how solitary walking on Bourbon Island brings about transformations in the lives of both Indiana and Ralph. While acknowledging the intertext of Rousseau's *Les rêveries du promeneur solitaire*, Sand employs the island topography to help Ralph and Indiana gain a new perspective on France and French social life and to discover a new sense of self in relation to France as they each walk along separate pathways, alone, in nature. For Indiana, high cliff vestiges near Saint-Paul provide views of the sea, bringing on hallucinations of Paris, while the forested ravines allow Ralph to find shelter and peace in his immediate surroundings. This now distant France unearths feelings of deep unhappiness in Indiana:

> [T]antôt elle vit une lame blanche s'élever sur les flots et décrire une ligne gigantesque qu'elle prit pour la façade du Louvre; tantôt ce furent deux voiles carrées qui, sortant tout d'un coup de la brume, offraient le

souvenir des tours de Notre-Dame de Paris . . . elle se prenait à palpiter
de joie à la vue de ce Paris imaginaire dont les réalités avaient signalé le
temps le plus malheureux de sa vie.   (254 [199])

[A]t times she would see a white breaker rise up from the ocean and
form a long line which she took for the façade of the Louvre; at times two
square sails, emerging suddenly from the mist, aroused the memory of
the towers of Notre-Dame de Paris . . . she would begin to quiver with joy
at the sight of that imaginary Paris whose realities had marked the most
unhappy time of her life.   (194)

Sand shows how the lay of the land, combined with the act of walking, leads
Indiana to abandon her desire for France through remembrance of her misery
there. Indiana's island walks also allow her a taste of independence from a restrictive domestic life:

Mais quand, vers le soir, la brise de terre commençait à s'élever et à lui
apporter le parfum des rizières fleuries, elle s'enfonçait dans la savane
laissant Delmare et Ralph savourer sous la varangue l'aromatique infusion
du faham. . . . Alors elle allait, du haut de quelque piton accessible, cratère
éteint d'un ancien volcan, regarder le soleil couchant qui embrasait la
vapeur rouge de l'atmosphère.   (253 [199])

When, towards evening, the land breeze began to rise and bring her the
scent of the flowering rice fields, she would go out into the savannah,
leaving Delmare and Ralph on the verandah to enjoy the aromatic faham
infusion. . . . Then, from some accessible peak, the extinct crater of a former volcano, she would go and watch the declining sun, which set the red
vapours of the atmosphere aglow.   (194)

Since solitary walking is the province of both women and men in Sand's novel,
I pause here and ask students for their observations on how gender, walking,
and place influence one another in *Indiana*. I ask them, for example, to identify
places in the novel where Indiana is portrayed as weak or irrational while walking alone and how this portrayal is influenced by place. In this analysis, my students and I follow Indiana's trajectory from France to Bourbon Island to France
and back as she bids farewell to the Ramières, flees Delmare, seeks out Raymon
at Lagny, and finally returns to the island with Ralph. While walking through
Paris before her first departure for Bourbon Island, for example, "elle sentit ses
jambes tremblantes prêtes à lui refuser le service" 'her trembling legs almost
refused to carry her' as she viscerally anticipates Delmare's anger and jealousy
(226 [175]; 171). Then when she returns to Bourbon Island with Delmare, his
paternalism continues to create a prison-like setting for her there even if they
have successfully escaped from metropolitan French society. When Indiana re-

turns by sea to France, violence has invaded the text through Delmare's kick to Indiana's forehead (269 [212]; 207) and the grotesque abuse by sailors leading to the death of Ophelia (282 [224]; 219).

Indiana's return to Paris from Bourbon Island in chapter 29 reconfigures women's travel to early-nineteenth-century Paris as a descent into the abyss: "être femme et se trouver là repoussée de tous, à trois milles lieues de toute affection humaine, . . . c'est le dernier degré de la misère et de l'abandon" 'to be a woman and to find oneself in such a place, a thousand miles from every human affection, . . . that is the last degree of misery and hopelessness' (300 [240]; 235). At this stage in her back-and-forth travels, Indiana embodies the identity crisis of French society under changing leadership as she ends up dazed, wobbly, homeless, and even hospitalized after digesting the news that the class hierarchy has significantly shifted.

In the end, since place does not in and of itself erase the idiosyncratic traits of individual travelers and because the Napoleonic Code extended to the colonies, Bourbon Island does not become a place of genuine possibility for Indiana until after the death of Delmare. Paris is characterized by despair and hopelessness, whereas Bourbon Island evolves in the novel from a site of memory to a *pays*, or homeland of return. Here Indiana and Ralph live transformed lives of personal liberty and "private happiness" near the Bernica ravine, working for the emancipation of slaves while keeping away from judgmental colonists residing on the island's periphery (342 [274]; 270). If Indiana felt constant weakness at Lagny, she and Ralph develop a more egalitarian relationship where the natural environment becomes the great protector of them both. Signaling her transformation in this landscape, the flower metaphor used to describe her in France is replaced by that of the volcano: "il n'y avait qu'une âme assez large pour répandre le feu sacré qui le vivifiat jusque sur l'âme étroite et glacée du pauvre abandonné" 'there was only one heart large enough to spread the sacred fire which animated it onto the narrow, icy heart of the poor abandoned one' (325 [260]; 256).

Ralph also thinks of France in negative terms during his long island walks:

> De son côté, Ralph était entrainé dans ses promenades vers les endroits sombres et couverts, où le soufflé des vents marins ne pouvait l'atteindre; car la vue de l'Océan lui était devenue antipathique autant que l'idée de le traverser de nouveau. La France n'avait pour lui qu'une place maudite dans la mémoire de son cœur. . . . Que n'eut-il pas donné pour arracher cet horrible souvenir à madame Delmare!   (255 [200])

> As for Ralph, in his walks, he was attracted towards dark, enclosed places where the winds from the sea could not reach him, for the sight of the ocean had become distasteful to him, as well as the idea of crossing it again. In his heart's memory, France had only an accursed place . . . what he would've given to tear its horrible memory away from Madame Delmare!   (195)

Deep in the Bernica ravine, where he enjoys close contact with birds, Ralph is able to abandon his formerly maudlin outlook on life. Sand lists a striking abundance of these birds: "les goëlands, les pétrels, les foulques, et les hirondelles de mer" and "la belle sarcelle de Madagascar, au ventre orangé, au dos d'émaurade" 'the seagulls, the petrels, the coots, and the sea swallows' and 'the Madagascar teal with its orange breast and emerald back.' She even follows the path of a "paille-en-queue, à brins rouges" 'red-winged tropic bird' from Mauritius to Rodrigues Island, tracing its flight around the Mascarenes and offering a lesson in Indian Ocean geography (257 [202]; 196). Like the island's steep, upward-rising cliffs, this proliferation of birds represents Ralph's renewed sense of freedom from societal demands in France and the judgment he describes in his confession to Indiana in chapter 30, when he tells her "on m'envoya vivre sur les rochers comme un pauvre oiseau des grèves" 'my parents sent me to live on the cliffs like a poor bird from the shore' (315 [252]; 248). In this long confession we learn of Ralph's own great sense of alienation and homelessness as a child rejected by both parents, who lived in exile in England and was married against his desire and living unfulfilled with Indiana and Delmare at Lagny. Solitary walking on Bourbon Island provides him with a sense of home that he is unable to find in society. And time spent in nature allows him to imagine a future life with Indiana.

A geographic approach to teaching *Indiana* enables an exploration of how the identities of the novel's central characters are intrinsically bound to place. At first, the island is introduced as a place of colonial enterprise, of exploitation of slaves and land. Sand then reveals through a tour of Indiana's bedroom chambers how the island is a central feature of Indiana's inner geography of longing. Then when Indiana, Delmare, and Ralph return to Bourbon Island she employs its landscape to express the possibilities and impossibilities of human transformation. We ultimately discover that the only two characters with real transformative possibilities, Ralph and Indiana, are shaped by the island's geography, whereas Delmare, who aims to shape it in the interests of colonialism, perishes.

This approach to teaching *Indiana* is particularly productive when it is taught alongside other nineteenth-century texts dealing with travel, displacement, and the self, such as Flora Tristan's *Les pérégrinations d'une paria. Les Meschacébéenes*, by the Louisiana Creole poet François Dominique Rouquette, contains poems written in a North American setting after the poet's return from living in France. Like Tristan, Rouquette provides rich material for examining questions of cultural hybridity, alterity, gender, and the influence of place on selfhood. Alternatively, students may be exposed to francophone journals of travel or other travel writings from the nineteenth century that represent colonized voices. In the end, this discussion of geography and its connections to identity render more complex students' interpretations of *Indiana* and other nineteenth-century texts of travel and exploration, in which place and embedded power structures deeply inform and transform the lives of characters.

Contextual Layers:
Teaching the Historicity of Sand's *Indiana* (1832)

James Smith Allen

Pendant que Raymon travaillait à établir sa fortune,
Indiana approchait des rives de la France. Mais quels
furent sa surprise et son effroi, en débarquant, de voir
le drapeau tricolore flotter sur les murs de Bordeaux!
Une violente agitation bouleversait la ville: le préfet avait
été presque massacré la veille; le peuple se soulevait de
toutes parts; la garnison semblait s'apprêter à une lutte
sanglante, et l'on ignorait encore l'issue de la révolution
de Paris.

—J'arrive trop tard! fut la pensée qui tomba sur madame
Delmare comme un coup de foudre.   (290–91 [232])

While Raymon was working at building up his fortune,
Indiana was approaching the shores of France. But how
surprised and alarmed she was when on disembarking,
she saw the tricolor flag flying on the walls of Bordeaux!
A violent disturbance was disrupting the town; the prefect
had been almost murdered the night before; on all sides
the populace was rising; the garrison seemed to be
preparing for a bloody struggle and the outcome of the
revolution in Paris was still unknown.

"I've come too late!" was the thought that struck
Madame Delmare like a lightning blow.   (226–27)

What did Indiana mean by arriving too late? Had the revolution of 1830 passed
her by? Not really, because the dramatic events of 27–29 July, which overthrew
the Bourbon restoration and empowered the Orleanist monarchy, were still under way nearly everywhere in France. She could easily have joined the crowd
in Bordeaux. Rather, Indiana considered it too late to protect the apparent love
of her life, an ardent supporter of the royal family, from the adverse effects of
the uprising. "Dans toute cette révolution, un seul fait l'intéressait personnel-
lement; dans toute la France, elle ne connaissait qu'un seul homme" 'In all this
revolution, only one item was of personal interest to her; in all France she knew
only one man' (291 [233]; 227), Raymon de Ramière, the object of her long and
dangerous voyage from Île Bourbon to Paris. She had not arrived in time to save
Raymon from history.

Such moments in George Sand's *Indiana*, the first novel to bear her pseudonym, deserve serious attention. They are no accidents. According to literary

historians, the introduction of specific dates and places in an otherwise sentimental romance is deliberate (Salomon, Introduction ix–xv; Bordas, *Éric Bordas* 20–58). Sand knows precisely what she is doing, weaving factual details into
an artfully crafted novel of unrequited love and its terrible consequences; her
compelling *roman à thèse* depicts the legal and social miseries inflicted on an
unhappily married woman enamored of a skirt-chasing cad. With this critical
realism, one in keeping with the novelist's stated intention in her preface of 1832
to show "la volonté aux prises avec la nécessité" 'desire at grips with necessity,'
Sand portrayed woman as a social as well as moral type, "l'être faible chargé
de représenter les *passions* comprimées" 'the weak creature who is given the
task of portraying *passions*, repressed' (40; 7; Sand's emphasis). After all, the
author is merely a mirror (37; 5), an apt metaphor that Sand perhaps borrows
from Stendhal's *Le rouge et le noir*, published in December 1831. No wonder
she calls her book "cette véridique histoire" 'this true story' in its first edition
(Didier, Notes 388n14; my trans.).

Because of Sand's historical achievement in this literary work, I argue, *Indiana* belongs in French history courses every bit as much as it does in surveys of
French literature. The novel is a revealing example in the history of realism, of
course, but it is also a document in the history of ideas, especially of Romanticism at its height in the early nineteenth century; the history of women and
their efforts to achieve equality, though not yet the first-wave feminism of the
fin de siècle; the history of social relations in a slowly industrializing economy,
which was marking new distinctions between classes as indelibly as did 1789;
and the history of colonial dominion outside the French *métropole*, a control
that grew rapidly after the renaming of Réunion in 1806 and again in 1814.
Above all, as the passage on the revolution of 1830 suggests, "cette chronique"
'this chronicle' (Didier, Notes 380n9; my trans.) powerfully imagines the changing landscape of French political life from October 1827, when the novel's action begins, to January 1832, when it concludes. It frames a pivotal point in
the constitutional monarchies (1814–48) with serious implications for stable
political order. For students to reach the core of Sand's historical moment, they
must peel back the contextual layers of this work, enveloped as it is in telling
and verifiable developments.

The most striking context evident in the novel is that of its (not very successful) resistance to Romanticism. Like other self-conscious realists—Sand sent
Honoré de Balzac an inscribed copy of *Indiana* a few days after it went on sale
in the bookstores (*Correspondance* 2: 86)—she was sharply critical of the Romantic movement, whose high point was marked by Alphonse de Lamartine's
admission to the Académie Française in 1830. A plethora of aspiring authors—
established ones, as well—found the deliberate flouting of literary convention
and the outrageous behavior of self-styled Byronic heroes good for sales (Allen
45–64). Sand had to contend with the likes of Victor Hugo's *Notre Dame de
Paris* in 1831, even though she fell victim to many of the same fashionable tendencies in *Indiana*: the pathetic fallacy imputing anthropomorphic feelings to

plants and animals (318, 256–57 [255, 201–02]; 251, 196–97); the pantheistic presence of a higher power underlying a natural religion apart from the Roman Catholic Church (248–50 [195]; 190); the magnetic fluids, first identified by Anton Mesmer, that define relationships in nature and society (227, 336 [176, 269]; 172, 265); the gothic evocation of moods from nocturnal settings far from human habitation (253–54 [198–200]; 193–95); even the invitation for readers to identify with the novel's characters, as two lovers did in their correspondence, signed "Indiana" and "Ralph," after they had read the book (Didier, *Notice* 360). Sand's realism was more asserted than realized, especially in the 1832 edition (Naginski, *George Sand: Writing* 53–56). At heart, the author was a literary romantic.

The intellectual ambivalence inherent in Sand's novelistic practice owes much to her affinities for the utopian Saint-Simonians (Sand, *Œuvres autobiographiques* 2: 195–96; *Story* 945). The trial of Prosper Enfantin and Michel Chevalier for violations of public decency concluded with prison time for both of them just three months after Sand's novel appeared. Their efforts to liberate women from bourgeois convention appealed to the writer's rebellious nature but also and more profoundly to her sympathies for the marginal, the poor, the repressed, "l'apathique désespoir qu'inspire la misère" 'the apathetic despair aroused by utter misery' (292 [233]; 227), which Indiana suffered at her most desperate moment, alone and without money in Paris (298–300 [239–40]; 234–35). Indeed, Sand's protofeminism was fed by Saint-Simonian notions of sexual equality as defined by gender roles rather than by legal rights, however compromised this position seems in retrospect (Offen 20–23). According to French law, for example, married women remained legal minors until 1904. What appears in Sand's novel, however, is less a fully developed ideology of women's rights—that took the women's movement another sixty years to conceive—than an instinct for the misfortunes of the weak, whatever their sex, in the context of new ideas about modern society.[1]

At the source of these ideas was a new social order arising from the long-term effects of what the historian E. J. Hobsbawm aptly termed the "dual revolution" (xv)—that is, the Revolution of 1789 and the Industrial Revolution of the ensuing decades. Beginning with the Bastille's fall, the dramatic dismantlement of the ancien régime moved many privileged aristocrats to emigrate, leaving their extensive properties, and those of the church, for nationalization and sale to new social notables like M. Hubert, Laure de Nangy's father by adoption (287–88 [229–30]; 224). The revolutionary and Napoleonic wars elevated still more disaffected veterans, some 12,000 of them like Indiana's uncle and husband, whose fortunes were made first in the Grande Armée then on half-pay in an industrializing economy (85 [53]; 48). When Delmare's factory fails because a Belgian creditor went bankrupt, his fate exemplifies a new capitalism dependent increasingly on international finance and commerce, one reaching as far away as Île Bourbon in the Indian Ocean, where former fortunes were rebuilt and new elites created. Meanwhile, the land and hand trades remained central to the livelihoods of older sectors of the economy—where Sir Ralph had secured his propertied interests—which left social hierarchies intact and widened the gap between rich and poor. The silk-weaving *canuts* of Lyon, not unlike the revolutionary mob in Bordeaux, revolted briefly against the industrial processes that threatened their way of life just months before Sand began writing her novel. Indiana's abrupt changes in material circumstances thus reflected an economic and social reality that she shared with many others in the period.

The novel's shift in setting from Paris to Île Bourbon in part 3 is revealing of yet another historical reality, that of colonial empire. A French possession since 1638, the island had been administered for a hundred years by the Compagnie des Indes, a royal concession based on trade in coffee and slaves. The Revolution of 1789, however, meant the promise of emancipation—the island established an effective autonomy for more than twelve years (1790–1803) and was renamed Île de la Réunion in 1793—but it failed in the face of opposition by French slave owners, including the likes of Indiana's brutal father (88 [56]; 51), who warmly welcomed the island's continued colonial status under the Napoleonic empire and the Bourbon restoration. From 1817 to 1831, Île Bourbon witnessed a doubling of its slave population, to seventy percent of the inhabitants, as the island's economy transitioned from coffee to sugar cane production (Combeau et al. 26–28, 152). Consequently, when Indiana and her tragic double, Noun, are described as Creoles "vivant au milieu des esclaves" 'living surrounded by slaves' (89 [56]; 51), the term was more than literary metaphor. It described the legal subjugation of a substantial colonial population, more than 70,000 people, in 1830.

The political implications of France's historical milieu are the most obvious in the novel (Bertier de Sauvigny 404–59). In chapter 14, Sand details her version of restoration politics according to three partisans: Raymon de Ramière, the legitimist defender of the restoration status quo; Colonel Delmare, the summarily pensioned Bonapartist officer in quest of France's former imperial glory; and Sir Rodolphe Brown, the British republican who endorses a vague, egalitarian utopia, a political sympathy instinctively shared by Indiana (174 [131–32]; 124–25). This selection, however, hardly does justice to all polemics in the period. In chapter 10, Sand also alludes to divisions between the *ultras*, "plus royaliste que le roi" 'more royalist than the king,' Charles X, on the one hand, and the *modérés*, who, like the *doctrinaires* led by Pierre Paul Royer-Collard in the Chambre des Députés, advocated political accommodation between propertied elites, on the other (128–29 [91–92]; 84–85). The *modérés* included the liberals like Louis-Philippe d'Orléans, the king of the French after 1830. Further to the left of Sir Ralph's republican dream were the utopian socialists like Pierre Leroux, later Sand's intellectual mentor, who sought to create a religion of humanity, and the revolutionary republicans like Auguste Blanqui, leader of the Société des Amis du Peuple, who was tried and convicted of insurrection in January 1832. As the narrator acerbically puts it, "on enferme les mêmes idées sous le nom de *jésuite*, de *royaliste*, de *révolutionnaire* et de *juste-milieu*" 'they clothe the same ideas with the names of *Jesuit, royalist, revolutionary*, and *happy man*' in a political map troubled by uprisings on all sides in 1832 (171 [129]; 121; Sand's emphases), from the supporters of the reactionary Duchess of Berry in the Vendée to those of the republican general Jean Maximilien Lamarque in Paris.

How nice it would be if historical reality were so tidy. Its varied layers of significance are so easily distinguished without reference to the tensions and conflicts within and between them. Among *Indiana's* tendencies described here, the blatant contradictions and discontinuities are also worth close study. Why, for example, do Indiana and Ralph not commit suicide together in good Romantic fashion? If Ralph is so rich—enough to sustain Delmare's bankruptcy and still buy the freedom of aged and infirmed slaves—why is he not an industrialist like Delmare and Hubert? How does the ardent Bonapartist Delmare tolerate the constant presence of the cynical legitimist Raymon and the dreamy republican Sir Ralph? The blurring of pat categories in Sand's novel is equally apparent in (and appropriate to) a literary work observing other conventions, such as the novel's characters, plot, and settings, which suggest more than historical structures, processes, and discourses. The imbrications of literature and history are what make Sand's text—initially printed in only 750 copies—of interest to literary scholars as well as to historians (Didier, Notice 357). On further examination, the novel develops its own historicity, which all students need to ponder, whatever their course of study. As Sand says in her *Histoire de ma vie*, "tout concourt à l'histoire, *tout est histoire*, même les romans" 'Everything converges in history, *everything is history*, even novels' (*Œuvres autobiographiques* 2: 78; Story 119; Sand's emphasis).

Delmare's personal trajectory, not just his family and social connections, bear witness to this truism. A self-made man, despite the timely assistance of Sir Ralph and his wife's aunt, Madame de Carvajal, the colonel seems to be based on Sand's disenchanting husband, Casimir Dudevant, another proud imperial veteran risen from the ranks and on half-pay during the restoration. But Sand has complicated this stereotypical figure hell-bent on dominating his wife and berating everyone who failed to recognize the glory and sacrifice of Napoléon's loyal army. Delmare is also a sincere liberal, whose faith in law and property make him much more akin to Benjamin Constant, the constitutional theorist par excellence during the empire and the restoration, than he is to Maréchal Michel Ney, the Bonapartist *à outrance* during the Hundred Days: "Toute sa conscience, c'était la loi; toute sa morale, c'était son droit" 'His only conscience was the law; his only morality was his right' (134 [96]; 89), in keeping with Napoléon's legal codifications. Moreover, Delmare is a determined industrialist, who understands well the mercurial operations of the market in his manifest success, guarding the secrets of his factory and, in his inadvertent failure, making good on his many debts before leaving for Île Bourbon. Clearly, the novel portrays Delmare as more than a marital thug; he represents the political compromises of a shrewd businessman.

Indiana's plot makes its historicity still more textual. For instance, Raymon's serial seductions of Noun, Indiana, and then Laure, which drive the novel's action nearly to the end, put him at odds with more than his politics. Like Aurélien de Sèze, on whom he is in part based, he must justify to himself the social compromise of paying court to all three women, each of whom marks a potential derogation of his aristocratic status. Noun is a servant, Indiana a bourgeoise, and Laure an orphan. Whenever Raymon skirts social as well as amorous disaster, he resorts to his mother, whose aristocratic credentials serve him better than his own. "Et puis Raymon était aussi embarrassé pour le choix d'une femme que pour celui d'une couleur politique" 'And then Raymon found it as difficult to choose a wife as to choose a political colour' (263 [208]; 202). Madame de Ramière has more scruples: "Mais soyez prudent, Raymon, et ne hasardez point le repos de votre vie entière pour une chimère d'ambition" 'But be prudent, Raymon, and don't risk the peace of your whole life for an ambitious day-dream' (265 [209]; 203). Although Raymon only hazards the thought of marrying a rich woman of lower social standing, his mother on her deathbed gives him permission to do so. In the end he prefers his choice of Laure de Nangy, who loves him too little, to his mother's choice of Madame Delmare, who loves him too much. The novel's action suggests that this was the social future of all French nobility after the July revolution.

The culminating and most complicated feature of Sand's novel, critics have long thought, is its ending on Île Bourbon (Salomon, Introduction xlvii–lii). It stands in sharp contrast to the miseries of Paris, from which Indiana and Sir Ralph escape to embrace the liberation of suicide in the cascading waters of their childhood idyll. Instead of leaping to their death at the Bernica ravine, they live to enjoy the natural harmony and beauty of a world far from the moral degradation of civilization, "dans un endroit extrêmement sauvage" 'in an extremely wild spot' (333 [267]; 263). Halfway between Saint Paul and La Saline, surrounded by striking mountains and streams, exotic birds and plants of every sort, Indiana and Sir Ralph revel in an idealized setting first celebrated by Jean-Jacques Rousseau and Jacques-Henri Bernardin de Saint-Pierre (Sand, *Correspondance* 2: 47) but also by the comte de Buffon, François-René de Chateaubriand, and Jules Néraud, the naturalist whose journal provided Sand her vicarious experience with Île Bourbon (Didier, Notice 367). In one stroke, Sand counters her novel's resort to realism, its attack on unjust laws and hypocritical society, its advocacy of an egalitarian republic, and its insistence on women's right to agency in love. By robbing Indiana of her independent voice in a timeless oasis—"notre chaumière indienne" 'our Indian cottage' (344 [275]; 271)—the author retreats from history entirely.

The feminist critic Naomi Schor has resolved this problem as well as anyone. "Idealism for Sand," she writes, "is finally the only alternative representational mode available to those who do not enjoy the privileges of subjecthood in the real" (*George Sand* 54). Sand's erasure of history is, in fact, an acknowledgment of its power to subjugate the powerless, whose voices are nearly always unheard in the master narrative, one conceived and written by white, upper-class men. Such literary elites praised Sand's novel when it first appeared in part because its accurate portrayal of social ills accorded well with their own perception of them. Omitted from both the novel and the reviews, however, were the deprivations of more than a hapless Indiana. Not one critic mentioned the cholera epidemic whose outbreak two months earlier had already killed thousands of impoverished Parisians, 18,500 altogether by October 1832. Perhaps the cholera had been too closely linked to the failure of the 1830 revolution to merit much more attention in the novels of bourgeois manners and mores, including Sand's (Kudlick 31–64). If the author had an uneasy relationship with the innermost layer of her historical context, she was not alone. This distance was not Sand's intention. As she reflected later on her work, "ce moment où j'ouvrais les yeux était solennel dans l'histoire" 'I opened my eyes at a solemn moment in history' (Sand, *Œuvres autobiographiques* 2: 195; Story 945). Little different from Indiana in the midst of a revolution, Sand was surprised but not dismayed by the layers of historical significance in her novel. It is not too late for us to recognize them, too.

NOTE

[1] According to Steven C. Hause and other historians, the modern notion of feminism as the advocacy of women's equal rights under the law, including suffrage, did not prevail in the women's movement until the twentieth century (Hause and Kenney 28–70).

Owning People: Human Property in *Indiana*

Peter Dayan

Of the many ideological struggles that make up the rich dynamics of *Indiana*, perhaps the easiest for our students to identify (because they have often encountered it before in literary study) is the conflict between Indiana's and her husband's views of the proper relationship between the sexes. The least visible of these struggles, for our students, tends to be one that particularly captured the attention of Sand's contemporaries: whether it is possible for true love to end in a happy relationship. Our students do not see this as a question at all. For them, true love is by definition a love that should lead to a happy relationship. That, however, was by no means the general view in the high Romantic era in which Sand was writing. The great novels of the time written by men (at least, so we see it now) describe magnificent love that inevitably ends in death, disaster, or disappointment. It is in its resolutely optimistic ending that *Indiana* seemed most to scorn this tradition and to refuse realism in favor of idealism.[1] The aim of this essay is to show how students can come to understand Sand's unique and fascinating answer to the question of whether true love can end well in this world, through a careful appreciation of power relations between the sexes in the novel; and the bridge between the two issues is the concept of human beings as property.

One sentence that students should certainly pick up on if they are asked to work on the relationship between the sexes as it appears in the early part of the novel is this description of Colonel Delmare: "excellent maître devant qui tout tremblait, femme, serviteurs, chevaux et chiens" 'an excellent master who made everyone tremble, wife, servants, horses, and dogs' (49 [19]; 15). What they will note is how the list places his wife in the same series as his horses, dogs, and servants, doubtless in contrast with their expectations. They may think that a hierarchical relationship properly pertains between an "excellent maître" and his servants or dogs, whereas between a man and his wife, there should be equality. I would, at this point, put two questions to them.

First: whose point of view does this sentence appear to express? I would hope that their answer to this would recognize the complexity of the narratorial voice here. On the one hand, the voice is indeed, formally, the narrator's. On the other hand, it certainly expresses the point of view of Delmare, for whom an "excellent maître" is by definition one whom wife, servants, and dogs all obey, and it is difficult not to feel that the way the sentence is organized implies some irony. The narrator does not unproblematically take Delmare's side, and the proximity of other points of view (none of the other main characters in the novel, after all, share Delmare's definition of the "excellent maître") invites us to view this affirmation with some critical distance.

My second question would concern the legitimacy of the hierarchy that this sentence sets up. This is the second occurrence of the word "maître" in the sentence; the first comes earlier, in the expression "maître de la maison" 'master of the house.' Delmare, being the legal proprietor of his house, is doubtless legitimately its master. He is also the legitimate proprietor of his horses and dogs and therefore their master. Does the same apply to his servants? Are they his property? Legally speaking, the answer is no. He is their master, but he is not their owner. They owe him obedience, but he cannot buy and sell them. The same applies to his wife. As we soon find out, Indiana does not agree that her husband should be her master; presumably the modern reader sides with Indiana here. But should he be the master of his dogs and horses? And should he be the master of his servants? These questions turn out to be more pertinent and more difficult than one might have imagined—and more difficult to separate from the question of the relationship between husband and wife. The status of master, whether it be of wife, animals, servants, or slaves, determines a particular kind of proprietorial attitude to the other. It is essential for today's students to understand that this proprietorial attitude is not simply to be seen as immoral, as wrong, as inadmissible, in the ideological context of the time—on the contrary. Delmare is never presented by the narrative voice as simply a bad man. In fact, he has high moral principles, which are carefully contextualized in the novel: they are those of the Napoleonic era, of which Delmare is the product; an era of glory, grandeur, and imperialism, in which hierarchical power relations are the cornerstone of society. Delmare's principles are opposed to another set, which are those of Indiana and, as we eventually discover, Ralph. This latter set refuses such power relations. The principles of Ralph and Indiana, in the novel, are consistently presented as idealistic, in the sense that they are politically unrealistic: they cannot form the basis of a conceivable social organization in France. This presentation of egalitarianism as unrealistic is common to most of the poets and novelists of the period. They generally agree that without masters, without the obedience of animals, servants, and wives, society cannot function, and the Revolution proved this if it proved nothing else. Where *Indiana* stands out from the realist mainstream is in the way it creates an ideal space in which masters do not enforce obedience. And in the creation of that space, a particular kind of power relation plays a critical role: slavery.

Slavery in the French colonies was abolished under the Revolution, along with so many other long-standing legal frameworks subordinating social inferiors to social superiors; from 1794 to 1802 there was no legal slavery on French-owned soil. In 1802–03, however, Delmare's hero Napoléon reestablished slavery in the colonies, and it remained in place until abolished, this time definitively, by the Second Republic in 1848—a decision that Sand supported. When *Indiana* was published, then, in 1832, under the July Monarchy, the history of the abolition and reinstatement of slavery seemed to confirm what most people thought: slavery was an institution that was natural in French society as long as it was governed by a king or emperor; only the republic had thought it could do without slavery, and history had proved this republican notion hopelessly idealistic, unworkable in the real world. Generally received wisdom in 1830 was that if the republic installed by the Revolution had lasted for such a short time (only twelve years), this was because the French nation could not function without the unquestioned authority of a monarch, backed by the spiritual authority of the church, and that unquestioned authority must be reflected, further down the social scale, in the subordination of wives to husbands, of servants to masters, and of slaves to slave owners.

This is precisely the argument at the heart of Raymon's defense of monarchism, in the debate that forms the political centerpiece of the novel:

> Raymon soutenait sa doctrine de monarchie héréditaire, aimant mieux, disait-il, supporter les abus, les préjugés et les injustices que de voir relever les échafauds et couler le sang innocent . . . Raymon . . . démontrait admirablement qu'un système plus large de franchises menait infailliblement aux excès de 93, et que la nation n'était pas mûre pour la liberté, qui n'était pas la licence.   (167–68 [124–25])

> Raymon supported his doctrine of hereditary monarchy, preferring, he said, to put up with abuses, prejudices, and injustices rather than to see scaffolds built again and innocent blood flow . . . Raymon proved admirably that a more broadly based franchise would infallibly lead to the excesses of 1793, and that the nation was not yet mature enough for liberty, which was not the same as licence.   (117–18)

For Raymon, equality may seem an admirable thing, but it must be subordinated to the need to preserve order in the state; otherwise, the result will be a new Terror. That order is synonymous with an established hereditary hierarchy. It requires an unquestioning acceptance of the hierarchical power relations established by law more generally, and no one is more unquestioning in his acceptance of that hierarchy than Delmare. His morality is based on the principle "Chacun chez soi"—in other words: each man must be master in his own home (132 [95]).[2] He must respect his equals and betters, but he is lord and master in the domain that the law assigns to him: "Il peut battre sa femme, maltraiter ses gens, ruiner ses enfants, cela ne regarde personne" 'He might beat his wife, illtreat his servants, ruin his children, that's no one else's business' (132 [95]; 87). That, at least, is Delmare's principle, and Indiana is keenly aware of it from the beginning. To her, it means that he considers himself her master, and this condition of subjection to a master is, to her, slavery. She does not consider the legal nuances that I have mentioned, the fact that slaves can be sold and, indeed, emancipated, whereas a wife cannot; all she sees is that another person has the right to oblige her by force to do his bidding, and this she finds intolerable. The word "esclavage" is used more than once by the narrator to describe Indiana's sense of her condition. Her revulsion at this condition quickly turns into revulsion against her husband, which renders her unable to see (or take advantage of) his virtues:

[L]'esclavage avait engendré dans ce cœur de femme une sorte d'aversion vertueuse et muette qui n'était pas toujours juste. Madame Delmare doutait trop du cœur de son mari; il n'était que dur, et elle le jugeait cruel.
(135 [97])

[S]lavery had undoubtedly made her feel a kind of dumb, virtuous aversion to him which was not always fair. Madame Delmare had too many doubts about her husband's heart; he was only hard and she thought he was cruel. (89)

On two occasions in the novel, Delmare uses force against his wife. On both occasions, it is in defense of what society would have recognized as his right as a husband; his right, particularly, not to be betrayed by his wife, who twice plots to leave him for Raymon. In doing so, she is rejecting simultaneously her husband (as an individual) and the institution of marriage as it existed at the time. She has, of course, no plans to divorce Delmare and marry Raymon, as that was legally impossible in restoration France. In planning to leave her husband, Indiana is not seeking a different status within society but rather defying the entire legal framework that defined family relations at the time. Her rebellions are therefore political acts. And the principle that she enunciates to justify them also hinges on the word "maître."

After her first abortive attempt to leave Delmare for Raymon, when Raymon has rejected her and she has returned to her husband's house, Delmare asks her where she has been. She refuses to say. He attempts to show who is master by squeezing her hand between his thumb and forefinger. This action, though it causes Indiana no injury, is a turning point in the novel. It is interpreted by all three persons present—Indiana, Delmare, and Ralph—simultaneously as Delmare's assertion of the fundamental principle that a wife must obey her husband and that he has the right to force her to do so and as an irrefutable demonstration that this principle is incompatible with their own sense of what is right and wrong. Ralph reacts by physically removing Delmare's hand from his wife's; which, under the traditional code of masculine honor, would certainly have given Delmare the right to strike Ralph or to challenge him to a duel. But Delmare does not: "Delmare eut envie de se jeter sur lui; mais il sentit qu'il avait tort, et il ne craignait rien tant au monde que de rougir de lui-même" 'Delmare wanted to go at him, but he felt he was in the wrong and he feared nothing in the world so much as being ashamed of himself' (233 [181]; 177).

Why, exactly, does Delmare feel he is in the wrong here? Has he not been behaving precisely in accordance with his own expressed principles? Does a husband not have both the legal and the moral right to force his wife to obey him? The answer is that Delmare, the former Napoleonic soldier who has lived on into the Romantic era, finds himself caught between two value systems. On the one hand, in principle he believes in hierarchy, in human property, and in the use of force to maintain order. On the other hand, he has not been able to help absorbing one of the fundamental values of his time, which is that a marriage should be based on love and that love cannot be enforced. His Napoleonic principles tell him he must discipline his wife; the romantic morality of his time tells him it is wrong to do so. The narrator's constant sympathy for Delmare is an acknowledgment of the difficulty of his position.

Indiana's moral posture is far less complicated. She has already made it clear that, for her, the Napoleonic Code that subjects wife to husband has no moral status whatever. Like the institution of slavery, it is based on the amoral principle that "might is right":

> Je sais que je suis l'esclave et vous le seigneur. La loi de ce pays vous a fait mon maître. Vous pouvez lier mon corps, garroter mes mains, gouverner mes actions. Vous avez le droit du plus fort, et la société vous le confirme; mais sur ma volonté, monsieur, vous ne pouvez rien, Dieu seul peut la courber et la réduire.   (232 [180])

> I know I'm the slave and you're the lord. The law of the land has made you my master. You can tie up my body, bind my hands, control my actions. You have the right of the stronger, and society confirms you in it. But over my will, Monsieur, you have no power. God alone can bend and subdue it.   (176)

After his attempt to force her to tell him where she has been, she continues:

> Ne pas régner sur la volonté d'une femme, c'est exercer un empire dérisoire. J'ai passé quelques heures hors de votre domination; j'ai été respirer l'air de la liberté pour vous montrer que vous n'êtes pas moralement mon maître et que je ne dépends que de moi sur la terre.   (233 [181])

> If you don't control a woman's will, your power over her is a mockery. I spent several hours beyond your power. I went to breathe the air of liberty, to show you that morally you're not my master and that I depend only on myself on the earth.   (177)

Two key words appear in both these passages: "maître" and "volonté." Delmare is master according to the Napoleonic Code. But that code and his mastery cannot control Indiana's will. Where the will is not engaged, love cannot flourish; the superior physical and legal power of the man gives him no advantage in this regard.

Raymon de Ramière knows this as well as Indiana. Unlike Delmare, he understands the romantic code of love and the importance of free will. The love he wants from Indiana is not that of a wife subject to her husband; it is that of a woman who gives herself. At another of the novel's turning points, Raymon, having been invited into Indiana's bedroom, and after a series of highly emotional events that I have not the space to investigate here, begins to embrace her. She, not wanting to go further, says:

> – Vous seriez donc capable d'employer la force avec moi?
> Raymon s'arrêta, frappé de cette résistance morale qui survivait à la résistance physique. Il la poussa vivement.
> – Jamais! s'écria-t-il; plutôt mourir que de ne pas te tenir de toi seule!
> (195 [148–49])

> "So you'd be capable of using force with me!"
> Raymon paused, struck by this moral resistance which outlasted her physical resistance. He quickly pushed her away.
> "Never!" he cried. "I'd rather die than have you against your will." (143)

The opposition between the physical and the moral is as clear here as it is when Indiana is faced with her husband. Raymon, however, unlike Delmare, is a man of his time, not a relic of the Napoleonic era. He knows that whatever the law may say, in love it is the will that counts, not physical domination, and the true joy of love comes only when both the man and the woman give themselves freely, under no physical constraint. If Raymon does not deserve Indiana and ends up trapped in an unhappy marriage, it is not because he does not understand what love is. It is because he is unwilling himself to give himself entirely to love. He is too attached to the monarchist society in which he lives and to the privileges that it bestows on him. Just as Indiana, in rejecting her husband, is rejecting not only an individual man but an entire social system, so Raymon, to deserve and accept Indiana's love, would have to abandon the society in which he feels so at home. This he will not do, so he rejects her and suffers the consequences.

The unfortunate Delmare, meanwhile, has demonstrated the literal truth of Raymon's maxim that it would be better to die than to use force against Indiana. On discovering her correspondence with Raymon (together with her journal of her love for him), in a jealous fury he knocks her down and kicks her. She soon recovers physically from this, but he never does. The "congestion sanguine" 'apoplexy' (270 [213]; 208) triggered in him by his rage and shame rapidly leads to his miserable death.

With Delmare dead and Raymon married to another woman, Indiana is left with only one man in her life: Ralph. He has no respect whatsoever either for the Napoleonic principles that led Delmare to use force against his wife or for the restoration morality that led Raymon to promise a love that he was unwilling to live out. Ralph the idealist republican has no interest in living by the rules of society. He spirits Indiana away to the "désert" of Bernica, where they live together, rejecting all three of the codes of human property that the novel has evoked. They spend their money, Ralph says, on freeing poor infirm slaves. Their servants are treated not as inferiors, subject to their masters, but as friends. And Indiana and Ralph live together unmarried. This triple refusal of the social order makes them social outcasts, but this is a status they, unlike Raymon, are happy to accept.

It may be remembered that at the very start of the novel, Delmare was described as the master not only of his wife and servants but also of his horses and dogs. The treatment of domestic animals forms a muted counterpoint to that of women and servants in *Indiana*. We learn in the first chapter that Delmare has killed his wife's spaniel. He makes it clear that he considers he had the right to do this; she makes it equally clear that for her it was an abominable act, symbolizing the absolute incompatibility between their worldviews and value systems. Toward the end of the novel, Indiana's other dog, Ophelia, is killed by the sailors who are to take her back to France; again, Indiana takes this as a sign that they belong to a world whose values she does not share. As the novel's conclusion describes Ralph and Indiana's ideal life in Bernica, there is no mention of any domestic animals, whether horses or dogs. And what of the relationship between human beings and wild animals? One of the central scenes of the novel (occupying chapters 13 and 14) is a boar hunt, in which Indiana participates with an enthusiasm that Raymon finds disquieting; Ralph, too, loves the chase. However, in the depiction of their new life in Bernica, there is no mention of what used to be their shared passion for hunting. Indiana and Ralph are not seen to take part in any acts that might seem to imply dominion over animals. Thus is another traditional hierarchy quietly abolished for their life in paradise.

I think that our students will readily appreciate the fundamental contrast between the values of Delmare and Raymon on the one hand and those of Ralph and Indiana on the other. They will interpret it as an opposition between an old order, imperialist or monarchist, in which love and happiness do not go together because hierarchical relations obstruct it, and a new republican order, not yet realized in Sand's time but to which the author looks forward, in which a new equality between the sexes and between social classes will make the realization of true love possible. Morally, the key to this new order would be the abolition of slavery, since a society that admits slavery must believe in human property, in the right of some to be masters of others. That interpretation would not be entirely false. However, it misses an essential point.

The relationship between Indiana and Ralph in Bernica is by no means an equal one. Ralph alone speaks to describe it to the narrator; Indiana is almost silent in the final scenes. But Indiana's silence is not only (though it is also) a mark of Ralph's possessive masculinity, contrasted with her submissive femininity. It is at the same time the expression of her superiority in a new hierarchy of the ideal.

What Ralph says is not that they have found a love that would require a different kind of society to be realized in public. Rather, it is that they have found a kind of love that cannot, in any circumstances, be expressed in public, a love that can only exist out of the reach of words:

Je ne vous parle pas de mon bonheur . . . ; s'il est des douleurs qui ne se
trahissent jamais et qui enveloppent l'âme comme un linceul, il est aussi
des joies qui restent ensevelies dans le cœur d'un homme parce qu'une
voix de la terre ne saurait les dire.   (341 [273–74])

I won't talk to you of my happiness. If there are sorrows which are never
revealed and which envelop the soul like a shroud, there are also joys
which remain buried in man's heart because an earthly voice cannot express them.   (269)

Happiness in love is to be imagined not as a result of changing society but by
leaving altogether the earthly realm that is governed by words. Ralph, in the
very act of talking around that of which he cannot speak, situates himself further from that happiness than Indiana, whose silence is the ultimate eloquence.
The novel began with a silent Indiana, flanked by a silent Ralph and a silent
Delmare, but that was the silence of boredom, generated by a mute rebellion
against the dynamics of human property backed by force. It ends with a silent
Indiana flanked by a vocal Ralph; now, her silence is one of happiness, generated by the absence of human property backed by force. Her only belonging
now is the result of a gift of herself made freely. If one looks at it thus, love in
Indiana appears more similar than one might expect to love in other great novels of the time, whether by Stendhal, Gustave Flaubert, or Honoré de Balzac or,
more generally, in the broad Romantic tradition, to which both the realist and
the idealist novel belong. Sand, like the masculine writers whom we now call
realist, steadily builds, over several hundred pages, a space that escapes words.
Only in that space can love be what it must be.

Languages are created by societies. Societies also, inevitably, create hierarchies, whose strength depends on various forms of human property, enshrined
in law and backed up by force—the extreme and paradigmatic form of human
property being slavery. Love depends on the refusal of such property through
an unforced and unenforceable gift of the self that cannot be regulated by society and cannot be expressed in any language. The writer's task is not to describe such love but to evoke a realm in which, beyond the possession of words
and beyond any words of possession, it might be imagined. This is, I think, a
fundamental principle underlying much of French literature—and not only in
the nineteenth century. However, it is one that is not obvious to students today.
Indiana is beautifully suited to leading them toward an appreciation of that
principle. First, I would set them the task of identifying the different points of
view of the various characters in the novel concerning the proper and admis-
sible use of force, in relationships between men, between men and women,
and between human beings and animals. Then I would ask them to identify the
advantages and disadvantages of each of these views and how the characters
justify them; it would be important at this stage not simply to allow the opinion
to prevail that Indiana is right and Delmare is wrong. Finally, I would ask why

it is in a "désert," on an island in the Indian Ocean, far from society, in isolation and apparent silence, under the protection of her male cousin, that Indiana's ideals seem to find their only home.

NOTES

[1] Schor's unforgettable and brilliant *George Sand and Idealism* sets out the contrast between the two traditions and presents *Indiana*, precisely, as potentially exhibiting, depending on the point of view of the reader, traits of both (51–53).

[2] Raphael's translation, "Everyone for himself" (87), misses this crucial meaning.

Reading Race in *Indiana*

Doris Kadish

This essay proposes a model for how students can be encouraged to read against the grain of literary texts, both primary and secondary, in search of the "non-dit" 'unsaid,' the deep-seated issues that authors are unable or unwilling to confront directly. The case in point is race in George Sand's *Indiana*. I argue that Sand, like other members of the white middle or upper class of her time, sought to avoid addressing the potential threat to society posed by others. At the same time, however, I discover a strong, albeit implicit, identification with and appeal on behalf of persons of color in Sand's novel. Students can learn from Sand's example that the interpretation of literature, and especially that of works from France's colonial past, is not a simple, straightforward process. As Anne Mc-Clintock insightfully reminds us, resistance to the imperial power that existed in Sand's time is often expressed in "contradictory and conflictual ways" (5). It is enlightening for students to see the workings of such contradictions and conflicts in *Indiana*. This essay focuses first on the erasure of race in the novel and its duplication in works of literary criticism in the 1970s and 1980s. Shifting gears, I then propose another reading of the novel aimed at ferreting out the resistance against racial oppression in *Indiana*. In this reading, it is possible to draw on the insights of more recent critics who directly address issues of race in *Indiana*. Their work provides another useful lesson for students: that literary criticism evolves and that what remained a "non-dit" at one time becomes grist for the critical mill in another.

The erasure of explicit references to race in *Indiana* rests in part on the confusing descriptions of both Indiana and Noun as "créole."[1] Indiana, the wife of the prototypical colonialist Colonel Delmare (literally, "of the sea"), is described as a "créole" in what would seem to be the sense of a white colonial ("Le blanc mat de son collier, celui de sa robe de crêpe et de ses épaules nues, se confondaient à quelque distance" 'The dull white of her necklace, of her crêpe dress, and of her bare shoulders, blended together from a distance' [80 (48); 43].) "Créole" also applies to Indiana's servant, Noun—"M. de Ramière était amoureux de la jeune créole aux yeux noirs" 'M. de Ramière was in love with the young creole with black eyes' (73 [40]; 36; trans. modified)—who appears for the most part in the text to be of mixed race. Her hair is referred to as being "d'un noir nègre" 'negro black' (192 [146]; 140; trans. modified), and her arms as "frais et bruns" 'young, brown' (104 [70]; 64). Aside from the curious use of "créole" and a sprinkling of hints about color, however, race hardly ever plays an explicit role in *Indiana*. Rarely is it made clear that it affects the main characters personally, despite the fact that the novel occurs at a historical moment when racial tensions and slavery were urgent and unresolved social issues in the French colonies and despite the fact that Noun is a servant. And yet I have found that most readers, both French and American, when asked their impression of Noun's color, will respond that she is not white; curiously, moreover, she appears as a person of mixed race in the illustration in the Garnier edition of the novel, although there is no acknowledgment in the introduction to that edition that race is an issue in either the illustration or the novel. The refusal in *Indiana* to acknowledge differences of color directly reveals an unwillingness in Sand's society, if not ours still today, to recognize the actual conditions in which persons of color live. Thus Noun's and Indiana's tragic love stories often seem to be merely the tales of any two Frenchwomen and not specifically those of two women from the colonies, where issues of race are to the forefront.

Indiana refuses in particular to acknowledge the sexual dichotomy established in colonial society between women of color and their white mistresses. The following description of Noun and Indian is representative: "Noun, grande, forte, brillante de santé, vive, alerte, et pleine de sang créole ardent et passionné, effaçait de beaucoup, par sa beauté resplendissante, la beauté pâle et frêle de madame Delmare" 'Tall, big, sparkling with health, lively, brisk, and overflowing with the full-blooded ardor and passion of a creole, Noun had a resplendent beauty which eclipsed Madame Delmare's pale, delicate beauty' (60 [29]; 25; trans. modified). To Indiana is granted the delicacy and light color of the mistress. To her servant is reserved animal-like strength and lustiness implying sexual availability typically associated by colonialists with black women slaves. Elsewhere that same sensuality reappears, as when Raymon is making love to Noun and thinking about the sexual opposition between her and her mistress:

> C'était Indiana qu'il voyait dans le nuage du punch que la main de Noun venait d'allumer; c'était elle qui l'appelait et qui lui souriait derrière ces blancs rideaux de mousseline; ce fut elle encore qu'il rêva sur cette

couche modeste et sans tâche, lorsque, succombant sous l'amour et le vin
il y entraîna sa créole échevelée.   (105 [70–71])

It was Indiana he saw in the vapors of the punch than Noun had just set
alight. It was she who was summoning him and smiling at him behind the
white muslin curtains, and it was again Indiana that he dreamed of on that
modest, immaculate bed when, succumbing to love and wine, he led his
dishevelled creole there.   (64–65; trans. modified)

Raymon blames the physicality of his "créole échevelée" 'dishevelled creole'
for his own abandon and debauchery ("succombant sous l'amour et le vin" 'succumbing to love and wine'); he interprets her seductiveness as solicitation ("le
nuage du punch que la main de Noun venait d'allumer" 'the vapors of the punch
than Noun had just set alight'; "c'était elle qui l'appelait" 'It was she who was
summoning him'). He further denigrates her, speaking of "l'ardeur insensée qui
consume les flancs de cette créole lascive" 'the mad ardor which inflames the
flanks of that lascivious creole' (106 [72]; 66; trans. modified).
    Yet paradoxically Sand also lumps the two women together to a certain ex-
tent and treats them both as inferior, along with all those who live in the colonies. The sexualization and diminution of women of color thus extends to all
"créoles," playing on the ambiguous multiracial sense of that term. In the following passage, for example, Raymon subjects Indiana to the same sexualization
as her servant:

[E]n reconduisant madame de Carvajal et madame Delmare à leur
voiture, il réussit à porter la petite main d'Indiana à ses lèvres. Jamais
baiser d'homme furtif et dévorant n'avait effleuré les doigts de cette
femme, quoiqu'elle fût née sous un climat de feu et qu'elle eût dix-neuf
ans; dix-neuf ans de l'Ile de Bourbon, qui équivalent à vingt-cinq ans de
notre pays.   (84 [51–52])

[A]s he escorted madame de Carvajal and madame Delmare to their carriage, he managed to raise Indiana's little hand to his lips. Never before
had a man's furtive, passionate kiss touched her fingers, even though she
was born in a burning-hot climate and was nineteen years old; and nineteen years old in Bourbon Island is the equivalent of twenty-five in our
country.   (46–47)

Although it is Indiana's sexual purity that is overtly proclaimed in this passage,
its covert message is her inherent propensity to the same excessive passion,
the same "lasciviousness," as Noun. The novel similarly emphasizes that both
women have the same luxurious, erotic dark hair: "S'il baisait ses cheveux noirs,
il croyait baiser les cheveux noirs d'Indiana" 'When he kissed her black hair, he
believed he was kissing Indiana's black hair' (104 [70]; 64).

The refusal to explicitly address racial issues is especially salient in the novel's implicitly negative message about mixed marriage and children of mixed race. When Noun, the servant, becomes pregnant by Raymon, the European aristocrat, Noun's death provides a solution to the problem of racial mixture. It is not surprising that Sand would have eschewed the radical solution to racial problems advocated at the time by others such as Henri Grégoire and Sophie Doin.[2] Sand states in the preface to the 1842 edition of *Indiana* that her goal was to find moderate solutions to social problems: "le moyen de concilier le bonheur et la dignité des individus opprimés par cette même société, sans modifier la société elle-même" 'how to reconcile the happiness and dignity of individuals oppressed by that same society without modifying society itself' (44; 11). Michèle Hirsch observes along similar lines that the political revolt depicted in the novel at the moment of Indiana's arrival in Bordeaux in 1830 seems to be dismissed as illegitimate in *Indiana* (125).

Sand's erasure of race lived on among certain of her critics up to the 1990s. Kathryn Crecelius provides a fascinating in-depth study of black and white imagery in *Indiana* (63–70), but astoundingly without ever acknowledging the possible relevance of that imagery for the issue of race. And in another important study, Leslie Rabine dwells on Noun as a lower-class woman but without looking as carefully at the issue of race as she does at that of class. Rabine states, for example, that "Sand makes the pure and desirable woman a white bourgeoise while the sensual and unattractive woman is a lower class Creole" ("George Sand" 13). The claim that Noun is unattractive is especially surprising since Sand stresses her beauty consistently in the novel. It is also surprising to find that Rabine treats Noun, whom Sand portrays as a respectable servant from the colonies, as a lower-class prostitute: "[T]he use of Noun in the novel demonstrates how the prostitution of lower class women was necessary to preserve the chastity of bourgeoise women. . . . Finally, in the novel, the lower class woman must be sacrificed to maintain the innocence of the bourgeoise woman and the stability of the social order" (14).

Shifting gears, I wish to turn now to my proposed alternative reading of *Indiana*, one that emphasizes resistance. In this reading I will attempt to discern elements of the "non-dit" 'unsaid' that may have puzzled or escaped the attention of the reader and of students of *Indiana*. The most obvious occurs in the title of the novel, which gives the ostensibly white heroine a name connoting both the nonwhite race of Indians and the novel's setting in the Indian Ocean. *Indiana* thus hints from the outset that the gap between whites and persons of color is not absolute and that the colonists' desire to maintain their racial superiority rests on less than solid ground.

Another salient aspect of the resistant side of *Indiana* is Sand's empathetic attitude toward the sexual oppression of the mistress and her servant and thus implicitly of women of all races. Both Noun's sexuality and her eventual childlessness are also Indiana's. Both are destined to play subservient roles as women; are treated similarly as slaves; are mistreated by the same unfeeling lover; and are cut off from power, language, successful marriage, and enduring progeny. Noun and Indiana serve less as models of the oppressed and the oppressor than as joint illustrations of slave women's sexual oppression. The refusal to assign to Indiana the traditional roles of wife and mother at the end of the novel can be viewed as a refusal to relegate Indiana to the biologically and socially reproductive role of mother that was assigned to black women in the colonies. Naomi Schor perceptively discerns in *Indiana* "a yearning to be delivered both from the base desire for carnal possession characteristic of male sexuality and the injustices of a man-made system of laws that enables the enslavement of both women and blacks"; and thus she sees in Sand's refusal to assign a reproductive role to Indiana a refusal to "legitimate a social order inimical to the disenfranchised, among them women" ("Idealism in the Novel" 73).

The resisting side of *Indiana* is also apparent in the many passages in the novel in which Indiana herself voices resistance to the analogous oppression imposed on women and slaves. The following passage is representative:

> [E]n voyant le continuel tableau des maux de la servitude, en supportant les ennuis de l'isolement et de la dépendance, elle avait acquis . . . une force de résistance incalculable contre tout ce qui tendait à l'opprimer. . . . Élevée au désert, négligée de son père, vivant au milieu des esclaves, pour qui elle n'avait d'autre secours, d'autre consolation que sa compassion et ses larmes, elle s'était habituée à dire: "Un jour viendra où tout sera changé dans ma vie, où je ferai du bien aux autres."   (89 [5])

> [T]hrough continually seeing the ills of slavery and enduring the vexations of solitude and dependence, she had acquired . . . an incalculable strength of resistance to everything that tended to oppress her. . . . Brought up in the wilds, neglected by father, and living surrounded by slaves whom she could help and console only with her pity and tears, she had become used to saying, "A day will come when my life will be completely changed, when I shall do good to others."   (51)

On occasion Indiana even serves as a spokesperson for ideas of resistance by slaves themselves to their oppressors, ideas that have a clear abolitionist ring:

> Dieu ne veut pas qu'on opprime et qu'on écrase les créatures de ses mains. S'il daignait descendre jusqu'à intervenir dans nos chétifs intérêts, il briserait le fort et relèverait le faible; il passerait sa grande main sur nos têtes inégales et les nivellerait comme les eaux de la mer; il dirait à l'esclave: "Jette ta chaîne, et fuis sur les monts où j'ai mis pour toi des eaux, des fleurs et du soleil."   (249–50 [196])

> God doesn't want his creatures to be oppressed and crushed. If he deigned to descend so far as to intervene in our petty concerns, he

would break the strong and raise up the weak. He would spread his large hand out over our unequal heads and make them level like the surface of the sea. He would say to the slave, "Cast aside your chain and flee to the mountains, where I have placed water, flowers, and sunshine for you."
(191; trans. modified)

In this passage, Indiana, refers to herself metaphorically as a slave and, through her use of the first-person plural "nos" 'our' in speaking together with black slaves of "nos chétifs intérêts" 'our petty concerns' and "nos têtes inégales" 'our unequal heads,' proudly proclaims her commonality with them.

Commenting on Sand's metaphorical use of the notion of slavery, Nancy Rogers rightly concludes that "Indiana joins the other rebellious runaway slaves so often depicted in the literature of the times . . . Indiana is branded as blatantly as any runaway slave recaptured by his master" (31). By choosing to live in the colonies and to live apart from white colonialists, both Indiana and the significantly named Ralph Brown can be seen as joining the ranks of a nonwhite community at the end of the novel. The novel closes, revealingly, with Indiana and Ralph devoting their efforts to helping black slaves—if not to escape slavery altogether at least to bear its burden with less suffering in sickness or old age: "La majeure portion de nos revenus est consacrée à racheter de pauvres noirs infirmes. C'est la principale cause du mal que les colons disent de nous. Que ne sommes-nous assez riches pour délivrer tous ceux qui vivent dans l'esclavage!' 'The major portion of our income is devoted to buying the freedom of poor, infirm blacks. That's the main reason for the bad things the colonists say about us. If only we were rich enough to free all who live in slavery!' (342 [274]; 270).

It is not surprising to find Ralph coupled with the racially impure Indiana and treated in many of the same ways as she is. Throughout the novel, Ralph is symbolically emasculated and feminized through analogy with women, slaves, and members of oppressed groups; we read, for example, that "Ralph n'avait connu de la vie que ses maux et ses dégoûts" 'Ralph had known only the ills and disappointments of life' (166 [124]; 117). No less than Noun and Indiana, he is a powerless and thus symbolically impotent victim of the masculine oppression of the colonialist system, which is consistently associated with slavery. Thus Ralph states: "Mon père . . . était prêt à me maudire si j'essayais d'échapper à son joug. Je courbai la tête; mais ce que je souffris, vous-même, qui fûtes aussi bien malheureuse, ne sauriez l'apprécier" 'My father . . . was ready to curse me if I tried to escape from his yoke. I bowed to my fate, but even you, who have also been unhappy, wouldn't be able to understand what I suffered' (323 [258]; 254). Unlike powerful masculine Europeans such as Indiana's husband, Delmare, and her lover, Raymon, Ralph is disparaged through his portrayal here in a symbolically feminine and slave-like guise as weak, submissive, silent, all-suffering, impotent, and asexual. Indeed, James M. Vest rightly captures the reader's overall impression of Ralph, designating him as phallically "oarless," in contrast with the oarsmen ("*ram*-eurs") who kill Indiana's defenseless female dog Ophelia and with Raymon de *Ram*-ière ("Fluid Nomenclature" 53). Denying the sexuality of male slaves, including the actual practice of castration, were facts of colonial life with which the literary desexualization of Ralph is consistent (W. Jordan 154).

Moreover, as a native of the colonies, Ralph too is a "créole." As Isabelle Naginski suggests, he is also an androgynous double of the feminine writer, "a working model for the author's double-gendered voice" (*George Sand: Writing* 65). And like Indiana, although he is white, his identity and hopes for the future are as rooted in the dream of the abolition of slavery and oppression as if he were black: "Ralph allait donc toujours soutenant son rêve de république d'où il voulait exclure tous les abus, tous les préjugés, toutes les injustices; projet fondé tout entier sur l'espoir d'une nouvelle race d'hommes" 'Ralph continued to support his dream of a republic from which he wanted to banish all abuses, all prejudices, all injustices, a plan based in its entirety on the hope of a new race of men' (167 [124]; 117). It is thus possible to see in the couple, Indiana and Ralph, a locus of combined masculine and feminine, white and nonwhite, resistance against the oppression and racism that for Sand characterizes the colonies generally and the colonialist colonel Delmare specifically.

The analyses of resistance in *Indiana* are intended to show students that literary works can be read in more than one way. They are also intended to show through the choice of secondary texts the importance of considering different critical perspectives. The perspective provided by feminist critics occupies a special place in this regard. If it has been possible to discern a discourse of resistance in *Indiana* it is largely because Schor and others who have followed in her wake have opened the way for readers to view *Indiana* as an emancipatory text of resistance.[3] That perspective has made it possible to see beyond the ideological compromises that Sand's characters make and acknowledge their willingness, albeit limited, to explore the means of fighting injustice that were available to the disempowered, blacks and women, in their time.

The nuances of resistance in *Indiana* have come under increasing scrutiny in secondary texts that directly address issues of race. Writing in 2000, Claudia Moscovici attends carefully to the connections in *Indiana* among the inextricably imbricated factors of class, race, gender, age, nationality, and sexuality. In "Espace colonial et vérité historique," Pratima Prasad provides an illuminating reading of the "colonial intertext" of *Indiana* in relation to Bernardin de Saint-Pierre's *Paul et Virginie*. Through a close reading that compares the two colonial texts—one dating from the eighteenth and the other from the nineteenth century—she enables us to measure the increasing, albeit still indirect, expression of racial issues in French literary history. She convincingly shows that at a discursive level the cultural processes that marked the colonization of the Indian Ocean islands can be discerned in Sand's novel (73). In addition, Prasad opens the reading of *Indiana* up to a less generic colonial reading and proposes one that is more focused on the discursive practices related to the Indian Ocean.[4]

Whereas several decades ago the issue of race was virtually silenced in criticism related to *Indiana*, one now finds productive differences of opinion bearing on specifics of the text. Calling attention to such differences can enrich class discussions of Sand's novel and the history of French colonialism. Consider Indiana's statement in the novel that Ralph "me vit venir à lui dans les bras de la négresse qui m'avait nourrie" 'saw me coming toward him in the arms of the negress who had been my wet-nurse' (157 [116]; 109). In "Representing Race," I concluded that the fact that Indiana was nurtured with the nonwhite, racially other milk of her wet-nurse made her partially nonwhite according to racist interpretations of her time, citing as support for my argument the fact that Portuguese Franciscans opposed admission of non-European-born inhabitants of the colonies into their order on the grounds that "even if born of pure white parents [they] have been sucked by Indian ayahs in their infancy and thus had their blood contaminated for life" (Anderson 60). In "Coloring Noun," Roger Little refutes my claim regarding Indiana, stating that a black woman's milk "cannot possibly make her 'partially' non-white" (27n23). Little's "cannot possibly" represents to my mind a dismissive and insensitive response to the subtle affective issues regarding women's bodies and reproductive processes. A more feminist response is provided by Véronique Machelidon in "Female Melancholy and the Politics of Authori(ali)ty." Attuned to Indiana's maternal loss and the transfer of oral affection to Noun, Machelidon emphasizes the sororal bond that unites the two women as "sœurs de lait" 'children nursed by the same mother.' Machelidon also takes issue with Little's assertion that Noun is undoubtedly "an admixture of Indian and Caucasian blood, with perhaps a dash of African." Machelidon contends that "Indian" refers to Noun's geographic origin (the Indian Ocean) rather than her ethnicity and supports my view when she says that "it seems uncontroversial to assert that Noun is colored and probably of mixed race" (43).

There is regrettably not room in the above snapshot of issues related to race in *Indiana* to include the larger historical perspective that teaching about slavery in Sand's works should provide. Students need to know that attitudes toward slavery and race changed with each decade of the late eighteenth and nineteenth centuries; thus the attitude toward race displayed by Sand in *Indiana*, written in 1830, differs from those in the many other works on the subject that she wrote throughout her long career (see Kadish, "George Sand"). Reading race in *Indiana* should not take place in a void. On the contrary, it should be the occasion for students to open their minds to the literary and historical complexities of race, slavery, colonialism, and transatlantic studies.

NOTES

Parts of this essay are adapted, with permission, from my "Representing Race in *Indiana*," which appeared in *George Sand Studies* in 1992.

[1] For more on the use of "créole," see Kadish, "Representing"; see also the essays by Berman and Machelidon in this volume.

[2] For these and other abolitionist writings, students are encouraged to consult *Francophone Slavery* (www.uga.edu/slavery).

[3] For an important contribution to feminist analyses of Sand see Massardier-Kenney, *Gender*.

[4] On the importance of including the Indian Ocean in considerations of Africa, colonialism, and the transatlantic slave trade, see Blum; Desai; Hofmeyr.

Teaching Race, Class, and Slavery in *Indiana*

Véronique Machelidon

Courses on representations of colonialism, race, and slavery in nineteenth-century French literature are likely to include rediscovered narratives by canonical writers such as Victor Hugo's *Bug Jargal*, Alexandre Dumas's *Georges*, Prosper Mérimée's *Tamango*, and the short but highly versatile *Ourika*, by Claire de Duras. Through rich critical attention amply demonstrated by the present volume, *Indiana* has emerged as one of George Sand's early masterpieces. Yet, despite its dual metropolitan and colonial settings and the abolitionist spirit of its winning team of characters, Ralph and Indiana, the novel remains a challenging candidate for a literary course on colonial and postcolonial studies. This may be explained both by the complexity of Sand's prose—her shifts in narrative technique, her use of free indirect discourse and irony—and by her play with literal and metaphorical meanings. While David Powell's carefully annotated French edition alleviates the linguistic challenge for students reading in the original language, it may not resolve the hermeneutic difficulty caused by the novel's complicated narrative technique and referential playfulness. Sand's ambiguity will continue to disconcert anglophone readers who are used to the greater explicitness of works of American literature, such as Frederick Douglass's *Narrative of the Life of Frederick Douglass, an American Slave* and Harriet Beecher Stowe's *Uncle Tom's Cabin*.

Including Sand's novel in an upper-level undergraduate course in French or world literature nevertheless brings significant rewards. It allows students to develop valuable analytic and critical skills, thereby meeting the learning outcomes of both the literature requirement and the critical thinking component that define the general education program in many liberal arts institutions. As an invitation to a critical rethinking of the ways in which race is constructed, deconstructed, and regulated in Western sociosymbolic systems, Sand's narrative is in fact an ideal literary case for "infusing critical thinking tools and strategies into existing courses and experiences" and providing "multiple opportunities for reflection, intellectual engagement, and action" ("Meredith").

As students reflect on the topic of race, *métissage*, color, visibility, and slavery in the framework of the novel, they begin to scrutinize uninformed views of race as a stable, discrete, and fixed category of identity that continue to circulate in media, politics, and society in the United States as well as in France. They become aware of the specific historical circumstances that defined race, class, colonial society, and slavery in various colonial empires, particularly in the French islands of the East Indies. They learn to question the validity of rigid binary oppositions (black versus white), which fail to do justice to Sand's complex treatment of race. Focusing on racial hybridity, identification, and (in)visibility and exploring Sand's participation in the contemporary nineteenth-century discourses on colonialism and abolitionism will challenge students to develop a more complex and critical view of racial identity as defined by historical, geographic, social, political, and economic circumstances. They can apply this newly gained insight not only to French colonial literature but also to racial issues in their own time and society.

In the historical context of early French colonization, race was a symbolic construction that eluded stable corporeal markers. Students learn to understand why Sand preferred to create racial indifference in her text: if the developing nineteenth-century theory of anatomical difference served to legitimate the enslavement of supposedly inferior races, racial identification could also be enlisted to destabilize colonial hierarchies and promote a different social order based on equality. To prepare the class for reading racial hybridity in *Indiana*, I begin with a brief introductory lecture on racial theory as it was emerging in the late eighteenth and early nineteenth centuries, with contributions from the pseudosciences of anatomy and craniometry. These discourses represented race as a biological site of difference based on somatic features like skin color, nose type, shape of the eyes, and brain size, among others—features that were supposed to be instantly visually recognizable. Illustrations of Julien Joseph Virey's *Histoire naturelle du genre humain* (1801), available on the Bibliothèque nationale de France's *Gallica* Web site, help students visualize developing racial hierarchies (http://gallica.bnf.fr/ark:/12148/btv1b2300617x). We focus on the drawing facing page 134 of *Histoire naturelle* (illus. 12 on the *Gallica* page), which contrasts the profiles of a classical statue of Apollo (at the top), a "nègre" 'negro' (in the middle), and an orangutan (at the bottom). This illustration reveals how racialist theories, based on supposedly visible anatomical differences, served to classify human beings into fixed types and to rank them from the inferior "negroid" type to the most "evolved" and therefore "superior" white race. Such a theory, predicated as it was on the purity of races, did not reflect the demographic reality at Île Bourbon (today's Réunion), where *métissage* took place at the very outset of French colonization, because of the scarcity of white women among the original settlers.

Having considered the historical specificity of racial discourses, we then turn to the novel. As homework, students are asked to locate descriptions of the main characters, including race, ethnicity, class, and political stance. They identify Raymon de Ramière as a white, metropolitan aristocrat and royalist; Colonel Delmare as a white, middle-class French industrialist; Sir Ralph Brown as a white baronet, island-born (i.e., creole) but with English blood and republican ideals; and Indiana Delmare as a white lady, also born in the colony, the unloved daughter of a ruined Bonapartist. Identifying her servant and friend Noun's social and racial status proves to be much trickier and elicits a variety of tentative answers. Readers cannot ascertain whether she came to France as a slave, an emancipated woman, or a free servant. To elucidate her ethnic origin, we consider her physical description: her "grands yeux noirs" 'big black eyes' (73 [40]; 36) contrast with Indiana's "grands yeux bleus" 'big blue eyes' (54 [23]; 19), and the narrator's emphasis on her taller size and robustness is opposed to

Indiana's sickly melancholy at the beginning of the novel. Both are defined by their "cheveux noirs" 'black hair,' yet only Noun's hair feels "sec et rude" 'dry and rough,' "froids et lourds" 'cold and heavy,' "d'un noir nègre, d'une nature indienne, d'une pesanteur morte" 'black like a Negro's, textured like an Indian's, heavy and lifeless,' when it is presented to Raymon as proof of his guilt (192 [146]; 140; trans. modified). But in case we lean toward a literal reading of the word "nègre," Sand quickly reminds us that the rougher, dryer texture may simply result from the maid's dismal fate. Cut from her dead body, Noun's hair "avaient déjà perdu leur moiteur parfumée et leur chaleur vitale" 'had lost its fragrant moisture and vital warmth' (192 [146]; 140). Moreover, Indiana, and not Noun, is named after the island in the Indian Ocean where both women were born, almost on the same day. The confusing allusion to Noun's "bras frais et *bruns*" 'young, *brown* arms' and to her "épaules larges et *éblouissantes*" '*dazzling*, broad shoulders' further puzzles the reader (103–04 [69–70]; 63–64; my emphasis). Faced with the hesitation between literal and metaphorical meanings and with the indeterminacy of color, students are left unsure of the maid's racial identity and skin color. Far from fixing racial difference through stable visual markers, the text entertains ambiguity through the use of attributes, such as "créole" (a term we research in its historical meanings), "Indienne" 'Indian' (81, 99 [49, 66]), and the curious "rose de Bengale" 'Bengal rose' (80 [48]; 43), that are indifferently applied to the two foreign women, who shared the milk of the same "negro" (or colored) wet nurse (157 [116]; 109).

Sand blurs color difference in favor of an emphasis on clothing and a play on sartorial identification. Thus the text identifies Noun's class and geographic origin through her "tablier blanc et son madras arrangé coquettement à la manière de son pays" 'white apron and head-scarf attractively arranged in the style of her native country,' which, in Raymon's eyes, define her as a "soubrette" 'lady's maid' (74 [42]; my trans.). When the narrator then compares Noun's coquetry with that of a *grisette* (a term used for metropolitan workingwomen), and when we recall that the "personnage vermeil et blond" 'pink and white character,' Ralph, is nevertheless named Sir Brown, we learn to take Sand's color allusions with more than a pinch of salt (51 [20]; 16). Through her particular use of color qualifiers (*blanc, brun, nègre, rose,* and *gris*), Sand seems to be questioning the very visibility of skin color and therefore of race as it was constructed by the racialist theories of her time. In conclusion, her play on literal and metaphorical meanings and her habit of questioning the relation between color attribute and signified may very well serve to defeat the reader's gaze and racial distinctions.

To facilitate students' acceptance of Sand's ambiguity, I provide them with excerpts from essays by Doris Kadish, Roger Little, Naomi Schor, and Pratima Prasad to explore how different critics have addressed and responded to Sand's refusal to fix racial identity. But instead of deploring Sand's lack of explicitness, the class learns to justify and valorize this literary strategy. One way to accomplish this is to look at representations of "indigenous slaves" reproduced in the informative book *De la servitude à la liberté: Bourbon des origines à 1848*

(Desport). Published in 1988 by the Comité de la Culture, de l'Education et de l'Environnement of the Région Réunion, it celebrates the island's heritage rooted in slavery and reproduces archival materials dating back to the first half of the nineteenth century. We first look at an 1848 lithograph by Louis-Antoine Roussin, the most prolific and best known Reunionese painter, of a well-dressed and distinguished pair, facing the viewer.[1] The man is dressed in elegant clothing, with light-colored trousers; a white shirt with buttons and raised collar; a dark, tight-fitting waist jacket with fancy pocket handkerchief; and a black top hat. In gentleman's fashion he is smoking what appears to be a cigar. His lady companion wears her hair in dark, smooth "bandeaux," according to nineteenth-century European style. She has a long madras shawl and an ample silky frock. Her face and shoulders, shaded by her fancy parasol, are slightly darker than the man's bright shirt, and both display refined facial features. The only clue to their social rank is their curious absence of footwear: they are standing barefooted on the pavement of some sort of plantation alley. We are surprised by the original caption, which identifies them as "Indigenous Slaves: Negress Housemaid and Black Servant" (77).

The next visual examined in class is a color lithograph drawn from life by Etienne Adolphe d'Hastrel de Rivedoux during his 1836–37 visit to the island and printed in Paris by Goffroy between 1840 and 1845.[2] It shows a woman of ostensibly humbler rank than the pair in the first image. She is wearing a simple but adorned blue dress, a pink shawl with a printed or embroidered border wrapped around her shoulders, and a distinct madras turban on her hair. On her left arm she is carrying a naked child. Both share the same whitish skin color. Only the bare feet and perhaps the woman's lips point to her class and her racial hybridity. It is unclear whether the child is hers or her master's. The illustration is entitled "Mulatto Slave from Bourbon Island" (62).

Both artists were born in France, enlisted in the French navy, and discovered Bourbon during their tours of duty. While d'Hastrel returned to France to publish his sketches of landscapes, costumes, human types, and engineering works, Roussin stayed on the island, where he married a creole woman and opened an art studio in 1843–44. Each artist intended to record observations done from life in the colony (*Louis Antoine Roussin*). If the two felt the same need to signal slavery through their subjects' lack of footwear, it is reasonable to assume that the population of the island was indeed so hybridized in the nineteenth century that sartorial signifiers had to be called to the rescue to reinscribe race and slavery in the absence of stable somatic difference such as color.

This assumption is confirmed by Frédéric Régent's *La France et ses esclaves*, which reveals that on Île Bourbon, unions across color lines were so frequent that "by 1717 there were only 6 families left where European blood had retained all its purity" (61). Sand's unwillingness to fix Noun's racial identity may therefore be interpreted on the basis of historical and geographic accuracy. Additional philosophical considerations may have reinforced her choice. Régent emphasizes how a colonial order based on the equation of slavery with color was progressively put in place in the Indian Ocean colony to justify power relations, social hierarchies, the superiority of white over black, and the economic order built on slavery. Through its *bureau des colonies*, French monarchy was instrumental in regulating and imposing "le préjugé de couleur" 'color prejudice and discrimination.' Indeed, color discrimination was instituted and policed to prevent the creation of "un front des libres de toutes les couleurs" 'a front uniting free men of all shades of color,' which would have resulted in the independence of the colony from the king's rule (197). Considered in this historical light, Sand's practice of racial invisibility served to undermine the very foundation of the colonial order, whose precariousness had been revealed by the brutal insurrection in Saint-Domingue and the ultimate independence of Haiti in 1804. (A simple handout with major events in the history of French colonialism and abolitionism can help students situate the intellectual and sociohistorical context of Sand's narrative.)

After emphasizing the role of race, color, and the construction of racial visibility in the preservation of French colonial interests, we turn to Sand's textual play on racial identification through masquerade. For our next class, I assign as homework a close reading of the two circular chamber scenes and ask students to examine the role of clothing in these episodes of seduction. Students discuss questions such as these: Which elements unify the two scenes? Who is masquerading as whom, for whom, and why? How do race and class function in the identification between maid and mistress? What are the concrete effects of the masquerade for the characters and for the reader? Does it subvert or reinforce race and class hierarchies? How is the plot affected by the disguise?

One common character serves to connect the two different scenes: Raymon de Ramière. His effect on the plot is to separate the creole doubles to better seduce, manipulate, or reject them according to his needs. The narrator relates Raymon's sexual power to his political, social, and symbolic seduction. A "champion de la société existante" 'champion of the existing social order,' he puts his pen and talent at the service of the constitutional but increasingly autocratic Bourbon monarchy (166 [124]; 117). As a "publiciste," or political commentator, he writes newspaper articles defending the status quo and the privileges of his class (129 [92]).

In the first of the two encounters in Indiana's circular chamber, the pregnant maid seeks to regain Raymon's love by elevating herself to his rank. To impress him and to secure a future for her unborn baby, she dons her mistress's attire in a gesture imitating colonial slaves, whose taste for adornment and refinement in clothing was regulated to preserve social hierarchies, according to a sumptuary decree of 4 June 1820: "Ils n'ont pas le droit d'arborer des bijoux d'or, des pierreries, des dorures, de la soie, des rubans ou de la dentelle. A la Réunion une ordonnance similaire est prise le 18 avril 1819. Elle oblige les esclaves à porter des étoffes communes et leur interdit de porter des bijoux." 'They are not allowed to wear gold jewelry, precious stones, gold ornaments, silk, ribbon or lace. On Réunion Island, a similar decree, passed on 18 April 1819, requires

slaves to wear clothes made of plain fabric and prohibits the wearing of jewelry' (Régent 145; my trans.). In the absence of stable color difference, these
royal decrees make clothing signify race and station. We observe how Noun
appropriates the sartorial identifiers of the upper class to overcome Raymon's
prejudices, with some initial success:

> Raymon fut saisi d'un étrange frisson en songeant que cette femme envelop-
> pée d'un manteau qui l'avait conduit jusque là était peut-être Indiana elle-
> même. Cette extravagante idée sembla se confirmer lorsqu'il vit apparaî-
> tre *dans la glace devant lui* une forme *blanche* et parée, le fantôme d'une
> femme qui entre au bal et qui jette son manteau pour se montrer radieuse et
> demi-nue aux lumières *éclatantes*.   (101 [67–68]; my emphasis)

> Raymon was gripped by a strange shudder at the thought that the cloaked
> woman who had led him there was perhaps Indiana herself. This absurd
> idea seemed to be confirmed when he saw a *white*, bejewelled figure ap-
> pear in the *mirror in front of him*, the ghost of a woman who, on entering
> a ballroom, casts aside her cloak to reveal herself, radiant and half-naked
> in the *brilliant* lights.   (61–62; my emphasis)

Not only does the bright light reveal Noun to be white, but the mirror unites
the two characters in a single frame, thus reinforcing their human equality and
the dangerous lack of class and color difference. But when the aristocrat's gaze
is troubled by identification across social and racial barriers, his moralizing categories immediately take over to separate maid and mistress, aristocratic lady
and lower-class exotic double. As students list the moral qualifiers now used
to debase Noun, some will recognize how moral stereotypes such as lasciviousness, immodesty, unbridled sexuality, unruliness, and mental disorder are
symptoms of what Sandra Gilbert and Susan Gubar called "the madwoman in
the attic," who had to be locked up and silenced to free the white, upper-class,
male protagonist. Racialist stereotypes were commonly used in the nineteenth
century to enforce social segregation. They served to demonstrate the inferior-
ity of the lower ranks and therefore justified the need for control by the upper
classes. (These racialist attributes were applied not only to Africans but also
more generally to the working class and to minorities.)

Through Noun's sartorial identification with her mistress, colonial and metropolitan hierarchies are temporarily shaken, then cruelly restored. Insight into
the workings of class and race discrimination is gained by the reader, but not
by the royal spokesman. We ponder the effects of this on Noun's plot: the colonial subaltern who transgressed the double barrier of race and class appears at
the end of part 1 fully objectified as a bundle of lifeless, indiscriminate clothing: "un morceau d'étoffes que le courant s'efforçait d'entraîner" 'a heap of
cloth, which the current was trying to pull along' (119 [83]; 76). She drowns in
the very stream that powers her master's factory, as if, for all the maid's color

indifference, Sand wanted to suggest that the abuse of the colonial other serves to support the economic operations of rising French industrialism.

When we move to the second circular chamber scene, I introduce the discussion by noting that the scene has been described as "a correction of the first, as though Indiana was avenging Noun's death" (Prasad, "(De)Masking" 108). How is it a correction of the first one? How does the sartorial identification operate in this scene? How does it continue Sand's questioning of racial hierarchies, which were used to support slavery? What is the effect of Indiana's masquerade on plot and characters? and on the reader?

In this repeat episode, racial cross-dressing is reversed and does not follow the pattern of social promotion described and prohibited in the colonial sumptuary laws. To ascertain her suspicions concerning Noun's death and Raymon's guilt, Indiana dresses up like her deceased maid, donning a "pelisse doublée de fourrure, . . . la même que Noun avait prise à l'heure du dernier rendez-vous pour aller à sa rencontre dans le parc" 'a fur-lined cloak; by a strange chance, it was the same one that Noun had chosen at the time of their last rendezvous to meet him in the grounds' (190 [145]; 139). She wears "un foulard des Indes noué négligemment à la manière des Créoles; c'était la coiffure ordinaire de Noun" 'a scarf of Indian silk, loosely [tied] round her head in the Creole manner. It was Noun's usual head-covering' (191 [145]; 139). Superimposing the two illustrations of female colonial fashion that were discussed earlier, students have an idea of what Indiana might have looked like. Her disguise is at once incomplete, hybrid, and ambivalent. She does not seek to impersonate fully her milk sister, but she mimics her maid, who had just tried to pass as white, upper-class, and metropolitan. As Indiana mixes clothing attributes from different racial and social groups, race becomes further and further removed from the pseudoscientific bedrock of somatic visibility. The seducer's power based on segregation is defeated, and he collapses to the floor in a faint (193 [147]; 141).

References to Noun's hair, which Indiana holds in her lap—and to its "nature indienne" 'Indian texture' and "noir nègre" 'black color like a negro's hair'—can now be interpreted as Sand's allusions to the novel's colonial context. When the white mistress identifies with her racialized creole servant, she reverses and subverts color and class hierarchies. The sumptuary code of the colonies, like Raymon's moral discriminations, was designed to assert class privileges and contain the slaves' and free colored people's longing for social promotion, a desire that jeopardized but was fed by the alleged superiority of white over black. Indiana's masquerade, on the other hand, represents social transgression downward and the moral superiority of colored over white, of servant over aristocrat, of innocence over guilt. It is sheer provocation of the established social order. For Sand's contemporary reader, who was familiar with colonial history and abolitionism, this scene can be read as a hidden but radical critique of the colonial class system based on slavery, race, and color.

To conclude our close reading of the two circular chamber scenes, we spend time reflecting on our own intellectual inquiry. We have proceeded from a fixed theory of identity to a more flexible concept of identification, which allows us to recognize how some characters move between different positions to question social and racial norms constructed, for instance, through clothing and to expose class prejudices disguised as moral values.

In the next lesson we follow Indiana's identification with her lower-class double, turning to the passage that represents the novel's most articulate statement on slavery and colonial abuse, namely, the famous letter that she sends to Raymon from Île Bourbon. By now students have become familiar with the writer's play with literal and metaphorical readings. Although Indiana is using slavery as a metaphor for her own abuse, her previous vindication of Noun's innocence and the origin of the letter invite a more literal reading also. The class examines how Indiana's letter moves from personal reproaches to a more general social critique. Students write down the vocabulary referring to power relations between master and slave, colonizer and colonized. Repeated oppositions between possessives ("vous," "votre," "vos," "mes," "leur," "leurs" 'your,' 'my,' 'their') structure the last part of her message, articulate Indiana's rejection of Raymon's aristocratic prejudices and immoral selfishness, and lead to her vindication of a utopian alternative society. She dreams of a new world where slaves throw off their chains and all ranks disappear, displaced by a generalized human fraternity in a nurturing and bountiful natural order blessed by God.

While students are quick to recognize the biblical accents of Indiana's message of equality, some of her accusations against Raymon will need to be explained. These include her denunciation of "les croyances de vos pères" 'the beliefs of your fathers' and "vos prêtres [qui] ont institué les rites du culte pour établir leur richesse et leur puissance sur les nations" 'your priests [who] have set up the rites of church worship to establish their power and wealth over the nations' (249 [195]; 190). In learning about the traditionally strong ties between the French aristocracy, king, and Catholic Church, the class is curious to discover the church's extensive and long-term implication in racial oppression in the French colonies. For instance, theologians referred to Genesis to define slavery as a divine punishment inflicted on black Africans (Sala-Molins 40; Hoffmann 69). As Canaan's descendants who had been cursed by Noah, they were considered a doomed race, and since blackness was traditionally associated with evil, pagan "negroes" were "meant" to be rescued by the white colonizer. Church services reinforced the social, moral, and political control of slaves. Through specific readings from the Bible and by making mass mandatory, priests inculcated unquestioning obedience to the white master. And as most religious and missionary orders in the French colonies also owned land and slaves, the Catholic Church's collusion with slavery and colonial oppression ran full circle. To explain Indiana's pointed critique of Raymon's self-serving conflation of monarchism and colonialism, it can be helpful to examine excerpts from the Code Noir (arts. 2 and 3). Originally promulgated by Louis XIV in 1685 for the colonies of the French Antilles, the code was later revised in the edict of 1723 to define master-slave relations in the Mascarene Islands.

As students begin to appreciate Sand's advocacy of identification across race, class, and color and her parallel play with literal and figurative meanings, they also learn to read beyond the letter and recover the hidden but sophisticated antiracialist and anticolonial subtext of her complex novel. At this point it is possible to refer to other works of Sand's time that students are likely to have read in other classes, such as Emily Brontë's *Wuthering Heights*, where similar practices of racial crossing and deconstruction are enlisted. Closer to our own time, the anonymous "Poème d'un Africain pour son frère blanc," which many students in the United States as in France will have read in high school or college, picks up on Sand's lead, turning "le préjugé de couleur" upside down and transforming it into an absurd joke. In an increasingly diverse American society, where minorities are quickly becoming majorities and ethnic identifications are blurred by *métissage* and immigration (witness the reelection of the first racially and culturally mixed president, born in Hawai'i of a white American mother and Kenyan father, raised first by an Indonesian father and then by a white grandmother with possible American Indian ancestry), Sand's critique of racial difference and visibility, her plea in favor of hybridity and creoleness make more sense than ever and teach us all to understand that bodies are made, not born, to matter.

NOTES

This essay picks up many of the same themes as my "George Sand's Praise of Creoleness: Race, Slavery and (In)Visibility in *Indiana*," published in *George Sand Studies* 28 (2009).

[1] A useful reproduction of this lithograph, without the bottom caption, can be found at *Potomitan: Site de promotion des cultures et des langues créoles* (http://www.potomitan .info/galerie/roussin).

[2] D'Hastrel's lithograph can be seen online at *Iconothèque historique de l'océan Indien* (http://www.ihoi.org/app/photopro.sk/ihoi_icono/home).

Subversion of a Stereotype:
The Tragic Mulatta in *Indiana*

Molly Krueger Enz

Female subjugation was a prevalent literary trope in the mid-nineteenth century. This time period also witnessed the rise of scientific racism that theorized a social role for the black race. In *Lettres sur la race noire et la race blanche* (1839), Gustave d'Eichtal outlines his perspective on racial and gender hierarchies:

> Le noir me paraît être la *race femme* dans la famille humaine, comme le blanc est la *race mâle*. De même que la femme, le noir est privé des facultés politiques et scientifiques. . . . Mais, par contre, il possède au plus haut degré les qualités du cœur, les affections et les sentiments domestiques. . . . Aussi le noir, être essentiellement *domestique*, comme la femme, a été jusqu'ici condamné comme elle à un esclavage plus ou moins rude. (d'Eichtal and Urbain 22–23)

> The black seems to me to be the *woman race* in the human family, as the white is the *male race*. Like the woman, the black is deprived of political and scientific abilities. . . . However, on the other hand, he possesses to the utmost degree the qualities of the heart, affections, and feelings of domesticity. . . . Moreover the black, being essentially *domestic*, like the woman, has been thus far similarly condemned to a rather harsh enslavement. (my trans.)

In her 1832 novel *Indiana*, George Sand analyzes the link between race and gender and highlights the theme of white male dominance. She demonstrates how married women in nineteenth-century France were governed by Napoléon's civil code and treated like slaves. According to Deborah Jenson in *Trauma and Its Representations*, "In *Indiana*, this theme of marriage as a form of slavery by analogy recurs with such numbing force that it produces a political mutation: the term *slavery* virtually sacrifices its meaning to the term *marriage*" (197). George Sand was born in 1804, the same year that the Napoleonic Code was established and that the nation of Haiti was created following the most successful slave rebellion in history. She was greatly influenced by the social and historical events of her time, so it is perhaps not unexpected that the oppression of women and slaves is a fundamental theme in her first novel.

When I teach *Indiana* in my upper-division French undergraduate course entitled The Exotic Other in Nineteenth-Century French Literature and Painting, we begin by analyzing the status of married women as dictated by Napoléon's civil code. I ask students to examine article 213, which states that a wife must obey her husband: "Le mari doit protection à sa femme, la femme obéissance à son mari" 'The husband owes protection to his wife, the wife obedience to her husband' (Code civil; Code Napoleon 59). Then we study article 1124 under the section that describes contracts, agreements, and ways to acquire property: "Les incapables de contracter sont les mineurs, les interdits, les femmes mariées, dans les cas exprimés par la loi, et généralement tous ceux auxquels la loi a interdit certains contrats" 'Incapable of contracting are minors, interdicted persons, married women in the cases expressed by the law, and all those generally to whom the law has forbidden certain contracts (Code civil; Code Napoleon 308). Students are typically surprised by the degree to which married women were stripped of their legal rights and treated as objects that could be possessed and dominated. According to the civil code, the husband controlled all the family's "property," which included his wife and children. Article 1388 defined the husband as the head of the family: "Les époux ne peuvent déroger ni aux droits résultant de la puissance maritale sur la personne de la femme et des enfants, ou qui appartiennent au mari comme chef, ni aux droits conférés au survivant des époux par le titre De la Puissance paternelle" 'Married persons cannot derogate from the rights resulting from the power of the husband over the persons of his wife and his children, or which belong to the husband as head, nor from the rights conferred on the survivor of the married parties of the title "Of the Paternal Power"' (Code civil; Code Napoleon 380). In our analysis of the civil code, students notice the repetition of verbs such as "to obey" and "to belong" and nouns like "obedience" when referring to women's roles. Much like the Black Code that was promulgated under Louis XIV, which equated slaves as objects to be purchased and abused by their plantation owners (Code noir), the Napoleonic Code allowed men to dominate and mistreat their wives.[1]

After our discussion of how a married woman is relegated to an object in the eyes of the law, students are better equipped to understand what influenced Sand in writing Indiana, which she outlines in the preface to the novel's 1842 edition: "Ceux qui m'ont lu sans prévention comprennent que j'ai écrit Indiana avec le sentiment non raisonné, il est vrai, mais profound et légitime, de l'injustice et de la barbarie des lois qui réagissent encore l'existence de la femme dans le marriage, dans la famille et la société" 'Those who have read me without prejudice understand that I wrote Indiana influenced by a feeling, unreasoned, it is true, but deep and legitimate, of the injustice and barbarity of the laws which still govern the existence of women in marriage, in the family, and in society' (46–47; 13). The connection between women and slavery becomes the basis for our analyses during the unit on Indiana.

Creoleness and the Ambiguity of Race

In our examination of the themes of oppression and liberty as they relate to race and gender, my students and I first study how the two main female characters, Indiana and Noun, are portrayed as doubles and how their lives parallel each

other: both characters are labeled as Creoles, both are nursed by the same
woman, both fall in love with and are rejected by Raymon de Ramière, and
both choose to end their lives by drowning (although Indiana ultimately does
not follow through with her decision). Although these similarities may seem
obvious, they are essential to understanding the intersections of race and gender in the novel. Before delving into a close reading of the physical and character descriptions of Indiana and Noun, students are asked to study the various
implications of the term *Creole* in critical works such as Christopher Miller's
Blank Darkness: Africanist Discourse in French and Carolyn Vellenga Berman's
Creole Crossings: Domestic Fiction and the Reform of Colonial Slavery. Culling
from these critical discussions of the term, we deduce that a Creole is a person
born or naturalized in a colony (generally a tropical dependency) but of either
European or African descent. A Creole can therefore be white, black, or mixed
race, colonizer or colonized. Miller, in particular, asserts that the term speaks of
"a double differentiation or exile and opens the question of race while distinctly
providing no answer to it" (93). In *Indiana*, the term is used ambiguously for
both female characters.

To gain a better understanding of race in *Indiana*, students are also asked to
read the critic Doris Kadish's article "Representing Race in *Indiana*." I then
explore with my students the ambiguity of Indiana's race and whether there
is a doubt about her whiteness, in part because of how she was nursed by a
"négresse" 'negress' (157 [116]; 109). In this regard, Kadish notes: "Indiana was
nurtured with non-white, racially 'Other' milk of her wet-nurse and thus is herself partially non-white, too" (24). Kadish adds that the expression "sœur de lait"
used in *Indiana* "carries racial connotations that heighten Indiana's association
with persons of color" (25). Moreover, Indiana takes on the appearance of a
person of mixed race in the bedchamber scene with Raymon after Noun's death.
Just as Noun attempts to appropriate her mistress's identity to win the heart of
her lover, Indiana similarly impersonates her former servant to test Raymon
and confirm her suspicions about his past relationship with Noun. The two seduced women thus frequently stand for each other in the text, suggesting that
they together represent an amorphous Creole identity.

The Trope of the Tragic Mulatta

To provide students with background on the literary figure of the mulatto,
I assign relevant excerpts of *Le nègre romantique*, by Léon-François Hoffmann, and *Neither Black nor White yet Both: Thematic Explorations of Interracial Literature*, by Werner Sollors, and ask students to write a half-page
summary of the figure for homework. In class, we discuss how mixed-race
characters were common in French Romantic literature, as authors grappled
with questions surrounding race and slavery. I explain the tragic mulatto/a stereotype, one of the oldest archetypes in American literature, which dominated

abolitionist reform fiction since the late 1830s. The American literary critic Sterling Brown, the first to outline the figure, in 1933, explains that it "stemmed from the antislavery crusade, whose authors used it partly to show miscegenation as an evil of slavery, partly as an attempt to win readers' sympathies by presenting central characters who were physically very much like the readers" ("Century" 339). He identifies a gender division in the figure and argues that the stereotype is not limited to male characters. In fact, it was more common for writers to portray the mulatta figure: typically the daughter of a black slave woman and a white father who is more predisposed to tragedy than her male counterpart. Brown posits, "The whole desire of her life is to find a white lover, and then go down, accompanied by slow music, to a tragic end. Her fate is so severe that in some works disclosure of 'the single drop of midnight' in her veins makes her commit suicide" ("Negro Character" 196). Critics such as Jennifer DeVere Brody, Sollors, and Marlene Daut have argued that the tragic mulatto/a stereotype is not limited to American abolitionist fiction. Daut posits that the stereotype "can also be traced to early nineteenth-century French colonial literature, where the trope surfaced in conjunction with the image of the Haitian Revolution as a family conflict" (2). She cites the example of Émilie Jouannet's *Zorada; ou La créole* (1801), whose eponymous heroine is the daughter of a white man and a black female slave from Saint-Domingue. Sollors declares that "the literary representation of biracial characters, whatever their statistical relevance may have been, does not constitute an *avoidance* of more serious issues, but the most direct and head-on *engagement* with 'race,' perhaps the most troubling issue in the period from the French Revolution to World War II" (235). In *Indiana*, Sand brings the theme of race to the forefront and adds to the international dialogue on the topic by representing her own tragic mulattas.

Indiana as Slave

Although at first glance it might appear that Noun is the more tragic of the two female characters because of her suicide, we discover in the classroom that it is in fact Indiana who best exemplifies the figure of the tragic mulatta because of her status as a married woman. Rather than replicate the tragic mulatta stereotype, Sand actually subverts it when she redeems Indiana's fate in the end.

Indiana is described throughout the novel as "the poor captive" and a "slave" who suffers first from the tyranny of her father; followed by that of her husband, Delmare; and finally by her lover, Raymon. The *Littré* dictionary, published between 1863 and 1872, relates the concepts of obedience and duty to the word *slave*, which is defined figuratively as someone who is dominated by emotions such as fear and love ("Esclave"). To explore the themes of slavery and women's rights in more detail, I divide students into small groups and assign each a critical text by Hope Christiansen ("Masters and Slaves"), Jenson (ch. 5 of *Trauma and Its Representations*), Leslie Rabine ("George Sand"), and Nancy E. Rogers ("Slavery as Metaphor"). For homework, each group must prepare a short *PowerPoint* presentation on the critic's main arguments so that the class gains a more complete understanding of the marriage/slavery analogy in *Indiana*. Together, we discuss how the more Indiana longs to be free, the more she remains bound by chains. Then I break students into two groups and assign each a character: Colonel Delmare and Raymon de Ramière. Each group must find and share relevant quotations or passages that highlight how Indiana is a slave, both literally and figuratively, to each male character.

The story begins with a description of Indiana's marriage to Colonel Delmare, "excellent maître devant qui tout tremblait, femme, serviteurs, chevaux et chiens" 'an excellent master who made everyone tremble, wife, servants, horses, and dogs' (49 [19]; 15). When Indiana married Delmare, she "ne fit que changer de maître" 'she had only changed masters' (88 [56]; 51), and the narrator reveals that she has never learned any law other than that of "l'obéissance aveugle" 'blind obedience' (89 [56]; 51). Furthermore, Indiana has witnessed "des maux de la servitude" 'the ills of slavery' and has experienced "les ennuis de l'isolement et de la dépendence" 'vexations of solitude and dependence' (88 [56]; 51). The association of Indiana with slavery is established from the very outset of the novel. Indiana has always been dominated and controlled by the male figures in her life, and her mistreatment is allowed and even promoted by Napoléon's civil code. Despite Indiana's solitude, the reader is provided a glimmer of hope as she waits for her "messie" 'messiah' and the day when "tout sera changé dans ma vie" 'my life will be completely changed' (89 [56]; 51).

I point out to students the way in which Sand plays with the meaning of the term *slave*, using it both literally and figuratively as a *mise en question* of the role of the woman. The word's ambiguity manifests itself from the beginning of Indiana's relationship with Raymon. Soon after meeting him, the narrator poses the question, "N'était-elle pas née pour l'aimer, cette femme esclave qui n'attendait qu'un signe pour briser sa chaîne, qu'un mot pour le suivre? Le ciel, sans doute, l'avait formée pour Raymon, cette triste enfant de l'île Bourbon, que personne n'avait aimée, et qui sans lui devait mourir" 'Was she not born to love him, this enslaved woman who was only waiting for a sign to break her chain, for a word in order to follow him? Surely the heavens had created for Raymon this sad child of Bourbon Island whom no one had loved and who, but for him, was bound to die' (90 [57]; 52). She hopes that they are able to establish a relationship based on mutual love and respect. Unfortunately, Indiana is not able to "break her chain," and her tragic romantic life continues. She desires a partnership with her lover, but Raymon quickly discovers "qu'il était le maître et qu'il pouvait oser" 'he was the master and could be daring' (93 [60]; 55). In a dramatic scene in which Raymon explains how his love will be different from that of her husband, he proclaims, "Indiana, vous m'eussiez trouvé là, à vos pieds, vous gardant en maître jaloux, vous servant en esclave" 'Indiana, you would have found me, at your feet, guarding you like a jealous master, serving you like a slave' (95 [61]; 56). He now equates himself as both a master who protects her and a slave who serves her. In appropriating both roles, Raymon gives Indiana the illusion of having the upper hand in the relationship.

After Noun's death, Indiana clearly explains her expectations for an equal balance of power: "Il faut m'aimer sans partage, sans retour, sans réserve; il faut être prêt à me sacrifier tout, fortune, réputation, devoir, affaires, principes, famille; tout, monsieur, parce que je mettrai le même dévouement dans la balance et que je la veux égale" 'I must be loved absolutely, eternally, unreservedly. You must be ready to sacrifice everything for me, fortune, reputation, duty, business affairs, principles, family, everything, Monsieur, because I would put the same devotion on the scales and I want yours to equal mine' (148 [109]; 101).

In a letter she later sends to her lover, Indiana reiterates her desire for equality. Raymon is surprised by Indiana's ability to resist him as well as her fortitude: "[I]l n'avait pas cru jusqu'alors qu'une femme qui s'était jetée dans ses bras pût lui résister ouvertement et raisonner sa résistance" '[H]e had never believed that a woman who had thrown herself into his arms would have been able to resist him openly and give reasons for her resistance' (200 [153]; 147). Indeed, in the secret of his own company, "il jura, dans son dépit, qu'il triompherait d'elle. . . . Il jura qu'il serait son maître, ne fût-ce qu'un jour, et qu'ensuite il l'abandonnerait pour avoir le plaisir de la voir à ses pieds" 'in his annoyance, he vowed he would triumph over her. . . . He vowed he would be her master and then he would abandon her so as to have the pleasure of seeing her at his feet' (200 [154]; 148). Soon after proclaiming to be her master, he reverses the master/slave relation again by begging her forgiveness and vowing to serve her: "À present, ordonne, Indiana! je suis ton esclave, tu le sais bien. . . . Je serai doux, je serai soumis, je serai malheureux" 'Command me, now, Indiana! I am your slave, you know that very well. . . . I shall be gentle, I shall be submissive, I shall be unhappy' (201 [154]; 148). Here, Raymon uses the art of seduction to play the role of the slave, pretending to be someone he is not in order to destroy Indiana.

Raymon is not the only character to employ the rhetoric of slavery. I suggest a close reading of the following passage, in which students discover that Indiana is at his beck and call. This occurs only after Indiana throws herself at Raymon, then flees Paris with her husband, and finally escapes and travels back to France:

> C'est moi; c'est ton Indiana, c'est ton esclave que tu as rappelée de l'exil et qui est venue de trois mille lieues pour t'aimer et te server; c'est la compagne de ton choix qui a tout quitté, tout risqué, tout bravé pour t'apporter cet instant de joie! . . . je viens pour te donner du bonheur, pour être tout ce que tu voudras, ta compagne, ta servante ou ta maîtresse.   (296 [236–37])

It's me; it's your Indiana; it's your slave, whom you recalled from exile and who has come a thousand miles to love and serve you. It's your chosen companion, who has left everything, risked everything, braved everything, to bring you this moment of joy. . . . I've come to bring you happiness, to be whatever you want, your companion, your servant, or your mistress.   (231)

Indiana's attitude toward Raymon seems to have changed from earlier in the novel when she attempts to test his love in her bedchamber. Here, Raymon clearly dominates Indiana, and she will go to all lengths to regain his affection and companionship. She no longer speaks of an equal partnership, but decidedly promises to be his slave and do what he asks. During our discussion of Indiana's relationship with Raymon, I also alert students to the introduction by Béatrice Didier to the Gallimard 1984 edition, in which she claims that Indiana's slavish relationship with Raymon is even more destructive than the domination by her husband:

Mais son esclavage est tout aussi grand, sinon pire, avec Raymon. L'amant, dans ce roman, et encore plus décevant que le mari, dans la mesure où l'héroïne attendant plus de lui. Et la société a fait que lorsqu'elle est sans mari et sans amant, vraiment seule, la femme est réduite à rien, et c'est un des sens du tragique épisode du retour à Bordeaux.   (26)

Her enslavement is equally as bad, if not worse, with Raymon. The lover, in this novel, is even more of a disappointment than the husband, given that the heroine expected more from him. Society ensured that as long as she is without her husband or lover, a woman is reduced to nothing, and this is one interpretation of the tragic episode of her return to Bordeaux.
                                                            (my trans.)

This "tragic" return to Bordeaux strips Indiana of her identity, and Didier equates the downfall of Indiana to that of her foster sister. Noun ends her life by suicidal drowning, but up until this point, Indiana is the character who best replicates the tragic mulatta figure in the novel. Unlike other nineteenth-century French literary heroines studied in this course, such as Atala and Ourika, Indiana's tragedy is tied to her status as a slave, a key component of the tragic mulatta stereotype.

A World Free from Oppression

After Raymon deserts Indiana, she has many near-death experiences, the most evident one being the suicide pact she makes with her cousin Ralph on return to their native island. As it turns out, Indiana and Ralph discover that they are soul mates, triumph over tragedy, and lead an idyllic life on Bourbon Island. I ask students to analyze the outcome of the novel by writing a one-page reaction paper to the following question: Why is there this near culmination in drowning, a near parallel to Noun, and then such an abrupt change of events? When students arrive in class with their written reactions, we break into groups, and they share their analyses and opinions with one another.

Together, we discuss how Indiana's ideal society is one in which everyone would be equal, free from "les tyrans, les injustes et les ingrats" 'the tyrants, the unjust, and the ungrateful' (250 [196]; 191). In this imagined dream world, which she admits is of "une autre vie, d'un autre monde" 'another life, of another world' (250 [196]; 191), God eliminates oppression and slavery: "il passerait sa grande main sur nos têtes inégales et les nivellerait comme les eaux de la mer; il dirait à l'esclave: 'Jette ta chaîne, et fuis sur les monts où j'ai mis pour toi des eaux, des fleurs et du soleil'" 'He would spread his large hand out over our unequal heads and make them level like the surface of the sea. He would say to the slave: "Cast aside your chain and flee to the mountains, where I have placed water, mountains, and sunshine for you" (249–50 [196]; 191). In this quotation, Indiana uses the possessive adjective *our* to relate the oppression imposed on women with that of slaves.

My students and I discuss Indiana's relationship with Ralph and the ambiguous conclusion to the novel. Despite the fact that the ending gives priority to Ralph's voice while Indiana's is silenced, it can also be read as a sort of liberation. Indiana finally returns to her native Bourbon Island, away from the oppression and hierarchy of the *métropole*. Although she was bound for the same tragic fate as Noun, she is perhaps spared because of her ability to break free from the bondage of marriage and oppression that governed her life up until this point. She now shares her life with Ralph, a fellow Creole who does not subordinate her: "Je fis de vous ma sœur, ma fille, ma compagne, mon élève, ma société" 'I made you my sister, my daughter, my companion, my pupil, my social group' (316 [253]; 249).

Throughout the novel Ralph is depicted as having feminine qualities and is compared with women, slaves, and other oppressed groups. Much like Indiana, who was abused by the male figures in her life, Ralph was also mistreated by his father, the all-powerful master: "Mon père . . . était prêt à me maudire si j'essayais d'échapper à son joug. Je courbai la tête; mais ce que je souffris, vous-même, qui fûtes aussi bien malheureuse, ne sauriez l'apprécier" 'My father . . . was ready to curse me if I tried to escape from his yoke. I bowed to my fate, but even you, who have also been very unhappy, wouldn't be able to understand what I suffered' (323 [258]; 254). Sand again employs the rhetoric of slavery by referring to Ralph's father's "yoke," or power. Regarding Ralph, I refer students back to Kadish's article:

> No less than Noun and Indiana, he is a powerless and thus symbolically impotent victim of the masculine oppression of the colonialist system,

which is consistently associated with slavery. . . . Unlike powerful masculine Europeans such as Indiana's husband Delmare and her lover Raymon, Ralph is denigrated through his portrayal here in a symbolically feminine and slavelike guise as weak, submissive, silent, all-suffering, impotent, and asexual.   ("Representing" 27)

On their native island homeland, Indiana and Ralph have become companions and partners. They have found peace and make it their life's work to provide all slaves on the island with freedom: "Que ne sommes-nous assez riches pour délivrer tous ceux qui vivent dans l'esclavage! Nos serviteurs sont nos amis; ils partagent nos joies, nous soignons leurs maux" 'If only we were rich enough to free all who live in slavery! Our servants are our friends; they share our joys, we tend their ills' (342 [274]; 270).

In *Indiana*, slavery is not limited to black or mixed-race characters but represents a metaphor for oppression, particularly the subjection of women by men and the societal rules governing women under the Napoleonic Code in nineteenth-century France. In her preface to the 1832 edition, Sand states that she created Indiana as a "type" who is "l'être faible chargé de représenter les passions comprimées, ou, si vous l'aimez mieux, supprimées par *les lois*" 'the weak creature who is given the task of portraying passions, repressed, or if you prefer, suppressed *by the law*' (40; 7). In the end, Indiana breaks free from patriarchal law and thrives in an environment based on mutual respect and understanding. If Sand were alive today, she would perhaps echo the questions posed by Eve Allegra Raimon in *The "Tragic Mulatta" Revisited: Race and Nationalism in Nineteenth-Century Antislavery Fiction*:

> If it is true . . . that such identity categories of race and gender cannot be isolated but instead express themselves through and in the terms of one another, then how is it possible for readers not to see themselves mirrored in racial as well as gendered terms in these narratives? For the tales to have accomplished their rhetorical aims, how could they not have called on their audience to identify with their heroines in *all* aspects of their subjectivities?   (27)

George Sand subverts the figure of the tragic mulatta to show that race and gender are inextricably linked in determining civil and social acceptance. The binaries of male/female, black/white, master/slave, and *métropole*/colony are brought to the forefront in *Indiana* as Sand calls into question the entire societal hierarchy of the mid-nineteenth century.

NOTE

[1] Students could be asked to complete a comparative analysis of the Black Code and the civil code as a homework assignment.

Indiana Debutante

Isabelle Hoog Naginski

An Ethereal Heroine

Chapters 4 and 5 in part 1 of *Indiana* recount in great detail Raymon's reentry into fashionable high society after a sentimental interlude in the country. At the ball given by the Spanish ambassador, Raymon finds himself the object of several women's gazes, including that of the sardonic Mlle de Nangy, who will later become his wife. More important, it is in this scene that Raymon wanders among the elegant attendees until he comes face to face with a young woman who is making her debut in the Parisian salons. Although married, the mysterious guest is nevertheless marked by all the attributes of the debutante—she wears a simple white dress, and her charming demeanor betrays her air of complete candor. Her appearance dazzles the young aristocrat:

> Les honneurs de la soirée étaient en ce moment pour une jeune femme dont personne ne savait le nom, et qui, par la nouveauté de son apparition dans le monde, jouissait du privilège de fixer l'attention. La simplicité de sa mise eût suffi pour la détacher en relief au milieu des diamants, des plumes et des fleurs qui paraient les autres femmes. Des rangs de perles tressées dans ses cheveux noirs composaient tout son écrin. Le blanc mat de son collier, celui de sa robe de crêpe et de ses épaules nues, se confondaient à quelque distance, et la chaleur des appartements avait à peine réussi à élever sur ses joues une nuance délicate comme celle d'une rose de Bengale éclose sur la neige. C'était . . . une beauté de salon que la lueur vive des bougies rendait féérique. . . .   (80 [48])

> At this moment, the honours of the evening were awarded to a young woman whose name no one knew, and who, by the novelty of her appearance in society, enjoyed the privilege of arresting everyone's attention. The simplicity of her dress would have been enough to make her stand out in the midst of the diamonds, feathers, and flowers which adorned the other women. Rows of pearls wound into her black hair were her only jewels. The dull white of her necklace, of her crêpe dress, and of her bare shoulders blended together from a distance, and the warmth of the rooms had barely managed to bring to her cheeks a delicate hue like that of a Bengal rose flowering in snow. She was . . . a drawing-room beauty, fairy-like in the bright light of the candles. . . .   (43)

As Raymon watches her dance, she appears to him a supernatural creature:

En dansant, elle était si légère, qu'un souffle eût suffi pour l'enlever.... Les contes fantastiques étaient à cette époque dans toute la fraîcheur de leurs succès; aussi les érudits du genre comparèrent cette jeune femme à une ravissante apparition évoquée par la magie, qui, lorsque le jour blanchirait l'horizon, devait pâlir et s'effacer comme un rêve.　　(80 [48–49])

As she danced, she was so light that a puff of wind would have been enough to blow her away.... At that time, tales of the supernatural were at the height of their popularity, and so connoisseurs of the genre compared the young woman to a charming spectre, magically evoked, which would become dim and fade away like a dream when day began to dawn. (43–44)

The allusion here may be to the "sylphide"—the eponymous heroine of the first Romantic ballet who, like Indiana, made her debut in the winter of 1832. The diaphanous and surreal existence of this debutante underscores the fashionable ideal of the time for ethereal women.

This is an excellent passage with which to start the first class discussion of *Indiana*. It is a pivotal scene appearing early on—in the first thirty pages—so that students who are just beginning the novel will have encountered it. They will recognize the first instance of the heroine's social gaucherie as well as the young man's Don Juanesque proclivities. They will also be able to ascertain how deftly Sand sets up the unequal relationship between the two main characters. As the novel progresses, the erotic duel between them will become a confrontation of two gendered sets of values: feminine naïveté, social ignorance, and credulity against masculine manipulation, social know-how, and verbal eloquence. Students will sense that the male character is at the top of his game as he embarks on his plan to seduce Indiana and sets in motion the coming tragedy. For in redirecting his attentions to Indiana, Raymon exacerbates Noun's sense of abandonment and precipitates her suicide, which takes place unusually early in the novel, at the end of part 1. Readers will also note the extent to which Indiana is starstruck, innocent in the extreme, ready to fall under Raymon's charm. This passage, then, can be studied as a pivotal scene that sets the wheels of the plot firmly moving forward.[1]

There are several ways an instructor can use this scene as a point of departure for a better understanding of the novel as a whole. First, it contains in miniature the love plot, which is based on illusion and on the seductive power of Raymon's discourse. Furthermore, it highlights the inequality between male and female social sophistication and knowledge. Raymon acts like a pro. Indiana is but a beginner, a debutante in the psychological as well as the social sense.

The scene is also a showcase for the heroine's virtues and faults. Readers can see how Sand constructs her heroine through a complex set of oppositions. Indiana is intellectually astute but socially inept. Her introverted temperament may give her a superior understanding of human nature, yet she is quite blind to a duplicitous character such as Raymon. For students who tend to look at the figuration of characters first, this passage is an apt illustration of Sand's conception of her heroine. Here is the budding novelist describing the prototype for Indiana in early 1832, at this stage called Noémi:

> [M]a Noémi c'est la femme typique, faible et forte, fatiguée du poids de l'air, et capable de porter le ciel, timide dans le courant de la vie, audacieuse les jours de bataille, fine, adroite et pénétrante pour saisir les fils déliés de la vie commune, niaise et stupide pour distinguer les vrais intérêts de son bonheur, se moquant du monde entier, se laissant duper par un seul homme, . . . dédaignant les vanités du siècle pour son compte et se laissant séduire par l'homme qui les réunit toutes . . . un incroyable mélange de faiblesse et d'énergie, de grandeur et de petitesse, un être toujours composé de deux natures opposées. . . .
> (*Correspondance* 2: 47–48; letter to Emile Regnault)

> My Noémi is a typical woman, both weak and strong; exhausted by the weight of the air and capable of carrying the sky; timid in everyday life, audacious on days of battle; sensitive, clever, and able to understand how to untangle the threads of daily life yet dumb and stupidly unable to distinguish the real interests of her own happiness, making fun of the entire world, allowing herself to be duped by a single man, . . . disdaining the vanities of the world for her own sake and allowing herself to be seduced by the man who embodies them all . . . an incredible blend of weakness and energy, of greatness and pettiness, a being forever composed of two opposite natures. . . .   (my trans.)

Sand's description can help students see how the debutante chapters illustrate the heroine's weaknesses. Readers can then be encouraged to identify contrasting scenes that highlight Indiana's strong points. The novel opens with such a scene, in which Indiana cares for the wounded Raymon, "avec un sang-froid et une force morale dont personne ne l'eût crue capable" 'with a sangfroid and moral strength of which no one would have thought her capable' (64 [32]; 28). The hunting scene later in the novel (ch. 14, pt. 2), in which the heroine's bold behavior elicits shock in Raymon, offers another instance. That Indiana's name becomes firmly associated with Diana, the virginal Goddess of the hunt, in those pages adds to Raymon's sense that the young woman's "intrépidité délirante" 'mad intrepidity' is out of character (162 [120]; 113).

In addition, the debutante pages contain the first protracted conversation between Raymon and Indiana and reveal the extent of the inequality of their respective rhetorical talents. Delmare speaks, Indiana shudders. She sputters a few banal words: "Ah! oui, monsieur . . . c'est vous!" 'Oh yes, Monsieur . . . it's you' (82 [50]; 45), then, afraid of having breached some social convention, falls silent and blushes. Raymon speaks with ease and at length, while she is only able to mumble a few additional words. When Indiana is leaving the ball, Raymon takes her hand and kisses it furtively. The young woman, completely overwhelmed by emotion, "abandons herself" to "the power of conviction of his spoken words."[2] Likened to a lawyer and to a preacher ("prédicateur"), Raymon is also depicted as a character who is powerful with words. This conversation of unequals prepares the way for the more elaborate one a few pages later, when Raymon forces his way into Indiana's apartment and embarks on a grand dithyramb of seduction (93–97 [60–63]; 55–58). This speech is worth analyzing carefully in its own right, as it contains a catalog of all the romantic clichés regarding women and love, thus showing Raymon to be as insincere as he is astute in his manipulation.

In these encounters between Indiana, described as "une personne étrangère au monde" 'a person unused to high society' (81 [49]; 44), and her seducer, students can begin to see how in Sand's fictional universe generally the character who has the power of speech exerts the most influence in the text. And in these early scenes, the heroine finds herself for the most part tongue-tied, incapable of speech. The debutante chapters are crucial, then, because they underscore a great tendency in Sand's fiction of privileging the speaking subject and giving spoken words at least as much importance as the character's inner monologues or epistolary ruminations, if not more.[3] This emphasis on the speaking voice reveals Sand's affinity for theatrical forms, of course, an affinity that she will exploit more fully later in her career. More important for us here, it underscores Sand's preference for orality, clearly associated with spontaneity and immediacy, over the fixed written word. Indeed, one of the underlying themes of this first novel is to show that the process of coming into literary power for Sand is achieved through mastery of the spoken language. Raymon's astonishing silencing at the end of the book, counterbalanced by Ralph's miraculous metamorphosis, can be understood in the light of this fictional law.

Indiana Seduced

In these early pages, Sand never actually refers to her heroine as a debutante.[4] Rather, Indiana is described as "une novice" 'a novice' (87 [55]; my trans.) and "[une] femme simple et neuve" 'this simple, inexperienced woman' (83 [51]; 46). Nevertheless the term is apt because it underscores the character's lack of astuteness in the social circles of her day. On a metaphoric level, the term *debutante* could be understood to refer to Sand, who, with the writing of *Indiana*, is embarking on her first solo literary journey. We know how vociferously Sand denied that Indiana's story was an unveiling of her autobiographical self: "*Indiana* n'était pas mon histoire dévoilée" '*Indiana* was not my story unveiled,' she insisted years later in *Histoire de ma vie* (*Œuvres autobiographiques* 2: 164; my trans.). Students can be made to see, however, that the debutante scene in which Indiana stands in awe before Raymon may well inscribe a depiction of the young Sand standing awestruck before the literary establishment of her time. She writes in her memoirs that in 1832 she was "émerveillée" 'filled with wonder' before a writer such as Balzac (2: 154).[5] More than the stereotypical Don Juan figure, Raymon is a gifted man of letters who possesses the power of words and is able to seduce his readers. It is his rhetorical potency rather than his sexual prowess that captivates Indiana and interests Sand. When pointing out this juxtaposition to students, instructors may wish to embark on a discussion of instances where a character can be understood not as a reflection of a real person in the writer's life, nor an instance of a character type, such as the ingénue or the evil seducer, but as the embodiment of an attitude of the author.

Many critics have noted that *Indiana*, surprisingly, does not seem to be a first novel or a novel of apprenticeship. Rather, it gives the impression of being the product of an established writer, of a confirmed talent. How could such a budding novelist express herself with the assurance of a mature author? Henry James, who analyzes this aspect of Sand's coming to writing, marvels at the vigor of this emerging literary voice when he writes:

> About this sudden entrance into literature, into philosophy, into rebellion . . . there are various different things to be said. Very remarkable, indeed, was the immediate development of the literary faculty in this needy young woman who . . . looked for "employment." She wrote as a bird sings; but unlike most birds, she found it unnecessary to indulge, by way of prelude, in twitterings and vocal exercises; she broke out at once with her full volume of expression.   ("George Sand" [1984] 717)

This "full volume of expression" refers of course to *Indiana*. And while we may, like James, admire the craftsmanship of this debut novel, I think it is also possible to discern in it a certain anxiety typical of an emerging writer. That anxiety is not so much felt in Sand's command of the language as it is hidden in the thematics of the novel, for, as we have just seen in the debutante pages, *Indiana* is a novel in which the deep subject is a writing debut. Sand inscribes this theme into her text through an examination of each character's language system. And so one can consider the novel as a succession of narrative experiments culminating in one character's coming finally into command of a narrative voice, a trajectory that clearly recapitulates Sand's discovery of her authentic authorial voice.

The debutante passage can readily be seen as an expression of the author's awe before the literary world she was exploring. In this sense, then, the heroine is a projection of the budding writer. Nevertheless, at the end of the novel, once Ralph has undergone his transformation into a poetic and psychologically astute storyteller, Indiana falls again into silence. At the end of part 4, it is Ralph who becomes the speaking subject of the narrative in a fifteen-page confession. And in the conclusion, it is Ralph who becomes the source of all the information the first-person narrator has at his disposal. So in a real way, in the last thirty pages, Ralph becomes the all-powerful character whose words control the narrative.

Coming to Writing

How does this fit with our idea of Sand inscribed into the text as a budding writer? I would propose that at the end of her text Sand has shifted her allegiance from Indiana to Ralph. She has now become Ralph, an identification that may seem problematic from a gender perspective. But such a claim is not simply a critical assertion, for there are indications in the text to support such a statement. Two sets of clues bear examination. The first has to do with Sand's use of the verb "veiller"—in the novel as well as in her memoirs—a verb that has two meanings, to stay up all night and to watch over someone.

As Sand embarked on her career as a writer, she adopted as well the act of "veiller" in its double meaning. Throughout her life she would write at night, and she had acquired the habit of being up at night as a girl, when she was caring for her invalid grandmother, and then as a young woman, when she watched over her children. Two passages in *Histoire de ma vie* illustrate the direct link in Sand's mind between the act of writing and the act of watching over a loved one:

> Voulant mener de front le soin de ma bonne maman, les promenades nécessaires à ma santé et mon éducation, j'avais pris le parti, voyant que quatre heures de sommeil ne me suffisaient pas, de ne plus me coucher que de deux nuits l'une. Je ne sais si c'était un meilleur système, mais je m'y habituai vite, et me sentis beaucoup moins fatiguée ainsi que par le sommeil à petites doses. Parfois, il est vrai, la malade me demandait à deux heures du matin . . . et je prenais le parti de lire et de renoncer à ma nuit de sommeil.   (*Œuvres autobiographiques* 1: 1091–92)

> Wanting to manage three areas at once—the care of my grandmother, the walks necessary for my health, and my education—I had decided, seeing that four hours of sleep were not enough for me, to go to bed only every other night. I do not know if I made the right choice, but I quickly became used to it, and felt much less tired doing that than sleeping in snatches. Sometimes, it is true, the patient would ask for me at two in the morning . . . so I would choose to read by her side and give up my night's sleep.   (Story 790)

Sand quite readily combines two unrelated occupations—that of keeping her grandmother company and that of reading and writing through the night. The caritative and the intellectual seem to coexist without conflict. And in the foundational scene of her coming to writing, a similar conjunction is set up. The young Aurore Dudevant, on the verge of embarking on a new life, is about to travel to Paris. She is still in Nohant on one of the last nights before her departure:

> J'habitais alors l'ancien boudoir de ma grand'mère. . . . Mes deux enfants occupaient la grande chambre attenante. Je les entendais respirer, et je pouvais *veiller* sans troubler leur sommeil. Ce boudoir était si petit, qu'avec mes livres, mes herbiers, mes papillons et mes cailloux . . . il n'y avait pas de place pour un lit. J'y suppléais par un hamac. Je faisais mon bureau d'une armoire qui s'ouvrait en manière de secrétaire et qu'un *cri-cri* . . . occupa longtemps avec moi. (*Œuvres autobiographiques* 2: 100; first emphasis mine)

> At that time I used what had formerly been my grandmother's boudoir. . . . My two children occupied the larger, adjoining bedroom. I could hear them breathe, and I could *keep watch* without disturbing their sleep. My boudoir was so small that, with my books, my herbarium, my butterflies, and my pebbles . . . there was no place for a bed. I made do with a hammock. My desk was in an armoire that opened like a secretary, and that a cricket . . . occupied for a long time as well.   (Story 881; emphasis mine)

Sand is involved in a *veillée* of two kinds—she watches over her children and devotes herself to her writing. The two actions of being at a loved one's bedside and writing late into the night have now become firmly merged in her psyche.

Turning to *Indiana*, students can recognize that Ralph is the character who is engaged in watching over the heroine, from the very beginning of the novel to its conclusion. Of the ten instances of the verb *veiller* in the text, six refer to Ralph (who watched over Indiana as a child and continues to watch over her in France and on her return with Delmare to the Île Bourbon), one to God, and one to Raymon's mother; the remaining two refer negatively to Raymon: he failed to watch over his mother, and he would have watched over Indiana in an unreal conditional tense. There are also several crucial scenes in which Ralph appears seemingly "ex machina" to save the heroine from her husband, from suicide, or from a fatal illness (116, 196, 227, 301 [81, 150, 176, 241]; 74, 144, 172, 236). In chapter 23, Ralph explains that he has been watching over Indiana for the past six months (237 [185]; 181). Since the Sandian reader knows that the action of *veiller* is linked to the action of writing, it is not surprising that Ralph at the end of the novel becomes its storyteller.

The Complex of the "Femme-Auteur"

The second set of clues involves the colloquial word "gaillard," a robust or strapping fellow. We may recall having encountered the term in a strange but triumphant declaration that Sand made to her convent friend, Laure Decerfz, in July 1833, in which she announced that "Mme Dudevant is dead"—in other words, that she herself has died: "A Paris Mme Dudevant est morte. Mais Georges [sic] Sand est connue pour un vigoureux gaillard" 'In Paris, Madame Dudevant is dead. But George Sand is known to be quite a guy' (*Correspondance* 2: 120; my trans.). How can students understand the novelist's proclamation of her own death?

Let us return briefly to *Indiana*. If we remember that Sand always had a deep-seated aversion to the image of the lady scribbler—what the French call "une femme-auteur," a woman who writes for women rather than so-called universal literature—then we will better grasp why Sand wanted at all costs to avoid being imprisoned in the ghetto of feminine literature, as she perceived that many of her predecessors had been. Sand wanted to be a part of *La revue des deux mondes*, to play a role in the Parisian literary world, to be the equal of the men of letters of her day. The aggressive remark she makes to her friend Charles Meuze in late January 1832, when she is at work on her debut novel, is symptomatic in this regard: "Ne m'appelez donc jamais *femme-auteur*, ou je vous fais avaler mes cinq volumes et vous ne vous en releverez jamais" 'Never call me a lady scribbler again, or I shall make you swallow my five volumes and you will never recover from the ordeal' (*Correspondance* 2: 16; my trans.).

And so we see in her correspondence that Sand sacrifices her own civic identity just as she will sacrifice her heroine in the last part of her novel. Sand sacrifices Indiana by silencing her and affiliates herself with Ralph. Indiana's voice is the voice of the "femme-auteur," and she is done away with, just as "Mme Dudevant" is. In her place, Sand's narrative reveals the verbal liberation of the androgyne Ralph Brown and in the telling manifests the emergence of the writer George Sand. Strikingly this newly born author called Sand, having declared his presence as "un vigoureux gaillard" in a letter to a friend, uses *gaillard* only once in *Indiana*, applying it precisely to Ralph and highlighting it, incongruously, in italics for good measure.[6]

Melancholic Indiana

Despite James's comments, one can find in Sand's debut novel elements that mark it as an apprenticeship piece. Especially noticeable in this regard is an outmoded system that the author uses as a way to give psychological coherence to her main characters—Indiana, Delmare, Ralph, and Raymon. That Sand herself considered her novel to be about four characters is clear in a letter that she writes to Emile Regnault in February 1832: "Mon livre est déjà jugé par moi. Il plaira à peu de gens. Il est d'une exécution trop sévère. . . . Ce sont quatre volumes sur quatre caractères . . . " 'My book has already been judged by me. It will please few people. It is too austere in its execution. . . . It consists in four volumes about four different characters . . . ' (*Correspondance* 2: 47; my trans.).

The fact that Sand wrote "caractères" rather than "personnages" indicates that she was thinking in terms of character types. Her fear that her novel would be judged "sévère"—I read this to mean rigid—suggests that she was using the theory of the four humors as the four structural pillars of her fiction. Like classical dramatic authors before her, such as Menander, Plautus, and Molière, the young author attempts to construct the main characters in a meaningful way by playing with the theory of the four humors. This medical theory, first formulated by Hippocrates and further expounded on by Galen, posited that the four fluids that were thought to make up the human body—blood, phlegm, yellow bile, and black bile—determined a person's psychological makeup. Someone suffering from a surplus of one fluid tended to display certain psychological characteristics. In this way, four main temperaments were identified: the sanguine, the phlegmatic, the choleric or bilious, and the melancholic. It is remarkable how powerful this theory was in the medical world, up until the middle of the nineteenth century. When we examine how Sand applied the theory of four distinct personality types to her main characters, we note that it is absolutely convincing in the case of the heroine and her cousin, works almost as a caricature for Indiana's brutish husband, and seems arbitrary or, at the very least, somewhat forced for the antihero, Raymon.

There is no doubt that Sand wanted to use Indiana to depict a feminized "mal du siècle" 'ailment of the century,' to make her the little sister of François-René de Chateaubriand's René.[7] The young author started with a melancholic heroine. Then, wanting her configuration of the four humors to work, she found it easy to create a choleric (or bilious) husband and placed him in opposition to her female character. We can surmise that the creation of Ralph as a typically phlegmatic Englishman evolved fairly easily after that. But what all this meant is that Sand was forced to associate the fourth humor rather arbitrarily with Raymon. Although the sanguine temperament at first seems to fit his figuration as an extroverted and suave seducer, his character becomes somewhat contradictory later in the novel.

It is striking how quickly, in the early pages of the novel, three of the characters are associated with a dominant humor. Thus Indiana, splenetic and prone to melancholy, suffers from an overabundance of black bile. Of the twelve occurrences of the adjective "mélancolique," seven are associated with her (three are ascribed to Ralph, two to nature). A vocabulary of melancholy fills the early pages, including "spleen," translated as "depression" (58 [27]; 23), and "mélancolie" (94, 61 [101, 67]) and "mélancolique" (56 [61]), both translated as "melancholy" (119, 83, 76). In stark opposition to Indiana stands her choleric husband, whose rages display the surplus of yellow bile in his system. While the word *colérique* does not appear in the text, there are many instances of words associated with the negative features of the bilious type, such as anger or rage. The word *colère* especially is significant: of the thirty-four instances of the word, eighteen belong to Delmare. In the early pages, we see this cluster of words designating the angry husband: "colère" 'anger' three times (65, 33, 29 [69, 33, 35]; 96, 63, 58) and "fureur" 'rage' once (66 [34]; 30). In contrast, Ralph's unusually calm and unemotional behavior marks him as a characteristic phlegmatic type. All four of the instances of the word *flegmatique* belong to him, and the word *flegme* is also present (55, 90 [24, 57]; 20, 52). So far, well and good. It is clear that the three characters fit their profiles with ease, and students can enjoy seeing how frequently words associated with the three humoral types are used by Sand.

But when it comes to the fourth character, readers cannot help feeling that he has been assigned the fourth humor, blood, almost by default. Although he is sociable, charismatic, and talkative, fitting the sanguine type, in the first half of the novel, in part 3 Sand seems to change her mind and makes him a more complex character, with both sanguine and bilious traits. Indiana has accorded Raymon a secret assignation. When he enters the darkened room, Indiana confronts him holding a mass of black hair in her hands and asking him if he does not recognize whose it is. Raymon is filled with horror. He falls into a chair, and the narrator informs us, "[t]ant d'émotions pénibles l'avaient épuisé. C'était un homme *bilieux* dont le sang circulait vite, dont les nerfs s'irritaient profondément. Il frissonna de la tête aux pieds, et roula évanoui sur le parquet" '[s]o many painful emotions had exhausted him. He was a man of irascible [bilious] temperament, with rapidly circulating blood and deeply irritable nerves. He shuddered from head to foot and fell to the floor in a faint' (192–93 [147]; 141; my emphasis). The association of Raymon with a bilious temperament is unexpected here. Furthermore, the symptoms of such a temperament that, in this instance, lead to fainting are not medically sound or convincing. The bilious type, according to the entry "bilieux" in the *Larousse du XIXe siècle*, often designates the temperament of an ambitious man who, when becoming ill, is more likely to have a greenish complexion, to fly out in a rage, or to fall prey to a fever or a nervous attack (or a "crise de foie" 'liver upset') than to faint. Before this scene, Raymon had been portrayed as a dashing young man of action, nimble on his feet, who could talk himself out of most difficult situations. These were all traits of the sanguine personality. This fainting scene seems out of character and prompts readers to wonder if this episode was perhaps composed more as a way to play with the spectrum of the four temperaments than to meet the exigencies of the plot. But perhaps Sand's choice becomes clearer when the reader learns later of Delmare's death by apoplexy, a death appropriate for a sanguine personality. These humoral clues, then, suggest that a change has taken place. It is as if the two male characters—Delmare and Raymon—had exchanged personalities in the second half of the novel.[8]

Students can be encouraged to see in *Indiana* a novel rich in meaning yet replete with contradictory elements. Despite its display of unusual mastery, it betrays, through the figuration of its heroine, that it is also a beginner's novel.

In their examination of the cast of characters, students can be made aware that a fictional being is not necessarily completely imaginary or based on an actual person in the author's life. Nor is the protagonist automatically a transposition of the writer. Indiana is not the young Sand, yet aspects of the heroine's behavior can be read as symptomatic of certain intellectual tendencies in the author. The novel, in its depiction of the social and political realities in 1830, deploys a series of realist stratagems, yet it already displays elements of Sandian idealism. While it is certainly a love story, *Indiana* is also a reflection on the craft of writing. It feminizes the fashionable Romantic melancholy of the day and also plays with the classical humoral system. In a very real sense, then, it allows for many different paths of critical assessment. As Sand's first solo novel, *Indiana* is a privileged text for students who are embarking on the discovery of her vast fictional universe and for those who want to understand better the development of the nineteenth-century European novel.

NOTES

[1] The importance of this passage will be further underscored in the "circular room" scene, when Raymon imagines he sees "dans la glace en face de lui une forme blanche et parée, le fantôme d'une femme qui entre au bal" 'a white, bejewelled figure appear in the mirror in front of him, the ghost of a woman . . . entering a ballroom' (101 [68]; 62).

[2] Indiana "s'abandonnait . . . [à] cette puissance de conviction [de] ses paroles" 'succumbed [to] [the] power of conviction . . . [of] his words' (83 [51]; 46).

[3] "Le plus honnête des hommes est celui qui pense et qui agit le mieux, mais le plus puissant est celui qui sait le mieux écrire et parler" 'The most honest of men is the one who thinks and acts best, but the most powerful is the one who writes and speaks best' (130 [93]; 85).

[4] Sand will reserve this appellation for another of her young and socially naive heroines, Consuelo.

[5] See also *Œuvres autobiographiques* 2: 159 and the beginning pages of her necrology of Latouche, where Sand recounts her beginner's mental "engourdissement" 'numbness' and her "ébahissement" 'astonishment' before her mentor's dazzling facility of speech ("H. de Latouche" 230–37; my trans.).

[6] Delmare is mocking Ralph's political ideas: "Parbleu! vous voilà bien, sir Ralph, avec votre philanthropie pratique! . . . Vous me ferez croire que votre fortune ne vous appartient pas, et que, si demain la nation en prend envie, vous êtes prêt à changer vos cinquante mille francs de rente pour un bissac et un bâton! Cela sied bien à un *gaillard* comme vous, qui aime les aises de la vie comme un sultan, de prêcher le mépris de richesses!" 'Oh, my goodness! That's just like you with your practical philanthropy! . . . You'll make me believe your fortune doesn't belong to you and that tomorrow, if the nation takes a fancy to it, you are ready to exchange your income of fifty thousand francs for a beggar's knapsack and staff. It's fitting for a strong chap like you, who's as fond of the comforts of life as a sultan, to preach contempt for wealth!' (123 [86]; 79).

[7] This is another instance of identification between Sand and her heroine: "Il me sembla que *René* [sic] c'était moi" 'It seemed to me that René was myself' (*Œuvres auto-*

biographiques 1: 1092; Story 790); "J'avais . . . cedé au goût du siècle, qui était alors de s'enfermer dans une douleur égoïste, de se croire René" 'I had probably given in to the taste of the century, which was then to bury oneself in egotistical suffering, imagine oneself a René' (2: 195; 945).

[8] For a slightly different reading of the play of humoral paradigms in the novel, see Grossman.

Indiana between Men:
Narration and Desire in George Sand's Novel

Aimée Boutin

Despite being named after its heroine, *Indiana* is a novel about men. Ostensibly about marriage and the condition of the mid-nineteenth-century Frenchwoman, as even the author's 1842 preface states (46; 13), the novel actually better represents the situation of men and masculinity at the dawn of the July Monarchy. *Indiana* describes three male characters' political ideologies, languages, and positions within that society, as well as the wounded masculinity that each of the three embodies. Its narration figures the homosocial bonds that underwrite late restoration society. "Triangular desire," a concept developed by René Girard in *Deceit, Desire, and the Novel* in which each heterosexual relationship is doubled by a competing homosocial relationship, figures the rivalry between men at both the thematic and narrative levels of the novel. This approach helps students understand how the narrative is constructed to draw attention to patriarchal relationships and to elicit the connivance of male narrator and narratee. Ultimately, however, a focus on the novel's male characters can lead to a better appreciation of Sand's feminism.

Whereas there is really only one central female character, there are three main male characters in the novel: Colonel Delmare, Indiana's husband; Sir Ralph Brown, Indiana's cousin and later her companion; and Raymon de Ramière, Indiana's lover. One could also identify a fourth central male character: the quasi-dramatized narrator who at times proffers his opinions in the first person, especially in the first edition dated 1832 (e.g., 83–84 [50–51]; 45–46).[1] Although each character is engaged in a heterosexual relationship with Indiana, the relations among men in the novel carry as much if not more weight than those between man and woman. Indeed, when I teach *Indiana* in a course on French women writers, I show how the novel maps two separate gendered spheres. The political debates in particular bind these men together in an exclusive public sphere. As, in the words of the narrator, "l'opinion politique d'un homme c'est l'homme tout entier" 'a man's political opinions are the whole man' (166 [123]; 116), each male character embodies a set of specific social, political, governmental, and linguistic ideologies. The novel uses these characters to comment on the years from 1828 to 1830, the "époque . . . où, sur le bord d'un abîme sans fond, la civilisation s'endormait, avide de jouir de ses derniers plaisirs" 'period . . . when, on the edge of a bottomless abyss, civilization was falling asleep, greedy to enjoy its last pleasures' (129 [92]; 85). Whereas Colonel Delmare represents the Napoleonic past, Ralph typifies the future republic, and Raymon the restored monarchy of Charles X. The narrator remains critical of all the characters and does not hesitate to emphasize their flaws.

C'était vraiment une chose curieuse que d'entendre les niaiseries senti-
mentales de Delmare et de M. de Ramière, tous les deux philanthropes
rêveurs, l'un sous l'épée de Napoléon, l'autre sous le sceptre de Saint
Louis; M. Delmare, planté au pied des Pyramides; Raymon, assis sous le
monarchique ombrage du chêne de Vincennes.   (169 [126])

It was a really strange experience to listen to the sentimental stupidities of
Delmare and M. de Ramière, both of them philanthropic dreamers, the
one under Napoleon's sword, the other under St Louis' scepter, M. Delmare standing firmly at the foot of the Pyramids, Raymon seated in the
regal shade of the oak of Vincennes.   (119)

As others have examined more closely, these nostalgic men, descendants of
François-René de Chateaubriand's René, represent the wounded masculinity
of individuals caught in a temporal vacuum.

Even more than the other two, Ralph embodies the displaced, splenetic Romantic hero. Misunderstood until we learn of his traumatic past (pt. 2, ch. 13), of
all the characters he undergoes the most dramatic psychological development.
The narrator, who retells the story he heard from Ralph on Bourbon Island
and who may indeed be no more than a front for Ralph, intentionally withholds
information about Ralph to disclose hidden depths that will open in the end to
reveal him as the novel's focal point. This growth is such that *Indiana*, in Peter
Dayan's words, "is indeed Ralph's story—not only the tale he tells but also the
narrative that constitutes him" (160). Although their personalities and ideologies differ, these three characters are united in their wounded masculinity and
in the homosociality that doubles all heterosexual relations in the novel.

A pattern of male friendship, entitlement, and rivalry determines the novel's
erotic triangles. In her 1985 book *Between Men: English Literature and Male
Homosocial Desire*, Eve Kosofsky Sedgwick expands on Girard's analysis of
erotic triangles in European fiction in *Deceit, Desire, and the Novel*. Whereas
Girard posits that rivalry and identification structure the relations between
members of the triangle regardless of gender, Sedgwick argues that the power
dynamics in a rivalry between men over a woman differ substantially from
those in an erotic triangle composed of two women and one man. Triangular
desire governs all relationships that involve Indiana, whether Delmare-Ralph-
Indiana, Raymon-Ralph-Indiana, Delmare-Raymon-Indiana, or Ralph–the
narrator–Indiana. Erotic triangles in *Indiana* in fact exemplify Sedgwick's observation that the bonds between male rivals are "stronger and more heavily
determinant of actions and choices, than anything in the bonds between either
of the lovers and the beloved" (21). Other triangular relationships also exist that
associate Raymon with two women—namely, Noun and Indiana or Indiana and
Laure de Nangy. Arguably, these do not have the same impact on the narrative
given the asymmetry Sedgwick posits between male and female homosociality.

Whereas female friendship and lesbianism exist in a "relatively smooth and palpable continuum" (23), male sexual and nonsexual bonds are radically opposed in modern society. Central to Sedgwick's thesis is the claim that the basic paradigm of "male traffic in women," or male homosociality, transmits and maintains the power dynamics that ground patriarchal society. For example, while we might expect that the secret romance between Indiana and Raymon threatens to undermine the patriarchal institution of marriage, the novel shows instead how Delmare's soliciting the aid of Raymon in harnessing his wife sustains patriarchal power.

Of all the relationships between men, that between Ralph and Raymon most intricately reveals the workings of male homosociality. Although Ralph and Raymon call each other "[m]on cher ami" '[m]y dear fellow' (165 [123]; 116), their male friendship masks their mutual frustration, jealousy, and rivalry over a woman. Yet it is the presence of male competition that makes Indiana worth pursuing in part 2 of the novel. Despite their dislike of each other, both Raymon and Ralph each save the other from harm's way. Ralph saves Raymon at the moment when the memory of Noun threatens to cause him to fall into the river (139 [110]; 93), and Raymon saves Ralph from committing suicide when he falsely believes that Indiana has fallen off her horse and died (163 [121]; 114–15). At times, it seems even that Raymon desires Ralph's desire more than Indiana's. In any case, he justifies to himself, "L'important, d'ailleurs, c'était de passer une nuit dans sa chambre, afin de ne pas être un sot à ses propres yeux, afin de rendre inutile la prudence de Ralph, et de pouvoir le railler intérieurement. C'était une satisfaction personnelle dont il avait besoin" 'The important thing was to spend a night in her room, so as not to appear foolish in his own eyes, so as to make Ralph's prudence ineffectual and to be able to laugh at him inwardly. It was a personal satisfaction he required' (181 [137]; 130). As he mounts the stairs at the end of part 2, Raymon exclaims: "Pauvre Ralph! . . . c'est toi qui l'as voulu!" 'Poor Ralph! . . . It's your own doing!' (187 [142]; 135). Here homosocial desire motivates heterosexual relationships.

One scene of rivalry between the two men deserves to be drawn to students' attention: the moment when Raymon anxiously discovers Ralph's portrait in Indiana's bedroom. He is enraged by the idea that Ralph possesses an imagined power to gaze at Indiana at will and unbeknownst to her:

> Il la surveille, il la garde, il suit tous ses mouvements, il la possède à toute heure! La nuit, il la voit dormir et surprend le secret de ses rêves; . . . quand elle se croit bien seule, bien cachée, cette insolente figure est là qui se repaît de ses charmes!   (109 [75])

> He watches over her, he protects her, he follows all her movements, she is his at any time! At night he can see her sleep and surprise the secret of her dreams . . . when she thinks she's quite alone and well hidden, that insolent face is there feasting on her charms!   (68)

As Naomi Schor has pointed out in "The Portrait of a Gentleman," the rivalry between Ralph and Raymon is entirely "ocular" and consists of "a struggle over who shall possess the exclusive right not to be gazed at by Indiana but to gaze at her" (125). According to Schor, by presenting a representation of male narcissism and by exposing the specularity of male desire, Sand criticizes "the very foundations of the representational system elaborated by patriarchal society" (126). The fact that the female protagonist is deprived of the right to look back at her observer ensures that homosocial relations, and the distribution of power they sustain, prevail.

The novel's ending prominently foregrounds issues of narration and homosocial desire. If, as Dayan argues, Ralph is the omniscient narrator of *Indiana*, he manipulates the characterization of Indiana to ensure her dependence—for example, when his narrative voice belittles her radical affirmation of desired independence in her letter to Raymon (251 [197]; 192). Ralph's story requires a weak woman whom he can save from the world (Dayan 160). That Ralph's story is predicated on female submission and silence duplicates the structure of male narcissism that we see throughout. Moreover, the narrative structure of the conclusion, whose intradiegetic narrator (a visitor to Bourbon Island) speaks in the first person, is but a device to allow for Ralph to tell his story to another man out of the now silenced Indiana's earshot (339 [271–72]; 267). In addition, one may point out to students the homosocial bond between the visitor and Ralph, evident from the outset in the young narrator's diffidence and "eager and indiscreet" curiosity about Ralph (336 [269]; 265). The "magnetic" relationship between the two men is echoed in the attraction the narrator feels for the botanist Jules Néraud, to whom he dedicates the conclusion and of whom he dreams while on the island. One may notice, too, following Véronique Machelidon's lead, that the young narrator and Ralph meet in a magical and frightening landscape figured as origin and as a maternal body, which further connotes their homosocial encounter ("Female Melancholy" 28–29). Although there are no direct addresses to the narratee in the conclusion, as there are in the first two parts, the ending implies a social contract between men that silences women. As Nigel Harkness cogently states, "the narrative is addressed to a male narratee through whom a male reader is interpellated and his acquiescence in an ideology of gender constantly solicited" (*Men* 46).

This solicitation is clearly played out in the narrator's attitude toward Raymon in parts 1 and 2, especially when the narrative voice attempts to justify the abandonment of Noun:

> La femme de qualité vous sacrifie vingt amants qu'elle avait; la femme de chambre ne vous sacrifie qu'un mari qu'elle aurait eu.
>
> Que voulez-vous? Raymon était un homme de mœurs élégantes, de vie recherchée, d'un amour poétique. Pour lui une grisette n'était pas une femme. . . . Tout cela n'était pas la faute de Raymon. . . . [F]aites attention: Raymon raisonnait fort bien et tout à fait dans l'intérêt de sa maîtresse.

Non, vous conviendrez avec lui que ce n'était pas possible, que ce n'eût pas été généreux, qu'on ne lutte point ainsi contre la société, et que cet héroïsme de vertu ressemble à don Quichotte brisant sa lance contre l'aile du moulin; courage de fer qu'un coup de vent disperse, chevalerie d'un autre siècle qui fait pitié à celui-ci.   (75–76 [42–43]).

The woman of rank gives up for you twenty lovers she had; the lady's maid only gives up for you the one husband she might have had.

What do you expect? Raymon was a man with polished manners, an elegant life-style and romantic love-affairs. For him, a working-girl was not a woman. . . . None of that was Raymon's fault. . . . But, take note, Raymon's reasoning was very sound and entirely in his mistress's interest.

No, you will agree with him that it was not possible, that it would not have been generous, that one cannot struggle against society in this way, and such virtuous heroics are like Don Quixote's breaking his lance against a windmill, an iron courage destroyed by a puff of wind, the chivalry of another century which arouses pity in this one.   (38–39)

The use of proverbial speech, direct questions addressed to the reader, and free indirect discourse cumulatively force the narratee to identify with Raymon's position and to forgive his behavior. These devices, combined with the oral narrative framework of the conclusion, lay bare the narrator's attempts to restrict the reader's interpretive freedom (Harkness, *Men* 46–54). The narrator has established a homosocial bond with Raymon, a character that from the outset "nous ne prétendons pas juger si rigoureusement" 'he has no intention of judging . . . very harshly' (73 [40]; 36). He then draws the narratee into his homosocial community, a community that assesses the value of a woman by counting the men she has been with. One might go so far as to say that the narrator has been seduced by Raymon's charm and eloquence, even though the overt performance of this indulgent stance may seem at times ironic:

Raymon avait l'art d'être souvent coupable sans se faire haïr, souvent bizarre sans être choquant; parfois même il réussissait à se faire plaindre par les gens qui avaient le plus à se plaindre de lui. Il y a des hommes ainsi gâtés par tout ce qui les approche.   (73 [40])

Raymon had the art of often being guilty without making himself hated, often unusual without upsetting people; sometimes he even managed to arouse pity in those who had the most reason to complain of him. There are men who are spoiled like this by all around them.   (36)

The irony is perceptible in such statements as "a working-girl was not a woman" or "it would not have been generous . . . one cannot struggle against society in this way"; but Sand's use of irony does not substantially alter the narrative's homosociality. If anything, it draws attention to the bond between men as a performance of homosociality (Petrey, "George" 144; Harkness, *Men* 46).

The novel's tacit cover-up of Noun's story resurfaces in the narrator's derogatory comments toward creole women. The discourse on creole women begins with references to Noun and Indiana's ethnic origins (they were born on Bourbon Island); although the word *Creole* was applied, without connoting color, to both white and nonwhite colonial subjects of either European or African descent born in the tropics, the novel makes a clear distinction between the sexual attributes of white and black, upper- and lower-class Creoles. Nevertheless, when the narrator refers to creole women, he invokes a common homosocial bond that assumes that Ralph, the narrator, and the narratee share a misogynist, racist, and colonial ideology that is explicitly not held by Indiana. Indiana's description of her god in part 3, chapter 23, and her participation in the emancipation of slaves sets her apart from the masculinist and colonial ideologies of Raymon, among others. On several occasions, the narrator opposes French or Parisian women and creole women, indicting creole women's credulity, naïveté, childishness, and ignorance (144, 153, 174 [105, 112–13, 131]; 98, 106, 124), and even pitting French and creole women against each other (150–51 [110]; 103). Ralph also makes clear his low opinion of women in general and of creole women (61, 174 [30, 131]; 26–27, 124) and Noun in particular (321 [257]; 253). These misogynist statements find their fullest expression in a passage about the foolish nature of all womankind, which follows Indiana's letter to Raymon mentioned above (251 [197]; 192). Such pervasive statements use the subject of women as a means to bond with other men. It is no wonder, then, that the novel is revealed as a story about Indiana's status as an object of exchange among three men.

These misogynist remarks, however, do not exist in isolation in the novel. *Indiana* allows for the free play of value systems wherein misogyny can coexist with feminism, conservative with socialist discourse, racist with anticolonialist discourse, homosociality with heterosexuality, realism with idealism. Students should be encouraged to reflect on the contradictions in Sand's "narrative androgyny" and "double-voiced" narration, to use Isabelle Naginski's influential terms (*George Sand: Writing* 3–4), which include commentary that is both critical and sympathetic toward women. The narrator's attitude toward Raymon is a good example of double-voiced narrative commentary. Despite being a man, the narrator has a mother's indulgence toward Raymon, who is compared with a spoiled child and whose selfish love for Mme de Ramière is seen by the knowing narrator as typical of all children's love for their mothers (141 [103]; 95). A progressive discourse also coexists alongside the misogynist and racist discourse on creole women. The analogy of slavery and marriage, references to the emancipation of slaves, and the critique of the patriarchal structure of the colonial plantation spell out a serious critique of the oppression resulting from patriarchy, marriage, and colonialism. Nevertheless, as Deborah Jenson and Pratima Prasad ("Espace colonial") have shown, the discourse on slavery is subject to "mimetic slippage" in the novel in, for instance, the metaphor of "willing" subjection to the enslavement of love, the displacement of black slavery by analogy, and the reinscription of Indiana's mastery vis-à-vis Noun's servitude (Jenson 208, 198).

Multivoiced narration introduces contradictions within the narrative such that *Indiana* eschews ideological coherence. Students will certainly want to grapple with some of the contradictions in the dual ending as well as in the tensions between the treatment of rivalry and bonding. The novel's male homosociality, which pervades the narrative at every level, is subtly shadowed by female homosociality. Critics have often discussed female doubling in *Indiana*, and some have suggested that there is little or no rivalry between women in the novel (Didier, Introduction 29). Indiana and Noun share a strong sororal bond given that they are *sœurs de lait* who nursed from the same black wet nurse (157 [116]; 109). Indiana, whose mother died, manifests a strong fascination for the motherly Mme de Ramière, who reciprocates the attachment. We could even see, as Machelidon does, relationships among women in the novel as operating along a metonymic chain back to the absent mother or as attempts to resist the oedipal relation and reconnect with the preoepidal mother (hence Indiana's persistant melancholy for an ill-defined lost object). Appropriate attention, however, should be given to the moments when the narrative stages the triangulation of desire and the rivalry between women (often instigated by one of the male characters), as in Indiana's relationship to Mme de Carvajal or to Laure de Nangy (another female character whose mother has died), who refers explicitly to the erotic triangle (297 [238]; 232). Most perplexing might be Indiana's statement that she does not want "une effrayante parité" 'frightening equality' with Noun (200 [153]; 147). Although the emphasis on sororal bonding leaves open other dialogic readings, pitting women against each other for the love of a man inevitably reinscribes feminine dependency on men and bolsters the homosocial argument. Yet, even if *Indiana* is a novel not about women but about men, it can still be an undoubtedly incisive critique of patriarchy by forcing readers to confront the powerful way homosocial desire shapes narrative form. As Sedgwick reminds us, "the status of women . . . is deeply and inescapably inscribed in the structure even of relationships that exclude women" (25).

NOTES

This essay is a pedagogical, English-language adaptation of an earlier piece that was published in Éric Bordas's *George Sand: Écritures et représentations*.

[1] Didier includes in the Folio edition many passages from the 1832 edition that were deleted from the 1856 Calmann-Lévy edition on which subsequent standard editions and translations are based (Notes).

One or Several Ralphs:
Multiplicity and Masculinity in *Indiana*

Charles J. Stivale

How does George Sand construct the male characters as masculine in her first
novel, *Indiana*, and how might such constructions serve usefully to introduce
students to the novel's narrative elements? Scholars have noted the conflicts
endured at the hands of men by *Indiana*'s two main female characters, Indiana
and her servant, Noun (e.g., Rabine, "George Sand" 2, 11; Schor, "Portrait" 114,
George Sand 53, Introduction xiii). Considering the constructions of masculinity, however, may yield greater clarity not only about why the female characters
endure such treatment but also about how a variable construction of masculinity
may determine the novel's progression and conclusion. Students might examine
the opposition of two rather stereotypical male types—the brutal Delmare and
the libertine Raymon. Whereas these characters offer little subtlety in their
masculine construction, they provide contrast with their male other, Indiana's
cousin Ralph, who seems to mutate throughout the novel. This internal textual
development, I argue, is a useful tool for introducing *Indiana* and the study of
narrative to students.

Since the term *masculinity* is fluid for any era and author, but especially for
the early nineteenth century, an adequate definition depends on various and
shifting biological and sociocultural concepts. During the decade preceding *Indiana*'s publication, two authors, Stendhal (notably in *Histoire de la peinture en
Italie* and *De l'amour*) and Honoré de Balzac (in essays such as *Physiologie du
mariage*), proposed diverse traits for constructing the masculine as vital flows of
energy. From these and other sources (e.g., Nye; Revinin; Sohn), one can derive
a fourfold set of masculine traits: vitality, virility, honor, and nation.[1]

These four traits reveal that Delmare and Raymon share with Ralph distinct
traits that situate them all within a vitalist conception of Romanticism.[2] Yet
Ralph's significant mutation is due as much to the narrator's particular learning
curve as it is to the novel's vital Romanticism. "One or several Ralphs" in my title
reflects a sense of Ralph's transformation. In this regard, students might track
the ways in which the narrator presents several perspectives on Ralph, especially in the section of the epilogue recounted by local island dwellers (334–35
[267–68]; 263–64). I must emphasize, however, that any transformations of
main characters in *Indiana*, male or female, occur solely from the narrator's
perspective. Thus students might also read *Indiana* to distinguish this mode of
narrative representation and track carefully how the reader is entirely tethered
to a myopic (not to say unreliable) point of view—the narrator's—throughout
the novel. Indeed, students could seek examples of tension between masculine
types due to the narrator's prejudice, evident in descriptions of the three male

characters from early in the novel (49, 51, 72–73 [19–21, 31–32, 40]; 15, 17, 22–23).

Besides Indiana and Noun, both marked as national others by their sex and their repeated descriptions as "créole," the sole character whose nationality stands out significantly is the "English" Ralph. Traits marking this national difference and masculine distinction are his consistent and almost invariable depiction by the adjective "flegmatique" 'phlegmatic' and the noun "sang-froid" 'phlegm,' or composure (90 [57]; 52). The narrator's prejudice extends to this latter trait, a classical humor marked by sluggishness and cold. The most telling display of "sang-froid" is Ralph's reaction (noted by the narrator) to what Ralph believes is Indiana's death from a riding accident: Ralph "prit son couteau de chasse, et, avec un sang-froid vraiment britannique, il s'apprêtait à se couper la gorge, lorsque Raymon lui arracha son arme et l'entraîna vers le lieu d'où partaient les cris" 'picked up his hunting-knife and with truly British *sang-froid*, was about to cut his throat, when Raymon snatched his weapon from him and dragged him to the spot where the screams were coming from' (163 [121]; 114; trans. modified). Nation, honor, and virility are all linked in this gesture, and the lasting irony is that the least honorable character (and Ralph's eventual rival), Raymon, prevents the suicide.

Immediately after this thwarted suicide, Ralph assumes his medical role, and, just as he had when Raymon was wounded by Delmare, Ralph does not hesitate to care for the injured man by means of "une saignée" 'a bloodletting' (163 [121]; 114). The evidently cold-blooded Ralph opts for the time-honored remedy of bloodletting, the goal of which, since Hippocrates, was to bring the four humors into balance (see Seigworth). For this fluid is clearly the substance in the relative absence of which Ralph is characterized and which, conversely, afflicts both Delmare and Raymon, not just when wounded, but in their daily lives.

But blood as a humor must be linked to another, that of bile, since they act in tandem to determine the behavioral traits of Delmare and Raymon. Raymon, logically the more hot-blooded, is described as "un homme bilieux, dont le sang circulait vite, dont les nerfs s'irritaient profondément" 'a man of irascible temperament, with rapidly circulating blood and deeply irritable nerves' (193 [147]; 141). Indeed, the narrator informs us that Raymon's fatal affair with Noun was not his fault: "C'était malgré lui que l'ardeur du sang l'avait entraîné dans de bourgeoises amours" 'it was in spite of himself that his passionate blood had dragged him into a lower-class love-affair' (75 [43]; 38). Yet Raymon is vitally transformed as he overcomes his "terreurs" 'fears' by recognizing Noun's ghost to be none other than the "maladroit espion" 'clumsy spy,' Ralph:

> Son sang glacé dans ses veines refluait maintenant vers son cerveau avec une violence délirante. . . . Raymon se trouvait audacieux et jeune comme au matin, lorsqu'un rêve sinistre nous enveloppait de ses linceuls et qu'un joyeux rayon de soleil nous réveille et nous ranime.
>
> "Pauvre Ralph! . . . c'est toi qui l'as voulu!"   (186–87 [142])

The blood which had been frozen in his veins now flowed back to his brain with frenzied violence. . . . Raymon felt young and daring as one is when, after being wrapped in the shrouds of a doom-laden dream, one is awakened and revived by a cheerful ray of sunlight.

"Poor Ralph! . . . It's your own doing!"   (135)

Delmare is also afflicted by blood, not just when his embarrassingly bellicose (and implicitly bilious) temperament lead him to wound Raymon in the park, but also as his aging body, afflicted by the cold and wet, gives him "de l'humeur" '[a] bad mood' due to "des rheumatismes" 'rheumatism' (50 [19–20]; 15). The narrator is at great pains at one point to defend Delmare as a product of "la vie des camps" 'life in military camp' (132–33 [96]; 88):

[Delmare] avait toutes les qualités et tous les défauts [des vieilles cohortes impériales]. Candide jusqu'à l'enfantillage sur certaines délicatesses du point d'honneur, il savait fort bien conduire ses intérêts à la meilleure fin possible sans s'inquiéter du bien ou du mal qui pouvait en résulter pour autrui. Toute sa conscience, c'était la loi; toute sa morale, c'était son droit.   (134 [96])

[Delmare] had all the good qualities and all the failings [of the old Imperial cohorts]. Childishly candid about some delicate points of honor, he knew very well how to do the best for his own interests without worrying about the benefits or the harm that might be the consequence for others. His only conscience was the law; his only morality was his right. (88–89)

So, like Raymon's burning impulses, Delmare's code of honor does him a disservice, and as the novel proceeds, Delmare's "nature guerrière et querelleuse" 'bellicose and quarrelsome temperament' manifests itself physically (166 [123]; 116). After an infuriated Delmare physically attacks Indiana, Ralph finds him "étendu par terre, le visage violet, la gorge enflée, en proie aux convulsions étouffées d'une congestion sanguine" 'stretched out on the ground, his face purple, his throat swollen, a prey to the suffocating convulsions of apoplexy' (270 [213]; 208). In contrast to that of the ardent Raymon, Delmare's blood flow seems altogether capricious: "Trop affaibli par l'âge et les fatigues pour aspirer à devenir père de famille, il était resté vieux garçon dans son ménage, et il avait pris une femme comme il eût pris une gouvernante" 'Too weakened by age and hardships to aspire to become a father, he had remained an old bachelor in his household and had taken a wife as he would have taken a housekeeper' (271 [214]; 209). And after Indiana's escape, Delmare's bilious condition leads to his death; Ralph informs Indiana, "je trouvai sa figure violette, son sommeil lourd et brûlant: il était frappé d'apoplexie" 'I found that his face was purple and his sleep heavy and feverish. He had already had an apoplectic fit' (302 [241]; 236).

Indiana also uses various vitalist traits to ensure her survival—as well as to achieve her ultimate utopian existence. Although she and Noun share a common heritage, Noun is described simply as "pleine de sang créole ardent et passionné" 'overflowing with the full-blooded ardour and passion of a Creole' (60 [29]; 25). In contrast, the narrator describes Indiana as "une âme impressionnable" 'an impressionable heart,' affected by "ses fibres délicates" 'her delicate nerves'; she is "un être faible" 'weak,' having "toutes les superstitions d'une créole nerveuse et maladive" 'all the superstitious feelings of a nervous Creole in poor health' (59 [28]; 24). Yet early on, when facing Delmare over Raymon's wounded body, Indiana responds to her husband "avec un sang-froid et une force morale dont personne ne l'eût cru capable" 'with a sang-froid and moral strength of which no one would have thought her capable' (64 [32]; 28). As with Ralph, one Indiana can conceal another, for she consistently aggravates her husband and startles Raymon with her humoral shifts. Indeed, Raymon is strangely affected by Indiana: "A la voir si confiante, si passionnée, si pure, . . . Raymon n'osait plus être homme . . . il se faisait vertueux comme elle" 'When he saw her so full of confidence, so passionate, so pure, . . . Raymon no longer dared to be a man . . . he became virtuous like her' (173–174 [131]; 124; trans. modified). Of course, Raymon soon recovers and "commençait à sentir qu'il était de son honneur de conduire [leur *amour*] à un résultat" 'was beginning to feel that his honour was involved in bringing [their love] to a favourable outcome' (178 [135]; 128), yet he is unable to thwart Ralph's strict (and cold) surveillance. Soon, readers witness a veritable battle of hot and cold humors, when Raymon's impetuosity becomes visible physically: "la pâleur de ses lèvres trahissait le tourment d'une impatience plus impérieuse que délicate. Il y avait de la brusquerie et presque de la colère dans ses baisers" 'his pale lips betrayed the torment of an impatience more domineering than tactful. There was a certain abruptness, almost anger, in his kisses.' In response, "Indiana eut peur. . . . Elle se réveilla et repoussa les attaques du vice égoïste et froid" 'Indiana took fright. . . . She recovered herself and repulsed the cold selfish attacks of vice' (221 [171]; 166). Her vocal response to this attack ends in a Ralph-like affirmation: "J'ai besoin de stoïcisme et de calme" 'I need stoicism and calm.' These words of resistance increase Raymon's "colère" 'anger': "Perdant tout à fait la tête dans cet instant de souffrance et de dépit, il la repoussa rudement, marcha dans la chambre la poitrine oppressée, la tête en feu; puis il prit une carafe et avala un grand verre d'eau qui calma tout à coup son délire et refroidit son amour" 'completely losing his head, hurt and annoyed, he pushed her away roughly, walked up and down the room, his heart heavy and his head on fire. He took up a water jug and gulped down a large glass of water, which suddenly calmed his agitation and cooled his love' (221 [171]; 167).

Alas, Indiana loses this apparent "stoïcisme et calme" and, facing her likely dishonor, nearly kills herself—saved at the edge of the Seine by the faithful Ralph. Still, she retains an instinct toward self-preservation that works against both Raymon and Delmare. As the narrator maintains, the discord with Del-

mare seems to have arisen from a basic misunderstanding since "Madame Delmare doutait trop du cœur de son mari; il n'était que dur, et elle le jugeait cruel"
'Madame Delmare had too many doubts about her husband's heart; he was only
hard and she thought he was cruel' (135 [97]; 89). Once she is forced to submit to Delmare's empire as they prepare to leave France, "Indiana était roide
et hautaine dans sa soumission" 'Indiana's submission was stiff and haughty'
(207 [160]; 154), and she seems to know precisely how to respond to his bilious
nature:

> Sa froide obéissance irritait le colonel . . . [et] en voyant le résultat
> de ses idées mal comprises, de ses volontés méconnues, [il] entrait en
> fureur. Mais quand elle lui avait prouvé *d'un mot calme et glacial* qu'elle
> n'avait fait qu'obéir strictement à ses arrêts, il était réduit *à tourner sa
> colère contre lui-même.* C'était pour cet homme, petit d'amour-propre
> et violent de sensations, une souffrance cruelle, un affront sanglant.
>   (208–09 [160–61]; my emphasis)

> Her cold obedience irritated the Colonel. . . . When he saw the conse-
> quence of his ill-comprehended ideas, of his misunderstood wishes, Del-
> mare would fly into a rage, but when, *with calm and cold words*, she had
> proved to him that she had only strictly obeyed his order, he was reduced
> to *turning his anger against himself.* For such a man, with his petty sense
> of self-esteem and yet violent sensations, it caused cruel pain and was a
> biting insult.   (154–55; trans. modified)

Indiana appears to act strategically on her vitalist instincts to combat this threat,
thus contributing to the influx of bilious fluid that will eventually kill Delmare.

But what about the several Ralphs? Students should judge this question in
the light of the novel's concluding chapters. The narrator hints throughout that
despite Ralph's cold, phlegmatic, and egotistical character, another Ralph lurks
just below the surface. When Ralph finally resolves to inform Indiana of Raymon's perfidy with Noun, "Ralph sentit son cœur se briser . . . mais l'infortuné
n'avait pas le don des larmes . . . [et] le sang-froid extérieur avec lequel il consomma cette opération cruelle lui donna l'air d'un bourreau aux yeux d'Indiana"
'[h]e felt his heart was breaking . . . but the unfortunate man had not the gift of
tears . . . [and] the external sang-froid with which he carried out this cruel operation made him seem like an executioner in Indiana's eyes' (184 [140]; 133).

What is underneath starts to emerge when Indiana later jumps into Ralph's
arms at his avowal of friendship: "Ralph faillit s'évanouir; car, dans ce corps
robuste, dans ce tempérament calme et réservé, fermentaient des émotions
puissantes" 'Ralph almost fainted, for in that strong body, in that calm, reserved
temperament, seethed powerful emotions' (243 [190]; 186; trans. modified).
This alternative Ralph reveals himself even more clearly during his promenades
on the island, following Indiana from afar:

> Il la fuyait plutôt que de chercher à la distraire. Dans l'excès de sa réserve délicate, il continuait à se donner toutes les apparances de la froideur et de l'égoïsme. Il allait souffir seul au loin. . . . Et pourtant la chasse et l'étude n'étaient que le prétexte dont il couvrait ses amères et longues rêveries.　(255 [200])

> He shunned her rather than tried to take her mind off it. In his excessive, sensitive reserve he continued to assume all the appearance of coldness and selfishness. He went far afield to suffer alone. . . . And yet hunting and nature-study were only the pretexts with which he covered his long, bitter reveries.　(195)

Finally, Ralph entirely takes charge of Indiana's life after her ill-fated trip to Lagny, and the pact to which they agree, suicide, requires a mutual training in "le receuillement d'un catholique devant les sacrements de son Église" 'the meditative attitude of a Catholic toward the sacraments of his church' (307 [244–45]; 241). There is a severe logic to the veritable discipline that they pursue together—to return to the "ravin solitaire de Bernica" 'the lonely ravine of Bernica' to leap into the falls—and this process produces serenity in Indiana (307–09 [245–46]; 241–42). In Ralph, "son âme, longtemps roidie contre la douleur, s'amollit à la chaleur vivifiante de l'espérance" 'his soul, long steeled to pain, softened in the reviving warmth of hope,' and this change opens him to his companion: "Pour la première fois, Indiana connut son véritable caractère" 'for the first time, Indiana came to know his true character' (309 [247]; 242; trans. modified). Ralph's previously negative quality now is revealed as positive, for he still acts with "un admirable sang-froid" 'wonderful self-possession' and insists that "il est nécessaire d'apporter un grand sang-froid au succès de notre entreprise" 'we need to bring the greatest self-possession for the success of our undertaking' (311 [249]; 245). After months of "recueillement" 'meditation,' Indiana's view of Ralph shifts:

> [L]'exaltation de[s] pensées [d'Indiana] avait grandi en proportion du changement opéré dans Ralph. Elle ne l'écoutait plus comme un conseiller flegmatique; elle le suivait en silence comme un bon génie chargé de l'enlever à la terre et de la délivrer de ses tourments.　(312 [249–50])

> [H]er thoughts had become more exalted in proportion to the change that had taken place in Ralph. She no longer listened to him merely as a phlegmatic adviser; she followed him silently as a good spirit who had been given the task of taking her away from the earth and delivering her of her woes.　(245)

And Ralph reveals that his lifelong disguise was necessitated by a well-calculated, personal strategy: "J'ai senti qu'il fallait élever autour de moi un triple mur de glace, afin de m'aliéner ton intérêt. . . . [J]e n'ai pas eu le droit de montrer même l'énergie de la colère et de la vengeance, car c'eût été me trahir et vous apprendre que j'étais un homme" 'I felt I must erect a triple wall of ice around myself, so as to alienate your interest in me. . . . I hadn't the right to show even the energy inspired by anger and the desire for revenge, for that would have been to betray myself and tell you I was a man' (324 [259]; 255–56).

Thus Ralph is only steps away from the narrator's (and the readers') perspective, whereas he remains true to himself, relying on his belief that "il n'y avait qu'une âme assez large pour répandre le feu sacré qui la vivifiait jusque sur l'âme étroite et glacée du pauvre abandonné. . . . Il n'était sous le ciel qu'une Indiana capable d'aimer un Ralph" '[t]here was only one soul large enough to spread the sacred fire which animated it on to the narrow icy soul of the poor abandoned one. . . . There was on earth only one Indiana capable of loving a Ralph' (325 [260]; 256; trans. modified)—that is, the true, reborn, and masculine Ralph, not his phlegmatic avatar. As if we needed further confirmation of this transformation, the penultimate description of Ralph with Indiana emphasizes fully the vitalist impulsion:

> Rendue à la vérité, à la nature, [Indiana] vit le cœur de Ralph tel qu'il était . . . car la puissance d'une si haute situation avait produit sur lui le même effet que la pile de Volta sur des membres engourdis. . . . Paré de sa franchise et de sa vertu, il était bien plus beau que Raymon, et Indiana sentit que c'était lui qu'il aurait fallu aimer.   (329–30 [263–64])

> Having returned to truth, to nature, [Indiana] saw Ralph's heart as it really was . . . for the power of his extreme exaltation had had the same effect on him as an electric battery on numbed limbs. . . . Embellished by his frankness and his virtue, he was much more handsome than Raymon, and Indiana felt he was the man she should have loved. (260; trans. modified)

And so, after "leurs lèvres s'unirent" 'their lips met,' "alors Ralph prit sa fiancée dans ses bras, et l'emporta pour la précipiter avec lui dans le torrent" 'Ralph took his fiancée in his arms and carried her off to plunge with her into the torrent' (330 [264]; 260).

But the epilogue extends their lives and tale through the first-person testimony of the narrator-traveler (Harkness, "Writing"), whose initial external impression of Ralph (336 [269]; 264–65) contradicts all the horrific tales recounted by local citizens. Moreover, his impression of Indiana, despite finding her rather ignorant and sad, nonetheless emphasizes a gaze that contained "une mélancolie qui semble être la méditation du bonheur ou l'attendrissement de la reconnaissance" 'a melancholy which seems to express a reflection on happiness or an emotion of gratitude' (337 [270]; 266). As the narrator-traveler concludes at the end of Ralph's tale, "[u]n cœur pur peut nous faire supporter l'exil; mais, pour nous le faire aimer, il faut une compagne comme la vôtre" '[a] pure heart can enable us to endure exile, but to enable us to love it, one needs a companion like yours.' To which Ralph responds: "Ah! dit-il avec un ineffable sourire, si vous saviez comme je plaigne ce monde qui me dédaigne" "'Oh," he said with an ineffable smile, "if you knew how I pity this society which despises me'" (343 [275]; 271). From the logical perspective of the couple's mutual movement toward serenity through the vitalist progression of "recueillement" 'meditation,' both Indiana and Ralph live in a kind of harmony, a balance that, according to the narrator (and implicitly in Ralph's view), would be impossible without Indiana. That is, their "recueillement" is symbiotic and leads to an almost Buddhist well-being and clarity of life purpose ("nos revenus . . . consacrés à racheter de pauvres Noirs infirmes" 'our income is devoted to buying the freedom of poor, infirm blacks' [342 (270); 270]).

It would seem, then, that in her first novel, Sand already suggests what Isabelle Naginski has called a "réalisme prophétique" ("prophetic realism")—that is, an idealist and vitalist path toward true balance and honor, in contrast to the expressions of temperament that so torment mankind ("George Sand et le réalisme"). In this sense, the epilogue is a necessary final section, because Ralph's testimony (shared, albeit silently but reflectively, by Indiana) affirms that the vitalist balance is achieved therein not just by the main characters but also by the narrator-traveler, who finally comes to recognize which Ralph and which Indiana he, and with him we readers, can fully appreciate.

Approaching the novel from the perspectives of masculine construction and vitalism, students can understand how the female characters' actions and reactions are informed by masculine constructs. Moreover, they can judge the contrast between each of the male characters, particularly the multiplicity of types implicitly presented throughout the novel and especially in the mutating Ralph. They also can assess the relation of these constructions and the narrator's distinct perspective, as well as the implicit interchange between the narrator and reader. These elements, finally, will help students better grasp how the plot, and especially the denouement and epilogue, are affected by these constructions and narrative facets. This expanded comprehension thus will give students greater awareness of Sand's craft in action and of the gender relations at the heart of this important novel.

NOTES

[1] Vitality may be understood through the vitalist balance of the four humors—blood, phlegm, choler, and bile—a constant in medieval and early modern medical discourse well into the nineteenth century. Virility consists (at the very least) of the display of manliness, often ostentatious, of male strength and allure, and, given its relation to a peer group, relates to honor, which usually entails a concomitant adherence to a strict code of loyalty and discipline, traditionally military and, in this era, often Napoleonic. Finally, nation may be understood to link vitality, virility, and honor through the prevailing

concepts of national temperament and milieu, inherited from Montesquieu and other Enlightenment thinkers. In my analysis here, I follow research developed by Harkness, who has addressed the masculine in terms of Sand's discursive choices within literary representation but also not as "the exclusive preserve of men" (*Men* 7, 9). Harkness also considers the problematic narrator in *Indiana*, whose voice depicts the male characters (42–64). See also Dayan.

[2] See Ruston for vital Romanticism in English literature.

Masculinity and the Performance
of Narrative Authority

Nigel Harkness

In her autobiography, *Histoire de ma vie*, Sand claims that she wrote *Indiana* "sans projet et sans espoir, sans aucun plan" 'without a purpose, without a hope, and without any outline' (*Œuvres autobiographiques* 2: 160; Story 921). Students grappling with the complexities of narrative structure and narrative voice in the novel may well feel inclined to agree, thereby attributing the shifting and inconsistent narrative position to the author's lack of experience and granting it no further significance in the novel. However, if one reads *Indiana* without taking into account the explicit gendering of narrative voice and the distance Sand introduces between herself and her narrator, one misses a great deal of the novel's complexity and fails to acknowledge its reflection on questions of gender and representation. A focus on the homosocial dimension of the exchange of Indiana's story between Ralph and the narrator in the conclusion brings the masculinity of the narrator to the fore and problematizes the heterodiegetic narrative position of parts 1–4 of the novel. This focus then serves as a basis for considering the ways in which the performance of narrative masculinity on Sand's part may have a subversive rather than mimetic function, for, like the other male characters, the narrator too participates in a set of power relations in which linguistic mastery is key. Encouraging students to read the conclusion alongside the preface of 1832—two textual spaces that mirror each other structurally and thematically—also helps spark discussion of the way in which the gender politics of the novel inflect narrative form.

Based on the typology of narrative voices that Gérard Genette elaborates in *Figures III* (*Discours du récit* [*Narrative Discourse*]), the narrator of the first four parts of *Indiana* initially appears as both extradiegetic and heterodiegetic, the omniscient and authoritative recorder of and commentator on events (thus apparently conforming to a model of realist narration that students may recognize from, for instance, Balzac). Then, some fifteen pages from the end, he is dramatized as part of the story and meets with the two main characters, thereby assuming an intradiegetic and homodiegetic position; furthermore, it is here that we learn that his narrative has a metadiegetic source, for it has been transmitted to the narrator by Ralph. The transition from the third-person narrative of the main body of the novel to the first-person construction "j'étais parti" 'I left' (331 [265]; 261), on which the conclusion opens and in which the French verbal construction agrees in the masculine singular, appears so abrupt and unmotivated that the reader's likely reaction is to see this figure as entirely separate from the narrator of parts 1–4. This problem is only resolved when the narrator informs us that Ralph "me raconta son histoire jusqu'à l'endroit où nous l'avons laissée dans le précédent chapitre" 'told me his story up to the point where we left it in the previous chapter' (339 [272]; 267). The first-person narrator of the conclusion thus hears the story from Ralph and is responsible for fashioning the latter's oral narrative as the novel we have just been reading. But if this resolves the question of the link between the narrative voices of the conclusion and the main body of the novel, it introduces further complexity, for, by dramatizing her narrator in this way and revealing the original source of the story, Sand undermines the illusion of narrative omniscience that has been constructed up to this point, subverts the narrator's objectivity and impartiality, and draws our attention to the homosocial exchange at the inception of the novel.

Whereas the authority and objectivity to which an omniscient narrative position lays claim are dependent on disembodiment and therefore on the narrator not occupying the same diegetic space as the characters, Sand's dramatization of the narrator in the conclusion has the effect of exposing him to the same type of scrutiny as the other characters and revealing his failings and prejudices. What, then, do we learn about the narrator in the conclusion? Ralph stresses the narrator's youth and inexperience, describing him as a "conscience naïve et pure que n'a pas salie le monde" 'pure, guiltless conscience untainted by the world' (342 [274]; 270; trans. modified). Furthermore, despite the narrator's sympathy for Indiana and Ralph and the apparent bond between them, his judgements reveal a number of social prejudices: Indiana's languid manner is "naturel aux créoles" 'natural to Creoles' (337 [270]; 266), and both Indiana and Ralph are judged according to criteria appropriate for measuring success in a Parisian *salon* as having "peu d'esprit" 'not . . . much wit' (337 [270]; 265). Before he leaves the island, he articulates views that are critical of their voluntary exile from society, accusing them of "mépriser l'opinion" 'despising public opinion' and arguing that "tout homme appartient à la société" 'every man belongs to society' (343 [274, 275]; 270). Although here he is presented as repeating the views of other people ("quelques moralistes" 'some moralists'), this episode nonetheless points to his propensity to align himself with, rather than situate himself in opposition to, dominant social views.

That these prejudices condition his view of his environment and undermine his reliability as interpreter of what he observes is highlighted in an episode early in the conclusion. Here the narrator is puzzling over the meaning of fossilized imprints on a basalt rock formation:

> Au front de ce monument étrange, une large inscription semblait avoir été tracée par une main immortelle. Ces pierres volcaniques offrent souvent le même phénomène. Jadis leur substance, amollie par l'action du feu, reçut, tiède et malléable encore, l'empreinte des coquillages et des lianes qui s'y collèrent. De ces rencontres fortuites sont résultés des jeux bizarres, des impressions hiéroglyphiques, des caractères mystérieux, qui semblent jetés là comme le seing d'un être surnaturel, écrit en lettres cabalistiques. Je restai longtemps dominé par la puérile prétention de chercher un sens à ces chiffres inconnus.   (332–33 [266])

At the top of this strange structure it seemed as if an inscription had been traced in large letters by an immortal hand. Volcanic rocks of this kind often show the same phenomenon. In the past, when their substance, softened by the action of the flames, was still warm and malleable, it received the imprint of the shells and creepers that stuck to it. These chance contacts have resulted in some strange patterns, hieroglyphic marks, mysterious characters, which look as if they had been cast there like the seal of a supernatural being written in cabalistic letters. I stayed a long time, under the sway of the childish pretention of finding a meaning in those mysterious marks.   (262)

In this passage, his informed and confident commentary on volcanic rock formations contrasts with the uncertainty of his discussion of the hieroglyphic marks and thus opposes the supernatural and the scientific. These hieroglyphic markings form part of the mysteries of a natural environment whose feminine otherness is constantly stressed (see Machelidon, "Female Melancholy" 28–29; Harkness, "Writing" 117–18), and because they fall outside his rational, scientific frame of reference, he dismisses as "childish" any suggestion that they might have meaning. This gesture is given added significance by way of the intratextual echoes that link this passage to the other moment of marking or imprinting in the novel, when Delmare discovers Indiana's diary and her letters to Raymon and in a fit of anger "la frappa au front du talon de sa botte" and "imprim[a] cette marque sanglante" 'kicked her on the forehead with the heel of his boot' and 'imprinted the blood-stained mark' (269 [212]; 207). While the ferocity of Delmare's actions here may be compared with the violence of the volcanic eruption, it is the lexical correspondence between these two episodes that is particularly striking: first, in the act of marking—the verb "imprimer" ("to print") for Indiana's body and the nouns "impression" and "empreinte" (both meaning "imprint") for the rock formation—and, second, in the place where the rocks and the female body are marked, the "front" 'forehead.' The linking of this episode to Indiana's body reinforces the idea that what falls beyond the narrator's ken is the otherness of femininity.

The impression that emerges from the conclusion is thus one of the narrator as a significantly compromised figure. This is reinforced by analysis of the preface to the 1832 edition of the novel. Sand's presentation of the novel here is far from straightforward, and the preface is a complex and even contradictory piece of writing, combining defensive and assertive rhetorical modes. Sand downplays the significance of the novel while also asserting its privileging of the real and the truthful over the fictional; she denies subversive intent, but, in countering accusations that the novel is attacking society, she is also signaling that such readings are possible (and the arguments she puts up here against them may seem less compelling than the weight of textual evidence from the novel). But one point appears constant in this preface, and that is the distinction Sand draws between the author and the narrator. The latter is always spoken of in the third person, whereas first-person constructions are reserved for the author (e.g., the dialogic structure of "vous me reprocherez" and "l'auteur vous répondra" 'you will reproach me' and 'the author will reply' [39; 7]). In the presentation of the narrator, his youth and inexperience are stressed: he is young and timid, a simple storyteller ("simple diseur") who lacks maturity and skill and talent ("fût-il plus mûr et plus habile" 'if he were more mature and more skilful'; "son talent, s'il en avait" 'his talent, if he had any' [38; 6]). His creative input into the story is also downplayed, for he is presented as the passive recipient of a ready-made story: "Voilà ce que vous pourrez conclure de cette anecdote, et c'est dans ce sens qu'elle fut racontée à celui qui vous la transmet" 'That is the conclusion you may draw from the story, and that was its meaning when it was told to him who passes it on to you' (40; 7; trans. modified). This fracturing of the authorial persona whereby the author erects the narrator as a screen between herself and the reading public may seem little more than a rhetorical strategy indicating the young author's lack of confidence. But this is undercut by the fact that in the second half of the preface Sand is more forceful in defending her work and takes ownership of it as author. We must therefore consider the possibility that the focus on the narrator has another function in the overall meaning of the novel and that by highlighting his role in this way, Sand is signaling it as both significant and problematic.

To most readers, however, the narrative voice of the first four parts of the novel evinces none of these signs of inexperience. *Indiana* can thus be read as a particularly interesting study in how narrative authority is constructed and performed. Susan Lanser observes that a narrative mode that is both heterodiegetic and extradiegetic "has been so conventionally masculine that female authorship does not necessarily establish female voice" (18). Indeed, in *Indiana*, although the narrator's masculinity is only unveiled in the conclusion, it has been implicit throughout the novel, and it is confirmed by constructions such as the masculine agreement of the adjective "absolu" in "vous me trouverez peut-être absolu" 'perhaps you will think I am dogmatic' (166 [123]; 116) and the narrator's alignment with a male "nous" when he writes, "[l]a femme est imbécile par nature; il semble que, pour contrebalancer l'éminente supériorité que ses délicates perceptions lui donnent sur nous" '[w]oman is naturally foolish. To counterbalance the outstanding superiority which her sensitive perceptions give her over us men' (251 [197]; 192).[1] Yet in Lanser's analysis, masculinity does not underwrite authority; rather, the two major elements of narrative authority are the extent to which a narrator situates himself in dominant social groups and conforms to dominant ideologies. We can see both these processes at work in *Indiana*.

Aimée Boutin has pointed to the centrality of a homosocial dynamic to *Indiana*, not only determining relations among the male characters (between whom Indiana is exchanged) but also inflecting the narrator-narratee dynamic, for, she argues, "le narrateur attire . . . le narrataire dans son camp homosocial" 'the narrator draws . . . the narratee to his homosocial camp' (128; my trans.).[2] It is also the narrator's positioning in the homosocial networks of the novel that underpins his authority, for in a series of direct addresses to the male narratee, the narrator solicits the latter's compliance with his views on the basis of a shared social position and gender. Students can be encouraged to look in detail at points where the narrator speaks directly to the narratee, as in chapter 10, when he discusses Raymon's politics.

I want to look briefly here at the opening pages of chapter 4, in which the ideological bonds linking Raymon, the narrator, and the narratee are invoked. After the initial "il vous est difficile peut-être de croire que" 'it is perhaps difficult for you to believe that' (72 [40]; 36), the narrator addresses a narrative "vous" 'you' no less than six times in three pages. In these interventions, the narrator counters potential dissent on the part of the narratee ("que voulez vous!" 'what do you expect' [75 (42); 38], "Faites attention" 'take note' [75 (43); 39]), responds to a lack of knowledge ("savez-vous que" 'are you aware that' [77 (44); 40]), refers his interlocutor to what he presents as widely held views ("la femme de qualité vous sacrifie vingt amants qu'elle avait" 'the woman of rank gives up for you the twenty lovers she had' [75 (42); 38]), and solicits agreement ("vous conviendrez avec lui" 'you will agree with him' [76 (43); 39]). The "vous" here is neither gender neutral nor gender inclusive, as evident in the assertion, "la femme de qualité vous sacrifie vingt amants" 'the woman of rank gives up for you the twenty lovers she had' (75 [42]; 38), in which "vous" has the grammatical function of the impersonal object pronoun but semantically refers to a group of men that includes the narratee. Throughout the novel, direct and indirect addresses to a male "vous" serve to situate the narrator and the narratee in a homosocial community, whose identity is constructed in opposition to femininity and from which women are excluded. This is precisely the function of the "nous" 'us' in a statement such as "c'est la violence de nos désirs, la précipitation de notre amour qui *nous* rend stupides auprès des femmes" 'it is the strength of our desires, the impetuosity of our love, which makes *us* stupid in our relations with women' (83 [50–51]; 45; my emphasis). This pronoun, which includes the narratee and by extension the male reader (while also excluding the female reader), hints at the consensus that underpins the homosocial space in which acts of signification and representation take place in *Indiana*.

The narrator establishes his authority through his citation from a body of social and cultural knowledge to validate the currency of his affirmations, particularly in relation to femininity (though, as Charles Stivale's essay in this volume shows, the narrator's presentation of male characters also draws on an ideology of masculinity—based on concepts such as vitality, virility, honor, and nation—that the narratee is assumed to share). In his comments on Indiana, the narrator repeatedly relates the specifics of her behavior to generalizations about women. Indiana would give her life for Raymon's love since "la femme est *faite* ainsi" '[t]hat's how women are' (274 [217]; 212), and, after the long letter in which she sets out her view of alternative social structures, he comments, "la femme est imbécile *par nature*" 'woman is *naturally* foolish' (251 [197]; 192; my emphasis).

With such constructions, the narrator repeatedly invokes biologically essential-
ist views to explain women's behavior. Indeed, misogyny becomes a means of
performing masculinity, for by affirming femininity as an identity characterized
by emotion, weakness (of body and mind), passivity, and dependence on men,
he constructs masculinity by contrast around reason, control, and intelligence,
thereby reinforcing masculine superiority.[3] These misogynistic comments also
cement the bonds that underpin the homosocial community, for they link the
narrator to the other male characters. Comparing the male characters' views
of women with those articulated by the narrator is revealing, for what emerges
from such a comparison is that beyond their differences and rivalries, they share
similar disparaging views of women. Delmare comments that "les femmes sont
faites pour obéir et non conseiller" 'women are made to obey and not to give ad-
vice' (204 [156]; 151), whereas Raymon criticizes women's extravagant emotion-
alism and comments that "les projets romanesques, les entreprises périlleuses
flattent leur faible imagination" 'romantic plans, dangerous enterprises appeal to
their weak imaginations' (203 [156]; 150). Ralph too harbors negative views of
women's capacity for rational thought, reflecting that "ces deux femmes [Indiana
et Noun] sont folles. . . . D'ailleurs toutes les femmes le sont" '[t]hese two women
are crazy. . . . Besides, all women are' (61 [30]; 26; trans. modified). Misogyny is
not only part of the glue that binds the homosocial community of male characters together; it also binds the narrator to his patriarchal brothers.

I have considered this process until now as one in which we see the mechanisms whereby narrative authority is constructed in a homosocial context. But
the narrator's performance of authority based on masculine superiority and
homosocial likeness is also undermined by those very mechanisms that would
affirm it. Even before his appearance as a character in the conclusion, the narrator has already established himself as part of the homosocial world of the
male characters of the novel. And his alignment with once dominant but finally
discredited individuals such as Raymon also compromises his credibility and
authority. A dual process thus operates in *Indiana*, whereby the narrator's authority is simultaneously constructed and undermined.

Indiana can be read as an example of Irigarayan *mimétisme*, or mimicry. For
Luce Irigaray, to mimic is to "assume the feminine role deliberately. . . . To play
with mimesis is thus, for a woman, to try to recover the place of her exploitation by discourse, without allowing herself to be simply reduced to it" (76).
Naomi Schor has proposed the following reading of Irigaray's theory whereby
a first mode of masquerade refers to "women's alleged talents at parroting the
master's discourse, including the discourse of misogyny," whereas in a second
mode, "parroting becomes parody, and . . . a canny mimicry" ("This Essentialism" 48). Mimicry would thus involve reproducing the discourse of patriarchy
in such a way as to undercut its authority. Read from this perspective, *Indiana* is
not simply a ventriloquizing of patriarchal attitudes on women through the use
of a male narrator, it is a "canny mimicry" of these attitudes that subverts the

124 PERFORMANCE OF NARRATIVE AUTHORITY

authority of the male narrative voice. The narrator's presentation of characters, his judgements of their actions, and his extrarepresentational acts (particularly his discourse on women) expose the homosocial structuring of his narrative and his misogynistic prejudices, and this excessive performance discredits him.[4]

In *Indiana* the narrator's position is constantly compromised. Sand seems to create the illusion of authority only then to subvert it and to expose the gendered strategies by which narrative authority is constructed. The same is true of her reflection on realist representation in the preface. Sand here tells the reader to blame society, not the writer, for social inequalities and injustices, for "l'écrivain n'est qu'un miroir qui les reflète, une machine qui les décalque, et qui n'a rien à se faire pardonner si ses empreintes sont exactes, si son reflet est fidèle" '[t]he writer is only a mirror which reflects them, a machine which traces their outline, and he has nothing for which to apologize if the impressions are correct and the reflection is faithful' (37; 5). This statement can be compared with Stendhal's more famous assertion in *Le rouge et le noir* that "un roman: c'est un miroir qu'on promène le long d'un chemin" 'a novel is a mirror taken along a road' (288; my trans.). Sand links the writer rather than the novel to the mirror and suggests that the authorial function is simply that of a mirror reflecting a preexisting reality or a machine capable of producing an exact copy of the social environment. But the theory asserted here is more complicated in practice. To unravel the ways in which the novel responds to and contradicts this statement, students should be encouraged to consider this statement alongside those points in the text when images of the mirror and mimetic copying recur. They can thus situate it against the way the mirror functions in chapter 7 as a space of male desire that deforms (as Raymon imagines seeing Indiana reflected in the mirror rather than Noun). The way it resonates with the episode of the hieroglyphs in the conclusion should also be considered. For these "empreintes" 'imprints' in the rock appear as a literal "décalque" 'copy' of the landscape, but one that is dependent on the mediating presence of the narrator to translate what is observed into language and thus to communicate its meaning. Furthermore, as the novel will also stress, language is neither neutral nor transparent:

> [La langue] est une reine prostituée qui descend et s'élève à tous les rôles, qui se déguise, se pare, se dissimule et s'efface; c'est une plaideuse qui a réponse à tout, qui a toujours tout prévu, et qui prend mille formes pour avoir raison. Le plus honnête des hommes est celui qui pense et agit le mieux, mais le plus puissant est celui qui sait le mieux écrire et parler.
> (130 [93])

> [Language] is like a queen turned into a prostitute who, demeaning and raising herself, plays all parts, who disguises herself and decks herself out in finery, dissembles and conceals herself; it is like a litigant who has

an answer to everything, who has always foreseen everything, and has a thousand ways of being right. The most honest of men is the one who thinks and acts best, but the most powerful is the one who writes and speaks best.   (85)

Language is depicted here not as a vehicle for the accurate reproduction of the external world but as part of a scene of seduction in which disguise, dress, and dissimulation operate and in which hypocrisy and artificiality displace truth and transparency. Moreover, the narrator does not speak from a position outside language. Rather—as the preface stresses with terms such as "diseur" and "conteur" (both translated as "storyteller" [38; 6])—language is his stock in trade. He too manipulates and seduces, uses language to exercise power, and thus cannot avoid contamination by the inauthenticity that is posted here as a feature of all language.

An approach that focuses on a detailed analysis of the narrator in *Indiana* allows students to make sense of the narrative complexity of Sand's first novel and to see how the narrator's position is constantly foregrounded and his authority compromised. Understanding *Indiana* thus involves to some extent reading beyond the narrator. Focusing on this problematic figure also provides opportunities for discussing the author's metatextual reflections on novel writing embedded in the text. Even if *Indiana* appears to bear the marks of a relatively inexperienced author still feeling her way, it has much to say about the female author's negotiation with the conventions of what would come to be known as the realist form and its gendered ideologies. *Indiana* emerges from such an approach as a significant novel that illuminates women's position in an early-nineteenth-century literary world that was increasingly dominated by men and that exposes the ideological and literary ramifications of a homosocial textual dynamic in which cultural authority is constructed as part of a narrative exchange that takes place between men and from which women are excluded.

NOTES

[1] In the first edition of the novel, these examples were part of a much larger network of comments in which the narrator spoke directly to the narratee or reader in the first person. Students can be encouraged to look at the variants given at the end of Didier's Folio edition of the novel (e.g., Notes 380n13, 381n16, 384n7). The effect of Sand's deletions is to enhance the realist illusion that the narrative transparently reflects the world since they minimize those points where the storyteller's art was most in evidence and where fictional conventions were foregrounded.

[2] See also Boutin's essay in this volume, which draws attention to the way the narrator is closely bound up with the patriarchal relationships of the novel and establishes and exploits his complicity with the narratee.

[3] As Charles Stivale shows in his essay, the narrator attributes Indiana's strength of character to her deployment of vitalist traits that pertain to masculinity.

[4] This reading of *Indiana* can usefully be compared with that offered by Françoise Massardier-Kenney, who examines the narrator's presentation of the different characters and shows how his authority is undermined by his attempts to read the characters through a stable framework of gender based on biological essentialism, whereas the novel is questioning the stability of gender boundaries (*Gender* 16–31).

Indiana and the Literary Island: Enlightenment Ideals, Nineteenth-Century Ironies

Kathrine Bonin

Indiana is often read from a forward-looking perspective; for instance, as Sand's first solo entry into the nineteenth-century Romantic novel or as an early example of socially engaged or feminist fiction. These are valid readings. But to help students understand some of *Indiana's* oddest paradoxes—especially its tricky conclusion—it is helpful to examine the novel in the framework of ideas under which Sand originally presented it to the reading public. Furthermore, given that many of her detractors, and even some of her admirers, have downplayed the seriousness of her writing by citing its "flowing" or "effortless" style (Schor, Introduction vii), it is all the more important to be aware of the philosophical and aesthetic theory underpinning her earliest independent work. During the writing of *Indiana*, Sand looked back to eighteenth-century literary models, as she revealed in a letter to her friend Émile Regnault:

> Mon livre est déjà jugé par moi. Il plaira à peu de gens. Il est d'une exécution trop sévère, pas le plus petit mot pour rire. . . . J'ai peur d'ennuyer souvent, d'ennuyer comme la vie ennuie. Et pourtant, quoi de plus intéressant que l'histoire du cœur humain quand elle est vraie ? Il s'agit de la faire vraie, voilà le difficile. . . . Beaucoup de gens diront, *ce n'est pas ça*, fût-ce écrit comme Bernardin, fût-ce pensé comme Jean-Jacques.
> (*Correspondance* 2: 47)

> My book already stands judged by myself. It will please very few people. The execution is too severe; it does not crack even the smallest joke. . . .

I am afraid it will often be boring, boring in the way that life is boring. And yet, what could be more interesting than the history of the human heart, when it is truthfully told? It is just a question of making it truthful, that's the difficult part. . . . Many people will say, *that's not it*, even if it were written like Bernardin, even if it were thought out like Jean-Jacques.

(my trans.)

Together, Jean-Jacques Rousseau and Jacques-Henri Bernardin de Saint-Pierre form a powerful tradition with which *Indiana* is in extended dialogue. This is the tradition of the literary island, begun by Rousseau with his pedagogic treatise *Émile ou de l'éducation* (1762), and continued by Bernardin with his best-selling novel *Paul et Virginie* (1788). Both authors promote the image of a secluded tropical island where human beings might be reared according to natural principles, kept apart from the corruptive influence of mainland, civilized mores. In this isolated island sphere, knowledge could (theoretically) be transmitted to the pupil directly through the senses, without the tools of a more worldly education such as maps, calendars, or books. Paradoxically, Rousseau argues that his hypothetical pupil Émile might develop a protective insular mentality—a mental and moral quarantine—through his intense imaginative engagement with a book: Daniel Defoe's *Robinson Crusoe* (1719). As Rousseau writes:

> Je veux que la tête lui en tourne, qu'il s'occupe sans cesse de son château, de ses chévres, de ses plantations; qu'il apprenne en détail non dans des livres mais sur les choses tout ce qu'il faut savoir en pareil cas; qu'il pense être Robinson lui-même.   (455; orig. spelling respected)

> I want [*Robinson Crusoe*] to turn [Émile's] head, I want him to be constantly preoccupied with his castle, his goats, his plantations; I want him to learn in detail not out of books, but by the things themselves, everything that one would have to know in such a situation; I want him to think that he himself is Robinson.   (my trans.)

Inspired by his friend and mentor, Bernardin de Saint-Pierre placed the young heroes of his novel in the interior of Île de France, an island in the Indian Ocean not far from Indiana and Ralph's childhood home in Bourbon. Like *Émile*, Bernardin's *Paul et Virginie* condemns the printed medium (the child protagonists grow up happily illiterate), and yet the novel also credits certain exceptional novels with the power to bring humankind together in a community of shared sentiment that transcends differences of race, class, or culture. This model of reading draws on the Enlightenment concept of sympathy, or the belief that all human beings are instinctively drawn to share the emotional state that they witness in others, especially a state of suffering or distress.[1]

Paul et Virginie dramatically demonstrates the transformative power of universal sympathy at the novel's catastrophic climax, when Virginie dies in a shipwreck in sight of Paul, her family, and a crowd of onlookers who are all powerless to intervene. One can ask students to compare Virginie's death with Noun's offstage drowning in *Indiana*, the allusion to Ophelia, as well as Indiana's various failed drownings; Sand's novel is clearly haunted by Virginie's death. In Bernardin's novel, the family's traumatic loss of Virginie transforms the disparate inhabitants of the island: a colony founded on maritime commerce and a cash-crop agriculture fueled by slave labor is now re-formed—and reformed—into a community united by shared grief. The point is dramatically underscored at Virginie's burial, which is a useful scene to read aloud in class. Virginie's mourners perform a diverse series of African and Indian funerary rites; as the narrator observes, "tant la perte d'un objet aimable intéresse toutes les nations, et tant est grand le pouvoir de la vertu malheureuse, puisqu'elle réunit toutes les religions autour de son tombeau" 'so greatly does the loss of a loved one interest all nations, and so great is the power of unhappy virtue, since it brings all religions together around its tomb' (183; my trans.). Whether they are African, Indian or European, rich or poor, slave or free, even good or bad: all witnesses to Virginie's death or attendees of her funeral know instantly how to "read" and respond to the event of her loss. Moreover, Bernardin hoped that this affective circle of mourners would extend beyond the pages of the novel to encompass its readers. Indeed, he seems even to have entertained visions of international détente founded on the widespread popularity of his best seller, declaring in the 1789 preface that "[j]'ai la consolation d'éprouver que la langue de la nature est toujours entendue, même chez les nations rivales, et qu'elle peut encore les rapprocher mieux que la langue des traités diplomatiques" 'I have the consolation of having learned that the language of nature is always understood, even among rival nations, and that it can bring them together better than the language of diplomatic treaties' (217; my trans.).

In this way, moral utility is central to the model of reading that both Rousseau and Bernardin promote with their shared image of the literary island. Of course, the idea that novels could teach their readers to be better people did not originate with Rousseau or Bernardin. Rather, the peculiar novelty of the natural, highly moral education provided by the island model is that, for these authors, reading the literary island is somehow coextensive with actually witnessing the events that the novel relates. Through sympathy, the line between reading and being there is blurred, just as the line between observing and knowing a thing vanishes in the island setting, as Diana Loxley has argued (7). It is this complicated image of reading that links *Indiana* most strongly to the tradition of the literary island. To get at this point, it is useful to ask students what Sand's novel reveals about Indiana's early education: Where does she learn? How does she know what she knows? One can draw students' attention to Indiana's letter to Raymon: "Si j'écoutais la voix que Dieu a mise au fond de mon cœur, et ce noble instinct d'une nature forte et hardie, qui peut être la vraie conscience, je fuirais au désert. . . . [J]'irais vivre pour moi seule au fond de nos belles montagnes; j'oublierais les tyrans, les injustes et les ingrats" 'If I listened to the voice that God has placed at the bottom of my heart, and to the noble instinct of a strong, bold nature which is perhaps the real conscience, I would flee to the desert. . . . I would live for myself alone in the heart of our beautiful mountains. I would forget the tyrants, the unjust, and the ungrateful' (250 [196]; 191).

Clearly Indiana believes that her desire to escape from the corruptions of the civilized world into island solitude comes from her natural instinct.[2] The novel's narrator, however, calls Indiana's instinct into question, observing that her desire stems not so much from conscience or nature as from her socially mandated subjugation to an abusive husband:

> Alors elle ne rêva plus que de fuite, de solitude et d'indépendance; elle roula dans son cerveau meurtri et douloureux mille projets d'établissement *romanesque* dans les terres désertes de l'Inde ou de l'Afrique. . . . Elle se faisait un monde à part qui la consolait de celui où elle était forcée de vivre.   (273 [215–16]; my emphasis)

> After this incident, Indiana dreamt only of flight, solitude, and independence. In her wounded, grief-stricken mind, she turned over a thousand plans for settling *romantically* in the desert lands of India or Africa. . . . She made for herself a world apart, which consoled her for the one in which she was forced to live.   (210–11; my emphasis)

The English edition translates the adjective *romanesque*, used several times throughout the novel, as *romantically*; but a more accurate translation would be *novelistic*: containing ideas or images characteristic of a novel. Indiana is characterized several times as "bookish"; instructors might ask students to look for evidence in the novel of what, and how, she reads. Not only the narrator but also Raymon take issue with Indiana's reading habits, complaining, "Où avez-vous rêvé l'amour? dans quel roman à l'usage des femmes de chambre avez-vous étudié la société, je vous prie?" 'Where have you dreamed about love? In what novel written for ladies' maids have you studied society, I ask you?' (217 [168]; 163). Viewed from this perspective, the voice at the bottom of Indiana's heart is not an instinct shared by all humankind but rather a set of the learned beliefs of a specific demographic, restricted to a disenfranchised and even denigrated gender and class. Moreover, the self-serving Raymon is adept at manipulating Indiana's *romanesque* ideals by counterfeiting the lover-messiah that he (quite accurately) guesses she has been awaiting throughout her adult life. In other words, and in stunning contrast to Rousseau's *Émile*, whose *Crusoe*-inspired fantasies protect him from society, Indiana's imaginary insular paradise leaves her culturally primed to become Raymon's dupe. *Indiana* clearly presents the literary island as an established part of contemporary culture—not existing in a protected space somehow outside culture.

The novel might have ended here, with its heroine's *romanesque* illusions thoroughly discredited, a precursor to Flaubert's *Madame Bovary*, as others have pointed out (Booker). But *Indiana*'s final few pages appear to rehabilitate the heroine's faith in Rousseauistic reading, island refuges, and lover-messiahs: the novel that opens with the ambition to mirror human life faithfully ends by imitating its literary island precedents in almost uncanny detail. Indeed, the novel's final words, "Souvenez-vous de notre chaumière indienne" 'Remember our Indian cottage' (344 [275]; 271), refer directly to the title of Bernardin's second novel, *La chaumière indienne* (1790; *The Indian Cottage*), in which a socially outcast couple finds happiness in the midst of an Indian jungle. It is interesting to ask students how they read these final words. Do they confirm that one may indeed hope to escape from civilized misery into a secluded tropical paradise? Or is this Sand's final ironic wink at readers, an acknowledgment that such utopias do not exist outside the realm of fiction? Does *Indiana* debunk or group itself among what the novel's heroine terms "ces riantes et puériles fictions où l'on intéresse le cœur au succès de folles entreprises et d'impossibles félicités" 'those optimistic, childish fictions in which the heart becomes interested in the success of crazy enterprises and impossible joys' (247 [193]; 189)? A compelling case might be made for either argument. In the fun of debating just how seriously we are meant to buy into Indiana's happy ending, however, one should not lose sight of the corollary point: that *Indiana*, with the first-person intrusions of its slyly ironic narrator and its self-conscious references to its literary antecedents, foregrounds the reading process, asking, in effect, how readers (naive or not) come to respond to a given work of fiction as though it were a truthful representation of the human experience. When one begins to allow for multiple, opposing readings of a novel, one disallows sympathy—that is, the literary island's representation of sympathy as an immediate and universal phenomenon that reduces the reading process to instant recognition of indisputable truths. Sympathy and irony in this sense are incompatible; narrative transparency is *Indiana*'s most subtle paradise lost.

Sand is not the only nineteenth-century French author who engaged with the tradition of the literary island, with its seductive promise of unmediated contact with things as they are. *Indiana*'s equivocal reprisal of Rousseau's and Bernardin's insular paradise bears comparing to Gustave Flaubert's short story "Un cœur simple" (1877; "A Simple Heart") and Charles Baudelaire's nonfiction essay "De l'essence du rire" (1855; "On the Essence of Laughter"). *Indiana* and "Un cœur simple" work well together on a syllabus that includes references to excerpts from *Émile* and *Paul et Virginie*. Baudelaire's essay on laughter may be of more limited interest to undergraduate students, but, given his famous hostility to Sand,[3] teachers of her works may be interested to know the ways in which both authors reprised the image of Bernardin's Virginie and the concept of a natural education.

Allusions to *Paul et Virginie* are not hard to find in "Un cœur simple"; Madame Aubain names her two children after Bernardin's main characters, and her small household recalls the matriarchal utopia of Bernardin's novel (comparisons might also be drawn to the social dynamic between Indiana and Noun). But the most interesting point of comparison lies in her servant Félicité's education. The familiar question, How does she learn?, may be applied to Félicité as well as to Indiana. Impoverished, unschooled, and illiterate, Félicité learns from observation of her surroundings, from direct contact with things as they are. She cannot read a map, never having been taught (per the natural education advocated by Rousseau and Bernardin) to make the cognitive leap from signifier to signified, from symbol to the thing represented. When confronted with the standard metaphors of the Roman Catholic Church (bird for Holy Spirit and so on), Félicité falls into idolatrous error, praying directly to the stuffed, worm-eaten body of her parrot. If asked to read aloud the final scene, in which Félicité lies dying of pneumonia (her lungs filled with fluid, she is drowning in a way that recalls Virginie, Noun, and Indiana's attempts), students inevitably laugh at the absurdity of Félicité's exalted dying vision of a gigantic parrot. Yet students readily acknowledge the story's pathetic side as well. From here, one can focus attention on elements of Flaubert's style that undermine efforts to locate a single, authoritative point of view from which the events of the story may be judged. Like *Indiana*, "Un cœur simple" mobilizes both irony and pathos in its response to the literary island's ideals of natural education and perfect narrative transparency.[4]

There is not much pathos in Baudelaire's wickedly funny essay on laughter, but Bernardin's Virginie makes an unexpected guest appearance here, as a foil to the diabolical figure of Melmoth the Wanderer.[5] Arguing that laughter is linked to humankind's original fall from grace, Baudelaire cites Virginie as a representative type of prelapsarian innocence. Whisking Virginie off to France, Baudelaire imagines her confronting a typical Parisian caricature:

> La caricature est double: le dessin et l'idée: le dessin violent, l'idée mordante et voilée; complication d'éléments pénibles pour un esprit naïf, accoutumé à comprendre d'intuition des choses simples comme lui. Virginie a vu; maintenant elle regarde. Pourquoi? Elle regarde l'inconnu. Du reste, elle ne comprend guère ni ce que cela veut dire ni à quoi cela sert. Et pourtant, voyez-vous ce reploiement d'ailes subit, ce frémissement d'une âme qui se voile et veut se retirer? L'ange a senti que le scandale était là.   (692–93)

> Caricature is double; the drawing and the idea: the drawing violent, the idea mordant and veiled, a complication of elements that are painful for a naive mind, accustomed to intuitively understanding things that are simple, like itself. Virginie has seen; now she stares. Why? She looks at the unknown. Besides, she barely understands what it means or what use it

serves. And yet, do you see that sudden folding of her wings, that shudder of a soul that veils itself and wants to retreat? The angel has sensed that scandal was there.   (my trans.)

Positing a natural, anterior human state to analyze aspects of contemporary culture is a familiar gesture. Indeed, Baudelaire's fable of Virginie in Paris reveals a canny understanding of the core tenets of the literary island, though the author seems to enjoy inverting them point by point. The sentimental tableau (such as Virginie's death scene) purports to be readily comprehensible to all viewers, requiring no specialized knowledge to understand at a glance and to enter sympathetically into the affective state of another human being. In contrast, caricatures are pictures that must be read and decoded. What Baudelaire terms the double nature of caricature, instead of bringing seeing and knowing together as closely as possible, imposes a gap between the two—one that cannot be crossed without an initiation into the culture for whom the caricature has meaning. Such an initiation fails to confirm the shared values of the human community and instead constitutes a fall from innocence into corruption; as Baudelaire concludes sinisterly, if Virginie stays in Paris long enough, she will learn and will begin to laugh (693). In short, here is an art form that does not try to serve moral purposes through a reaffirmation of universal human values.

"Supposez un philosophe relégué dans une isle deserte" 'Let us suppose that a philosopher is relegated to a desert island,' Rousseau invites readers of *Émile* (429; orig. spelling respected; my trans.); it is an invitation accepted by Bernardin and the nineteenth-century heirs to the literary island legacy. Rousseau's meditation on issues of epistemology, ethics, and the role of art, mapped onto an imagined opposition between mainland and island, created an enduring image that resonated with very diverse authors—Sand and Baudelaire are not often noted for their points in common, for instance. What links Sand, Baudelaire, and Flaubert is that their reprisals of the literary island all highlight the readers' role in creating meaning in the text: the ideal narrative transparency of universal sympathy gives way to complex issues of hermeneutics. Introducing student readers of *Indiana* to these concepts provides them with the context to a novel whose scope is broader than a mere love triangle in a tropical setting. Sympathy and irony are not easy or obvious opposites, but their conflict in *Indiana* is central to understanding the novel and to recognizing Sand's original contribution to the history of ideas.

NOTES

This essay presents in a pedagogic context ideas that were originally published in "The Edifying Spectacle of a Drowned Woman: Sympathy and Irony in *Indiana*" in *George Sand Studies* 28 (2009), with the kind permission of *George Sand Studies*.

[1] For more about Rousseauistic reading, see Darnton; Caplan.

[2] The reference to "the bottom of my heart" again recalls *Émile*, in particular the Savoyard vicar, who cites his own "régle facile et simple . . . dans la sincérité de mon cœur" 'rule of the heart,' by which he judges the truth value of anything he reads (570; orig. spelling respected; my trans.).

[3] In "Mon cœur mis à nu" ("My Heart Laid Bare"), Baudelaire writes, "Elle a le fameux *style coulant*, cher aux bourgeois" 'She has the famous *flowing style*, dear to the bourgeois,' and extends the metaphor unpleasantly by calling Sand "cette latrine" 'that latrine' (411; my trans.).

[4] Flaubert famously denied the use of irony in "Un cœur simple," in a letter to Mme Roger des Genettes: "Ce n'est nullement ironique comme vous le supposez, mais au contraire très sérieux et très triste. Je veux apitoyer, faire pleurer les âmes sensibles, en étant une moi-même" 'It is not at all ironic the way you think, but on the contrary very serious and very sad. I want to move to pity; to make sensitive souls cry, as I myself am one' (28–29; my trans.). For more on irony, pathos, and the Sand-Flaubert relationship, see Schor, "Idealism" (Hollier).

[5] In pairing Virginie with Melmoth, Baudelaire overlooks (knowingly or not) Melmoth's love interest, Immalee, yet another beautiful European girl reared in virtuous solitude on an island in the East Indies; see Maturin's Gothic classic, *Melmoth the Wanderer* (1820).

Codes Visible and Invisible:
A Law and Literature Approach to *Indiana*

Lynn Penrod

> If society did not bind women with all manner of chains
> while men go unshackled, what would there be in my life
> to keep anyone from loving me?
> —Germaine de Staël, *Corinne* (1807)

The juxtaposition of law and literature is both interesting and rewarding in teaching George Sand's *Indiana* in an undergraduate literature course. Whereas most of my second- and third-year law students have an adequate background in the basic differences between common law and civil law, my literature students do not (although some have a keen interest in learning more about law, since they are often considering law school as a future career). Literature students, for their part, have often had experience in textual analysis and have not yet encountered the rather dulling effect of reading nothing but case reports during many years of study. Yet, in virtually all law and literature classes, both literature and law students are equally ill-informed about the basics of French legal and social history and thus become easily confused when reading a nineteenth-century novel like *Indiana*. Providing an appropriate context for the reading of the text thus becomes the instructor's primary task. Basic differences between civil and common law, the legal status of women during Sand's time, the importance of understanding the significance to each of us in our daily lives—these general discussions pave the way for creative analyses by students.

Students often have a variety of questions after their first reading of *Indiana*: Why is the tone so often melodramatic? Why do the relationships between the principal characters seem so emotionally fraught? Why would an author write a second preface to a work ten years later? In response to these confusions, some contextual information, or what lawyers like to call further and better particulars, can give student readers clues that can lead to a more nuanced interpretation of the text. There are several ways in which the legal context of *Indiana* can be useful in approaching the text, depending on whether the teaching audience is made up primarily of law students or of literature students. In this essay, I focus on literature students, but my usage of the concept of codes can be easily varied and emphasized differently to suit a specific student audience.

Since France is a civilian law jurisdiction, the very concept of code as it relates to the law becomes critical as we observe how the aftermath of the French Revolution and the development of the Code Napoléon (later the Code Civil) affected the society and people appearing in Sand's novel. And while this particular legal code is a visible one—that is, a legal printed document presented in book form and available to all—there is another code that is also at play in

Indiana, one that is less easy to describe accurately, for it remains below the surface of everyday life, understood only intuitively and never written down. This invisible code, which the historian William Reddy has described as a code of honor, is also an important key to a fuller understanding of the narrative world of *Indiana*.

The Visible Code

A preliminary class discussion of *Indiana* focuses on a snapshot of the writer as well as a brief freeze-frame of the historical period in which she and her work are immersed. When Sand published *Indiana* in 1832, she was twenty-eight years old, had been married (rather unhappily) for nine years to Casimir Dudevant, and was the mother of two children. She grew up in a France where both her family situation and the country's political situation had been for most of her life tumultuous, to say the least. During Sand's life, France had already experienced the rise and fall of the Napoleonic empire, which had succeeded the final decade of the French Revolution and the Directory. After Napoléon, the country saw the return of the monarchy to France (the Bourbon restoration), a period that would last until 1848. Just as one is born into a language, one is also born into culture and into a particular historical time. And although it may be stating the obvious, we are also born into law and into a particular legal system, whether or not we are consciously aware of its influence on virtually every aspect of our lives. The legal system into which Sand was born would have a significant impact on both her life and her work.

Most English-language readers of Sand live in common law jurisdictions where courts have the authority to make law based on the concept of precedent and the rule of stare decisis. Common law jurisdictions trace their beginnings primarily to England, where common law courts had the authority to make (create) law where no legislative authority existed and where the court could interpret a statute to ascertain its meaning. In a general sense, then, the reasoning used in common law jurisdictions is case-based, and courtroom procedures are adversarial. Most anglophone students understand this system intuitively and can explain how laws are enacted and then interpreted by courts and how cases are decided by reference to previous cases. Once that discussion is completed, we move to the less familiar civil law system.

In contrast to common law systems, a civil law system is based primarily on Roman law. Laws are often collected and codified, not interpreted by judges, as they are in common law. In a civil law system, legislation is seen as the primary source of law, and the court system is inquisitorial rather than adversarial. Precedent does not bind a civil law court, and judges, instead of being appointed from among lawyers, are trained specifically as judges. It is oversimplistic to state that, whereas in a common law jurisdiction the law is accumulated over time through the precedent establishment of case-by-case decisions rendered by the courts, civilian law jurisdictions tend to find the law in a book or a code—yet those are the distinguishing features of the two systems. In the twenty-first century the two systems have drawn much closer to each other. The discussion of the civil law system is always an interesting one, as students grapple with the idea of the law in a book.

The codification of French law under Napoléon I in the early years of the nineteenth century makes the legal underpinnings of *Indiana* important, especially those related to the situation of women in terms of marriage and divorce. For students to understand women's legal status in 1832, we need to go back in time, before the French Revolution, to the ancien régime. During the ancien régime, there had been no possibility of divorce in Roman Catholic France. Thus France's very first divorce law (20 September 1792) marked a radical departure from the past and even by today's standards was extraordinarily liberal. In the words of Michèle Plott, "It made divorce affordable even to the very poor, it was equally available throughout France, and it was not based on any double standard of sexual morality that would have put women at a disadvantage." It "reflected the Revolution's commitment to the rights of the individual and its antipathy to Roman Catholicism." The 1792 law acknowledged the principles of marital breakdown in which neither spouse would be named the guilty party to the divorce. Mutual consent to divorce was possible and in cases of "incompatibility of temperament" either spouse could obtain the divorce unilaterally with a six-month waiting period (Tulard, Fayard, and Fierro; my trans.). Specific grounds for divorce included immorality, cruelty, insanity, condemnation for certain crimes, desertion for at least two years, or emigration. Thus, from 1792 to 1804, persons who found themselves in an untenable or unhappy marriage could divorce quickly and easily.

The liberal provisions of the first divorce law were greatly curtailed by the Code Napoléon of 1804, however, under which they became both more restrictive and more bureaucratically complicated. The grounds for divorce were reduced to adultery, ill-treatment, and condemnation to certain degrading forms of punishments. Divorce by mutual consent now required the permission of family members, and the ground of incompatibility was eliminated completely. In addition, and more important for readers of *Indiana*, a sexual double standard was introduced into the law. A man could be divorced from his wife if she committed simple adultery, but a man could be convicted of adultery only if he brought his mistress into his home. And divorce was made more expensive and more difficult procedurally. These changes in the code's divorce laws strengthened the position of men and patriarchal authority in the family.

Divorce remained a possibility in France until 1816, when it was abolished completely, since Roman Catholicism was reinstituted as the state religion under the restoration. After 1816, the only legal option for partners in a marriage that had broken down was judicial separation. After the revolution of 1830, there were several attempts made to reestablish divorce, through a reversion to the 1792 law or to the more restrictive 1804 law. In the four successive years from 1831 to 1834, the chamber of deputies passed such a bill, only to have it rejected by the chamber of peers. As Plott notes, "France's aristocracy clearly rejected any return to the revolution; their vote against these divorce bills was as much a rejection of the revolution's heritage as of divorce's social effects."

The Code Napoléon, given its pan-European scope, would become a model for many nineteenth-century law codifications. The code is "a literary as well as a legal masterpiece; its language is clear and precise, concise and direct," and its provisions are "neither vague nor subtle; qualifications, limitations, and exceptions are kept down to a bare minimum; confusing casuistry and sterile abstractions are entirely absent. . . . Its provisions are neither too reactionary nor too revolutionary and strike a successful balance between a prudent liberalism and an enlightened conservatism" (Holmberg). Although divorce was no longer a subject in the civil code by the time of Sand's work on *Indiana*, the restrictions imposed by the 1804 version relating to the obligations of husband and wife were certainly still in force. The Code Civil remains even today the basic source of French law, informing the way in which daily life is regulated and providing legal rules for social and familial relationships. Sharing parts from book 1, *Of Persons*, such as title 5 (*Of Marriage*) or title 6 (*Of Divorce*), gives students a chance to see the format, language, and style of the provisions.

In her preface to the 1832 edition of *Indiana*, Sand provides a clue to her opinion of the law in her description of the novel's narrator:

> Perhaps you will do him justice if you agree that he has shown you the misery of the person who wants to free himself from legitimate restraint, the utter distress of the heart that rebels against its destiny's decrees. If he has not shown in the best light the character that represents the law, if he has been even less favorable to another who represents public opinion, you will see a third who represents illusion and cruelly thwarts the vain hopes and crazy enterprises of passion. Finally, you will see that if he has not strewn roses on the ground where the law pens up our desires like sheep, he has cast nettles on the paths which lead us away from it.   (7)

The law, represented in *Indiana* most clearly by Colonel Delmare, is seen from the outset as confining, enclosing our desires "like sheep," and trying to free ourselves from law is to follow a path strewn with nettles, a source of pain, rather than roses, a source of beauty and happiness. It is significant, too, that Indiana is described by her creator as a "type"—"woman, the weak creature who is given the task of portraying passions, repressed, or if you prefer, suppressed by the law" (7)—and as a generic woman is assigned the role of representing passions, something that the law would seek to control. Indiana, pictured as a generic woman subjected to the total authority of law, provides a contrast to another female character in the novel, Laure de Nangy, who "calmly and philosophically" accepts the fact that Raymon is more interested in her money than in her love:

She had too much good sense, too much knowledge of the real world, to have dreamed of love side by side with two million. . . .

Mademoiselle de Nangy had therefore quite made up her mind to submit to marriage as a social necessity, but she took a malicious pleasure in making use of the liberty she still had and in imposing her authority for a while on the man who aspired to deprive her of it. No youth, no sweet dreams, no brilliant, deceptive future, for this girl who was condemned to undergo all the miseries of wealth. For her, life was a stoical calculation and happiness and childish illusion, against which she must defend herself as against a weakness and an absurdity.   (226)

We know that the law demands the subservience of all married women, whether they are the likes of Indiana or the likes of Laure. Indiana experiences pain and unhappiness at her subservience, whereas Raymon's future wife seems to have accepted her lot, even if rather cynically. And perhaps, too, we can see here just how powerful the law can be, with Indiana on the one hand often described as ignorant of the letter of the law yet constantly hypersensitive to her submissive position in her marriage, and Laure, on the other, just as much an exchange commodity as Indiana, realizing that she has only authority to deal with Raymon up until the time of her submission to him in marriage.

Ten years later, in the preface to the 1842 edition of *Indiana*, George Sand no longer speaks ambiguously about the law but takes the position of writer-advocate: "Long after writing the preface to *Indiana*, under the influence of a remnant of respect for organized society, I was still seeking a solution to this insoluble problem: *how to reconcile the happiness and dignity of individuals oppressed by that same society without modifying society itself*" (11). She describes the writer as a "prudent defender, not trying too hard to excuse his client's faults, and appealing far more to the clemency of the judges than to their austerity, the novelist is the true advocate of the abstract beings who represent our passions and our sufferings before the tribunal of force and the jury of public opinion" (11). We note here Sand's conflation of both visible and invisible codes. Not only does the Code Civil, the visible code, serve to oppress certain individuals in the society it regulates, but the "jury of public opinion" finds its authority through a different yet equally powerful code (what Reddy terms a code of honor). Sand explains in her 1842 preface that she wrote *Indiana* "influenced by a feeling, unreasoned, it is true, but deep and legitimate, of the injustice and barbarity of the laws which still govern the existence of women in marriage, in the family, and in society. [Her] task was not to write a treatise on jurisprudence but to fight against public opinion, for it is that which delays or promotes social improvements" (11–12).

It is important to note, however, that significant events in Sand's life had occurred during the decade separating *Indiana*'s two prefaces. During the year of *Indiana*'s composition and first preface, Sand was a married mother of two. But she was also a romantic rebel and had at least symbolically escaped her marriage prison by taking several lovers and moving to Paris with one of them, Jules Sandeau, to live a bohemian life. The conduct of her husband was hardly blameless; he preferred "hunting, drinking, and carousing" rather than "sharing life's experiences with his wife" (Powell, Introduction 8).

Although divorce in the France of 1832 was no longer in the book, judicial separation did remain as a remedy for marriage breakdown. Indeed, Dudevant had signed an agreement in February 1835 to separate from his wife that fall but then began to have second thoughts once he realized that he would not be able to stay on at Nohant as lord and master and would be forced to accept the income from his Paris property in exchange. Perhaps, in addition to wishing to retain his control of his wife's property, Dudevant also wished to avoid the public humiliation of being revealed as a betrayed husband. But after a particularly upsetting and public argument in front of guests at Nohant on 19 October 1835, Sand herself decided to file for a legal separation, even though this action was risky. If her lifestyle (notably, her adulterous affairs) were to be made public in open court, Sand would be at risk of losing her children as well as control of her property. A double standard was definitely the order of the day, not only in the fictional world of Madame Delmare but also in the real-world France of the same period. Sand's husband's affairs would be seen as minimal compared with her own misconduct.

The Invisible Code

After students have an idea of the ways in which the visible Code Civil had affected the legal situation of women in France, we move to a discussion of a second code that lies beneath the overt text of the Code Civil and concurrently informs our reading of the text.

In the preface to his book *The Invisible Code: Honor and Sentiment in Post-revolutionary France, 1814–1848*, the French social historian William Reddy summarizes the various legal codes that came into force in the early years of the nineteenth century: "The abolition of privilege, equality before the law, the right of due process, freedom of contract—these and other principles of 1789 were enshrined in definitive form in the codes, in terse, easy to understand French" (xi). Reddy also confirms a sharp decline in the legal status of women since fathers and husbands had absolute control over women and their property. He concludes, "The Codes provided the structure of a new male public sphere of open competition, on which talent and merit were to receive their due and in which property and money would flow freely from hand to hand in response to the pressure of supply and demand, and from which the family and women would be firmly excluded" (xi).

Yet Reddy argues that another code existed at this time as well, "an invisible one that was also transmitted to the future by the work of the Napoleonic years, a code of honor" (xi). This underlying code plays an important role in any modern-day reading of *Indiana* since it allows us to understand the motivations behind some of the more puzzling aspects of the text (the themes of suicide, the somewhat ambiguous roles played by Raymon's mother and the salon of Madame de Carvajal, or the relationship between Indiana and Ralph). Although the concept of honor was presumed to be a thing of the past following the Revolution, the code of honor described by Reddy had a familial-marital dimension and a public-political dimension as well. These two dimensions are most clearly illustrated in *Indiana* by Sand's dual gendered triangles: the female trio Indiana, Noun, and Laure and the male triad Delmare, Raymon, and Ralph. The dual codes, visible and invisible, read in concert, allow us to think creatively about the shifting relationships in the text.

This new code of honor, although written nowhere, was enforced by the numerous and public law courts of the postrevolutionary era, which interpreted the articles of the Code Civil dealing with marriage as a guide for the protection of family honor (and in many other ways as well). But this code of honor was also enforced in other ways, especially by men's extremely strong emotional responses, their feeling of shame that could overwhelm their better judgment (Reddy xii). According to Reddy's archival research on court cases involving legal separations between 1814 and 1848, some men failed to defend themselves in the (shameful) arena of the public courtroom against separation requests by their wives, whereas for women "honor could often seem less important than emotional fulfillment; sentimental attachments were what women prized most or mourned most if they went sour" (xii).

Reddy questions how this difference between men and women had come about and focuses his study on the hypothesis of a complementarity in the way honor and emotion (or sentiment—as the female realm of feeling was labeled—or passion, if we use Sand's vocabulary) were conceived of and experienced by early-nineteenth-century French men and women:

> This complementarity hinged on the idea that male shame was not a feeling, at least not a part of the female lexicon of "sentiment," and that therefore men, who regulated their behavior on the basis of honor, acted more rationally than women, were free of the bewildering play of feeling, able to see and think with greater clarity and consistence. The male public sphere thus anchored its legitimacy on the false notion that, by excluding women, just as when they excluded children or the insane, men were excluding the irrational. The idea that private feeling could be contained or eliminated from public deliberation or action—in spite of its evident falseness—ran very deep, as it still does today, for that matter.   (xiii)

Although Reddy is a historian and focuses on broad areas of the social history of restoration France, his study offers students a useful perspective on the fictional world of Sand's *Indiana*, helping them understand the actions of all three main male characters, as well as giving them an appreciation of a woman writer like George Sand.

Reading with the Codes

Reading always involves the deciphering of codes—linguistic, thematic, symbolic, or cultural—and *Indiana* allows for several coded readings, on many levels. The all-too-easy binary oppositions between reason and sentiment, honor and dishonor, public and private, male and female must all be reconsidered to fully appreciate the force of *Indiana* as a text both descriptive of the complexities of its time and yet always straining to provoke remedial social action. As the narrator describes Indiana, these complexities become clear:

> In marrying Delmare she had only changed masters; in coming to live at Lagny she had only changed prisons and places of solitude. She did not love her husband, perhaps only because she was told it was her duty to love him and mental resistance to every kind of moral compulsion had become a kind of second nature to her, a principle of conduct, a law of conscience. No one had tried to teach her any other kind of law than that of blind obedience.   (51)

External evidence, both historical and autobiographical, indicates that Sand had an agenda in writing *Indiana*. We can certainly analyze the text according to our views of realism, Romanticism, feminism, socialism, or even what Naomi Schor calls "the difficult emergence of Sandian idealism from the realist paradigm constituted by Balzacian realism" (Introduction xii). In addition, there is ample textual evidence to support a reading of the two codes: an underlying influence of the visible code (the impossibility of divorce; the lack of legal remedies available to women in unhappy marital situations) and a conscious or even unconscious grappling with the changing invisible code (the mutable concepts of honor; the relationships between men and women of the day).

The three main male characters are delineated as representatives of different political and social moments and ideologies at the end of the restoration: "Delmare is the embittered cashiered Napoleonic soldier, Raymon, the opportunistic legitimist, Sir Ralph, the idealistic democrat" (Schor, Introduction xiii). Yet, as Schor reminds us, at issue is not simply the masculine and public political concepts of what honor is or ought to consist of but how that concept gives meaning to the lives of the women with whom men are connected, whether through the institution of marriage or through an emotional attachment of love (illusory or realist). Reddy would most certainly agree with Schor's assertion that "what makes Delmare such a compelling figure is not his adherence to some sort of Balzacian social typology but rather his instantiation of an idea, the Law, which reduces women to the status of objects of exchange and to the abjection of virtual slaves" (xiii).

The concept of honor and the public face that this invisible code demands for men underlies many of the dynamics of Indiana's male trio: Delmare's jealousy and angry outbursts (emotional and stereotypically feminine responses) are closely linked to the public loss of personal honor. Raymon's honor is intimately linked of course to his political and social position and its concomitant necessity of marrying appropriately. Sir Ralph and Indiana's relationship provides an interesting hybrid of honorable submission to both a male and a female code of honor, in that Indiana has already unsuccessfully attempted to disobey both the visible and invisible codes that law and society have imposed on her.

As for the three main female characters, Noun, the creole servant and double of Indiana, presents the reader with a variation on the subordinate, almost inhuman, position of women in nineteenth-century France. Under the Code Civil, as Renee Winegarten has pointed out, "in the eyes of the law, a girl came first under her father's protection, then under her husband's. Only when these natural protectors failed her could she appeal to the law to take their place" (176). Thus Noun is absolutely without legal recourse when her liaison with Raymon reaches its unhappy end, and suicide seems to be the only possible end for women in her situation. Both Laure and Indiana retain their subordinate positions in society, even if their individual manners of living as subordinate are different.

Indiana provides fascinating insights into the complex and ever-changing legal and social landscape of the first half of the nineteenth century in France. Complex interrelations between public and private spheres, men and women, and the visible code of the law and the invisible code of honor provide the plot with a social and historical context that enhances the twenty-first-century reader's study of the novel. This complexity, particularly that introduced by the two complementary codes, adds to the ongoing interest of this text for contemporary readers.

Teaching *Indiana* in English

Françoise Massardier-Kenney

Instructors wanting to teach *Indiana* in English will find several translations written in different periods and for different audiences. In the nineteenth century, the novel was one of the most popular of its time, in both French and English. The rise of realism and naturalism brought a lull in Sand's reputation, but her renewed popularity in academic circles, beginning with feminist scholars in the late twentieth century, led to two retranslations. As an analysis of the major translations of *Indiana* will show, the modern translations, published as part of a feminist reevaluation of Sand, actually tone down the presentation of the female character as victimized, whereas the earlier, traditional translations unexpectedly intensify the description of the main character as a woman who is oppressed and who is therefore justified in freeing herself. Comparing these translations will allow instructors to analyze how differences in the stylistic nuances of a translation influence readers' understanding of the character and plot and how the fabric of a translation reflects the translator's view on Sand's style.

The first English translation of the novel, translated anonymously, appeared in 1845 and was presented as "[a]n original translation from the Fourth Brussels edition." On the title page, the name of George Sand was followed by Madame Dudevant, in parentheses, and the title was preceded by "Beautiful French Romance." This translation included the 1832 preface and a short note by the anonymous translator.[1] It was published in New York by Dillon and Hooper, a newspaper publisher. The second translation was undertaken by George W. Richards in 1850 and published by T. B. Peterson and Brothers in Philadelphia in an unabridged edition titled *Indiana, a Love Story, with a Life of Madame Dudevant (George Sand)*. This version included a biographical and critical preface written by the translator and excerpts from laudatory appraisals by a range of authors, such as the well-known French historian Jules Michelet, William Thackeray, John Stuart Mill, and Heinrich Heine. New editions of the translation appeared in 1870, 1881, and 1888. A new translation by George Burnham Ives appeared in 1900, in a series titled Complete Masterpieces of George Sand, published by George Barrie and Son in Philadelphia. This translation, like the other volumes in the series, was translated by Ives and had neither a preface nor an introduction; it was reprinted in 1975 by Fertig, in 1978 by both Academy Chicago Press and Cassandra Press, in 2010 by Nabu Press,[2] and in 2011 by Kessinger Publishing. Then, in the second part of the twentieth century, two new translations appeared within one year of each other: one in 1993, by the American translator Eleanor Hochman and published by Signet, with an introduction by Marilyn Yalom, a specialist of women's writing, and the other in 1994, by the British academic Sylvia Raphael and published in the Oxford World Classics series, with an introduction by Naomi Schor, a prominent nineteenth-century French literature scholar.

The first translation by Richards is based on the original edition of *Indiana* (1832) and includes the long authorial comments that Sand removed in the 1842 edition, but it does not include her prefaces to the 1832, 1842, or 1852 edition. The Ives, Hochman, and Raphael translations include all the prefaces and are based on the 1852 edition. Three of the translations are easily accessible: the Richards and the Ives texts can be accessed electronically,[3] and the Raphael translation was reissued in 2008 and is available in paperback and as an electronic book. The Hochman translation, however, is out of print and unavailable electronically.

Choosing which translation to use can present a challenge for the instructor, since the texts differ in many ways. Consider, for example, the following versions of *Indiana*'s short second paragraph:

> Ce personnage, beaucoup plus âgé que les deux autres, était le maître de la maison, le colonel Delmare, vieille bravoure en demi-solde, homme jadis beau, maintenant épais, au front chauve, à la moustache grise, à l'œil terrible; excellent maître devant qui tout tremblait, femme, serviteurs, chevaux et chiens. (49 [ed. Didier; 48 words])

> This man, much older than the others, was the master of the house, Colonel Delmare, a brave old soldier; once handsome, but now too large, with a bold forehead, gray mustachio, and terrible eye; before whom all trembled, wife, servants, dogs, and horses. (17 [trans. Richards; 43 words])

> This person, who was much older than the other two, was the master of the house, Colonel Delmare, an old warrior on half-pay, once a very handsome man, now over-corpulent, with a bald head, gray moustache and awe-inspiring eye; an excellent master before whom everybody trembled, wife, servants, horses and dogs. (4 [trans. Ives; 51 words])

> This person, who was much older than the other two, was the master of the house, Colonel Delmare, a retired army officer, who had once been handsome but now was heavy and bald with a grey moustache and a fierce look; he was an excellent master who made everyone tremble, wife, servants, horses, and dogs. (15 [trans. Raphael; 55 words])

> This person, much older than the other two, was Colonel Delmare, the head of the house; a retired soldier on half-pay, once handsome but now overweight, with a grey mustache and a harsh expression, he was an excellent master before whom everyone—wife, servants, horses, and dogs—trembled. (31 [trans. Hochman; 48 words])

Even a cursory glance shows an instructor that all the versions but Richards's are as long, or longer, than the French source text. The compactness of Richards's translation corresponds to a difference commonly found between English language texts and their French originals, which tend to contain considerably more amplification and are longer as a consequence. That difference between Richards's translation and the others proves to be a pattern, and an instructor will want to assess and explain its effects. The same cursory glance will also prompt an instructor to note that the earlier translations repeat the word "old," a purposeful repetition. In addition, Richards is the only translator to use "man" instead of "person."[4] He also removes the reference to "on half-pay," while Ives keeps the "on half-pay," and the twentieth-century translators substitute the adjective "retired." This small difference too is part of a pattern worth explaining: in the descriptions of the husband, the earlier translators emphasize his age, a negative characteristic. An instructor can also point out that none of the translators picks up on what "demi-solde" suggests—that is, a former soldier of Napoléon's army. This is important because Sand immediately identifies each male character with a political position. A good way to make students aware that each translation presents a version, an interpretation, of the text is to ask them what other lexical differences they notice in this excerpt and what they think their effect is. For instance, an instructor can point out that Richards removes the ironic comment "excellent maître" and changes the word order (he puts "dogs" before "horses") and ask about possible reasons (an obvious one is to obtain a harmonious sentence whose rhythm echoes that of Sand's).

To decide which translation to select, an instructor would instinctively want to consult reviews, but reviews of the *Indiana* translations do not contain comments on the translations; they focus instead on Sand's themes and characters. Similarly, if the instructor were to turn to reference works on translation, the entries on Sand would not provide much guidance. The entries in two standard reference works on translations in English, *The Encyclopedia of Literary Translation into English* and *The Oxford Guide to Literature in English Translation* (both published by Oxford University Press in 2000 [Tilby; France]), display a marked reluctance to fully convey Sand's significance and do not describe the translations of *Indiana*. For instance, Michael Tilby, after suggesting, erroneously, that Sand's work in English had a restricted readership (1225–26), selectively quotes Patricia Thompson, so as to disparage the translations of Sand's works into English and misrepresent Sand's importance.[5]

Thus an instructor might turn to the focus of the course as a basis for selecting a translation. All four translations are by competent translators who have produced highly readable texts, and the choice will depend more on the purpose of the course than on the intrinsic quality of the translation. In a course on nineteenth-century European literature, the instructor might want to select an older translation (probably Richards's or Ives's), one that will give the students a sense of the flavor of an older period and an indication of Sand's place in the literature of that period. For an undergraduate gender studies course in which thematic concerns are primary, the twentieth-century translations might be preferable, especially one with an introduction geared to students (Raphael's) or to the general public (Hochman's). A translation based on the 1832 edition (Richards's) would be appropriate in a course on women's writing, since it includes Sand's original comments on writing. If the course focuses on the representation of women, however, Ives's translation, which is particularly attentive to the victimization of women characters, might be the better choice.

In addition, instructors presenting a foreign work in translation must attend to the cultural and literary conditions that give the work its place in the literary landscape of its country of origin and that accompany its transfer into the target culture. Instructors will want to provide information on the translators, mentioning the circumstances in which the translations were made and their characteristics, to make students aware of the cultural and literary contexts in which particular translations are produced. For instance, the admiration for Sand's style displayed in the early translations by Richards and Ives must be contrasted with the views of the later translators, whose lesser appreciation of a literary style characterized by "naturalness" informs their translations and influences readers' reaction to the text. Instructors can alert their students to the different conceptions of language and style that influence the practice of different translators by selecting specific examples for discussion.

Richards, *Indiana*'s earliest known translator, was "one of the best French scholars in this country," according to the *WorldCat* record of the 1850 Peterson edition, and "a member of the Philadelphia bar." *Indiana* is the only book that he translated, but apparently Richards knew nineteenth-century French literature very well.[6] His introductory essay, "Life of Madame Dudevant," shows a deep knowledge of Sand's works and refers to many of her novels. It provides a brief account of Sand's life and a summary of the ideas expressed in her works that ends with a reference to "the beauty and brilliancy of her style" (16).[7] It also gives the reader an indication of Richards's purpose in translating *Indiana*: "she is about to have a fair hearing among us in an English translation of her works, which will be judged according to their real merits—the people, not the quarterly critics, being the judges" (3). To ensure that fair hearing, Richards advocates on behalf of Sand's work with statements about her "consummate studies of characters, lifelike, breathing, natural" and her attachment to "democratic faith" (12). In sum, he presents Sand as a great writer, "the great female genius" (3), whose style "exhibit[s] a wonderful knowledge of character and acuteness of observation" (13). The other paratexts (excerpts from reviews written by important contemporaries) also establish Sand as a great writer and moralist. Thus it is no surprise that Richards's translation strives to render Sand's style and pays close attention to the natural effect of this style and to the rhythmic means through which it is achieved.

Ives was, among other things, a very prolific American translator.[8] He not only produced nineteen volumes of Sand's works but also translated the *Comédie humaine* and numerous works by Guy de Maupassant, Alphonse Daudet, Victor Hugo, Prosper Mérimée, Eugénie de Guérin, Théophile Gautier, Gustave Flaubert, and Michel de Montaigne, among others. This productivity indicates that Ives knew nineteenth-century authors extremely well and that he dealt with the styles of a wide range of writers. He was also the author of *Text, Type and Style: A Compendium of Atlantic Usage*, published in 1921 by the *Atlantic Monthly Press*.[9] A further testimony to his importance on the American cultural scene is the fact that his personal library was catalogued. Unlike Richards's translation, Ives's 1900 translation includes neither an introduction to Sand nor a comment by the translator, which suggests that, by 1900, Sand's reputation in English had been established and needed no introduction. Thus Ives's goal in translating Sand was not to introduce her work and make her acceptable to an American audience. Indeed, his translation reflects the status of Sand as a major writer, and there is no effort made to adapt her writing to the standards of American English syntax. Even the short excerpt presented above shows that Ives expanded Sand's sentences instead of compressing them.

From the mid-nineteenth century, when Richards's translation first appeared, until the 1900s, when Ives was beginning his translation of Sand's works, Sand was considered a master stylist and a major writer, alongside Honoré de Balzac and Hugo. When Hochman and Raphael translated *Indiana* in the 1990s, Sand's works had been rediscovered by academics after a long period of oblivion. It may be assumed that the Richards and Ives translations were aimed at an educated general public in the United States, whereas Raphael's Oxford World Classics translation is intended for an audience of teachers and students of French literature. Hochman's translation, in the popular Signet Classic paperback series, is aimed at the general public, as the holdings in public libraries seem to indicate. Further, while the Ives translation was published at a time when there had been a considerable number of reviews of Sand's works, modern scholarship on Sand was inexistent. The Hochman and Raphael translations benefit from scholarship focusing on Sand. Instructors should note, however, that this scholarship is almost entirely focused on themes that concern modern academics (race, class, gender, historical and cultural studies, etc.) and provides little discussion of the stylistic means through which these themes might be conveyed. This lack of interest in style may explain some of the paradoxes exhibited in the translations.

Hochman has translated modern works such as the best seller *War of the Buttons*, by Louis Pergaud, as well as classics such as Alexandre Dumas's *Three Musketeers* and Émile Zola's *Germinal*. In addition to collaborations with her husband, she is the coauthor of the Kettridge French/English dictionary; she is also the author of a book on women in American fiction, *Fictional Females, Mirrors and Models*, and of several romance novels (published under a pseudonym). Her interest in popular fiction is reflected in the novels she has translated (all novels that were extremely popular when they were published, *Indiana* included). Although Hochman provides a single-paragraph translator's note explaining that the Bourbon Island described by Sand really existed (xv), the note does not mention any issue related to translating the text into English, which is typical of translations into English.

Unlike Hochman, Raphael is an academic; she has also translated several nineteenth-century works for the Oxford World Literature series, among them

Germaine de Staël's *Corinne*, a few works by Balzac—*Eugénie Grandet, Cousin Bette*, and short stories—as well as another novel by Sand, *Mauprat*. Raphael's translations include introductions by well-known scholars specializing in these authors and whose biographies are provided by the publisher of the series. But again there is no translator's foreword or any mention of the translator, a stark reminder of what the translation studies scholar Lawrence Venuti has termed "the translator's invisibility." Although the translator is not completely invisible—the cover announces "A new translation by Sylvia Raphael," and the "explanatory notes" are assumedly her work[10]—readers do not learn why the retranslation was made, how it differs from the previous translations, or what the translator's aims were.

Knowing in what circumstances the translations were produced, what Antoine Berman calls the "horizon" of the translations, prepares the instructor to identify patterns in the translated text (5). Depending on the focus of the course, the instructor might have students first look at Sand's introduction and preface to the 1832 edition. These short texts are strategic, since Sand refers in them to the controversy surrounding the publication of her novel, and she uses them to establish her authority as a writer. She does this through, among other things, her syntax, using a number of complex sentences and making ample use of the semicolon. The way the translators treat Sand's paratexts follows a pattern. Sand uses six semicolons in the 1832 preface, twenty-two in the introduction. The translation by Ives respects Sand's syntactic structure, using seven semicolons in the preface and twenty-two the introduction, whereas the Hochman greatly reduces the number of semicolons (five and six), and Raphael uses even fewer (one and four). Typically, more semicolons tend to be used in English than in French, which means that Ives makes a conscious attempt to "[move] the reader toward the writer," to use Friedrich Schleiermacher's famous phrase, to adhere to the syntactic structure when possible, despite Sand's syntactic complexity (42). On the other hand, the modern translators simplify Sand's syntax and adapt it to modern English-language readers' expectations. In fact, the noticeable simplification of the sentences contributes to the slippage through which the image of Sand as a natural writer becomes that of a simple writer. Such comparisons allow readers to see the effect that Sand's long and complex sentences create and to understand that recent translations embody the underlying critical view that Sand's writing is less sophisticated than that of her contemporaries, at least at the syntactic level.

Similar patterns of simplification occur in the translation of the novel as well. Compression is typical of translation from French into English, a response to the French tendency toward amplification mentioned above, and one can see from a comparative study of ten representative passages that Richards systematically compresses (nine times out of ten). Ives, however, instead of compressing the text as one would expect, tends to expand it (five times out of ten), whereas Raphael and Hochman do so less frequently (three times out of ten in both translations). Raphael expands the text in passages where Ives has also expanded, but Raphael's expansions are compressions of Ives's translation. This relation indicates that the Raphael translation was as much influenced by the Ives translation as by the French source text. An instructor using the Raphael translation may wish to mention that it is mediated not only by the specific cultural context in which it is produced but also by the previous translation.

In addition, whereas Ives, Raphael, and Hochman stay very close to the text, even when compressing and expanding, Richards occasionally modifies the text to emphasize a point. Consider the following passage: "Mais, mordieu! il me payera cher l'affront que je ressens au fond du cœur. Et cette femme qui le soigne et qui fait semblant de ne le pas connaître! Ah! comme la ruse est innée chez ces êtres-là . . . " (69–70). Ives's version is fairly literal: "But, *mordieu!* he shall pay dear for the insult, which I feel in the depths of my heart. And that woman nursing him, who pretends not to know him! Ah! how true it is that cunning is inborn in those creatures!" (25). Richards omits the "who pretends not to know him" and transposes the "mordieu" into an additional sentence (italics mine): "'But he shall pay dearly for this affront, which I will bitterly resent—and this woman, who is now nursing him. Cunning is truly a part of the sex.' *Gnashing his teeth till they were almost broken, he said no more*" (32–33). While the modern reader might find that Richards has taken too great a liberty, Richards was probably aware that the strength of "mordieu" would be lost on the reader, and his addition (or transposition) emphasizes the brutality of Delmare and the victimization of Indiana. Ives's "mordieu" will require checking in the dictionary, since the swearword "by the death of God" is now obsolete.

The two modern translations stay close to the source text. Raphael renders it by "But, by God! He'll pay dearly for the insult which I feel to the depths of my heart. And this woman who is looking after him and pretends not to know him! Oh, how innately cunning these creatures are" (33), and Hochman by "I assure you he will pay dearly for his offense. And that woman who nurses him and pretends not to know him—ah, how true it is that all those creatures are instinctively cunning!" (47). Students will notice that these last two excerpts tone down the depiction of Delmare as a brutal man.

Instructors can also point out that the existence of previous translations creates a tension in subsequent ones. Whereas Raphael's version updates Sand's language to fit new readers (at least the expectations of the readership that the publisher's marketing department has targeted), it is also influenced by the earlier, less modern, lexical choices of the Ives text. For instance, the idiom "chercher midi à quatorze heures" (which means to unnecessarily complicate things) in the preface is translated literally by Ives ("it looks for noon at 2:00 o'clock"), which is consistent with his attempt to bring the reader to the author, and as "it looks for midday at two in the afternoon" by Raphael, which makes the text ambiguous rather than idiomatic. Hochman, however, changes the structure of the sentence and removes "comme disent les bonnes gens" ("as people say") but provides an accurate rendering: "critics are never content to judge what is directly in front of their eyes but go out of their way to look for what is not there" (17).

Similarly, the rare inaccuracies found in Ives are kept in Raphael's translation. In Sand's 1852 preface to the novel, the sentence "si un bravache fait le mata-more, c'est une insulte contre l'armée" is translated by Ives as "if a bully plays the swashbuckling soldier, it is an insult to the army" (viii) (probably because the equivalence of "bravache" and "bully"—an erroneous one—is proposed in several bilingual dictionaries) and by Raphael as "if a bully behaves like a swash-buckling soldier, it is an insult to the army" (3). But "bravache" means braggart, not bully, as does "matamore" ("braggadocio" or "swaggerer"). Hochman pro-vides the accurate version, probably because of her background as a lexicogra-pher, "if a swaggering soldier behaves like a bully, it is an insult to the army" (17–18). In the same way that a work in the original language is inevitably read through the prism of the previous scholarship or reviews that have introduced it, a text in translation refracts other translations, other readings.

Instructors must also be aware that the translations present different im-ages of Sand at the lexical level, although not necessarily the ones expected by the reader. Raphael's and Hochman's language is obviously more modern than Richard's mid-century American or Ives's late Victorian language. The more current English actually better parallels Sand's French. Indeed, one of the well-known consequences of the monitoring of the evolution of French by the Aca-démie Française is that standard written French tends to evolve more slowly than English. Modern readers of the French text are therefore less likely to find it quaint than will modern readers of Ives's English version, although American students may be surprised by Raphael's Britishisms. More surprising, however, is the way that Ives and, to a lesser degree, Richards encourage the reader to feel sympathy for Indiana by emphasizing the terms that describe her status as an innocent, oppressed victim. When Sand introduces her characters in the beginning of the novel, for instance, the French reads, "enfoncée sous le man-teau de cette vaste cheminée de marbre blanc incrusté de cuivre doré; si vous l'eussiez vue, toute fluette, toute pâle, toute triste" (50)[11] which is translated by Richards as "near that vast chimney of white marble, encrusted with gilt copper—pale and sad, leaning her elbows on the *menacing* head of an andiron of polished steel" (18; note the addition of "menacing"); as "*buried* under the mantel of that huge fire-place" by Ives (4); as "*[d]eep* in the chimney corner" by Raphael (16); and as "*dwarfed* by the mantel of that huge white marble fireplace adorned with burnished copper" by Hochman (32). The connotations of "buried" and "menacing" are clearly ones of oppression and invoke physi-cal threats. This lexical semantic pattern continues throughout the description of Indiana. The description "toute fluette, toute pâle, toute triste" (50)—liter-ally, "frail, pale, and sad"—is compressed into "pale and sad" by Richards (18), who removes the softening adjective "fluette," and intensified to "slender, pale, depressed" by Ives (4); Raphael renders the phrase as "so slender, pale, and sad" (16), and Hochman as "slim, pale, sad" (32). The distinction between depressed (that is, made oversad by circumstances) contrasts with merely sad. The description continues: "Elle toute jeune" (50)—literally, "she quite young"—which Richards omits, translating only "by the side of her old husband" (18); it becomes "a mere child" in Ives (4), "so young a girl" in Raphael (16), and "a young girl" in Hochman (32). Again, "a mere child" stresses the vulnerability of Indiana while "young" merely states her age. Finally, "femme frêle et souffreteuse" becomes "young and suffering woman" in Richards (51), "that pale and unhappy woman" in Ives (5), "frail and sickly woman" in Raphael (17), and "so frail and ill" in Hochman (32). Instructors might point out that the French adjective "souffreteux" means either deprived of necessary things or suffering, rather than merely in poor health, and that later the word "maladive" ("sickly") will be used (59), thus showing Sand's careful choice of adjectives to describe her characters.

Thus we have a paradox: the modern translations, which are published during the period of a feminist reevaluation of Sand, deemphasize the victimization of the female character, whereas the early translations intensify her description as a victim of oppression who is justified in freeing herself. Again, comparing the descriptions of Indiana in these different translations not only allows instructors to analyze the process by which the reader's understanding of the character and the plot are influenced by differences in the stylistic nuances of the description, but it is also a way to show how the fabric of a translation reflects the translator's view on Sand's style. A translator who assumes that Sand's style is natural (i.e., simple), will tend to minimize the thematic patterns of the novel; conversely a translator who admires Sand's prose is more likely to notice the stylistic means through which the themes of the novel are expressed. The following translations of a descriptive passage about Indiana (with pertinent sections emphasized) show well the varying degrees to which she is valorized:

> [Raymon] ne se doutait pas . . . que, dans cette femme si frêle et en apparence si timide, résidât un courage plus que masculin, cette sorte d'intrépidité délirante qui se manifeste parfois comme une crise nerveuse chez les êtres les plus faibles. Les femmes ont rarement le courage physique qui consiste à lutter d'inertie contre la douleur ou le danger; mais elles ont souvent le courage moral qui s'exalte avec le péril ou la souffrance. Les fibres délicates d'Indiana appelaient surtout les bruits, le mouvement rapide et l'émotion de la chasse, cette image abrégée de la guerre avec ses fatigues, ses ruses, ses calculs, ses combats et ses chances.   (162 [120])

> [Raymon] . . . knew that this frail, and, apparently, delicate woman *had that masculine courage*, which sometimes appears like *nervous crises* in the *most feeble beings. The physical courage of women* rarely enables them to struggle against agony or grief; but *they have that moral courage*

which rises superior to peril and danger. Her imagination was excited by the noise, rapid movement and emotion of the chase; this miniature of war, with its stratagems, fatigues, calculations, combats and chances.
(107 [trans. Richards])

Raymon did not . . . suspect that in that frail and apparently timid woman there abode a more than masculine courage, that sort of *delirious intrepidity* which sometimes manifests itself like a nervous paroxysm in the *feeblest creatures. Women rarely have the physical courage which consists in offering the resistance of inertia to pain or danger; but they often have the moral courage* which attains its climax in peril or suffering. Indiana's delicate fibres delighted above all things in the tumult, the rapid movement and the excitement of the chase, that miniature image of war with its fatigues, its stratagems, its calculations, its hazards and its battles.   (128 [trans. Ives])

Raymon . . . did not suspect, either, that this apparently frail, timid woman possessed a more than masculine courage, the kind of *mad intrepidity* that can sometimes be manifested as a nervous crisis in the *weakest creatures. Women rarely have the physical courage* which lies in fighting passively against grief heightened by peril or suffering. Indiana's delicate nerves responded above all to the sounds, the swift movement, and the emotion of the hunt, which is like a war in miniature with its fatigues, its subterfuges, its calculations, its fights, and its luck.   (113 [trans. Raphael])

Raymon had no idea that . . . this frail, timid woman was capable of a more than masculine courage, a kind of *frenzied bravery* that sometimes manifests itself in the *weakest people* and is occasionally mistaken for *nervous hysteria. Women rarely have the physical courage* with which to confront pain or danger, but those same challenges often enable them to rise to heights of moral exaltation. Every fiber of Indiana's being responded to the tumult, the animation, all the thrilling activities of the hunt, which with its strategies, calculations, sorties, unpredictable outcomes, and exhaustion is a miniature version of war.   (125 [trans. Hochman])

The different word choices (e.g., "delicate," which refers to a physical condition, versus "timid," which is a negative psychological or moral characteristic; "crisis" versus "hysteria") contribute to create a positively or negatively and stereotypically coded portrait of the character.

In addition to the representation of the oppression of women, another theme in *Indiana* is eloquence and the deliberate manipulation of language. It is thus instructive to look at the ways in which the use of the familiar "tu" form, which is employed strategically in the French text, is rendered by the translators. The narrator describes Raymon as someone who speaks extremely well and is quite persuasive. When Raymon attempts to seduce Indiana, Sand has him put his linguistic resources to work; in particular, he switches from the respectful "vous," which signals a certain distance, to the familiar "tu," which acts as a signal that he is pressuring Indiana. Compare the following passage of the novel with its English translations:

> "Je *te* jure," lui dit-il, "d'être à toi corps et âme, je te voue ma vie, je te consacre mon sang, je te livre ma volonté; prends tout, dispose de tout, de ma fortune, de mon honneur, de ma conscience, de ma pensée, de tout mon être."
> "Taisez-*vous*," dit vivement Indiana, "voici mon cousin."
>
> (149; my emphasis)

> "I swear to be yours soul and body. I vow to your service my whole life. I consecrate myself entirely to you; to you I sacrifice my blood; to you I consecrate my will. Take all; dispose of all: my fortune, my happiness, my honour, my soul ifself."
> "Be silent, here is my cousin."   (97 [trans. Richards])

> "I swear," he said, "that I will be yours body and soul; I devote my life, I consecrate my blood to you, I place my will at your service; take everything, do as you will with my fortune, my honor, my conscience, my thoughts, my whole being."
> "Hush!" said Indiana hastily, "here is my cousin."   (114 [trans. Ives])

> "I swear to be yours body and soul," he said. "I dedicate my life to you, I devote my blood to you, I abandon my will to you. Take everything, everything is at your disposal, my fortune, my honour, my conscience, my thoughts, my whole being."
> "Be quiet, here's my cousin," said Indiana agitatedly.
>
> (101 [trans. Raphael])

> "I swear," he told her, "to be yours body and soul. I give you the rights to my life, my blood, my will. Take and dispose of everything—my fortune, my honor, my conscience, my thoughts, my whole being—as you see fit."
> "Careful, be quiet," Indiana said, interrupting him. "My cousin is coming."   (114 [trans. Hochman])

While the familiar "tu" cannot be translated literally in English (the use of "thee" would be archaic), the instructor can point out that there are standard ways to express the familiarity it is meant to signal, ways that these translators do not use. One possibility, for example, is to use compensation, a translation strategy that allows the translating of a syntactic or grammatical category that does not exist in the target language through lexical means. In this instance, adding a term of endearment ("my darling," "my love") would take care of expressing the familiarity conveyed by "tu." Similarly, when Indiana responds with the formal "vous" form of address, using "sir" would immediately signal her rejection of Raymon's familiarity. None of the translators addresses the switch from familiar to formal in this instance or in the other occurrences of "tu" in direct speech. It is surprising that Richards fails to do so, since on many other occasions he does not refrain from making additions or omissions.

The translators also vary in their handling of "vivement," a variation that conforms to the descriptive pattern mentioned earlier. Richards removes it altogether and uses a short, curt sentence to express Indiana's reaction. Ives chooses the neutral "hastily"; Raphael prefers "agitedly," which is in keeping with her representation of Indiana as a weak figure; and Hochman uses a grammatical transposition, "interrupting," which is both idiomatic and accurate, again a characteristic of her translating style.

But the translators do work with the issue of the familiar form when it is explicitly brought up by the narrator: "il s'aperçut que lorsqu'il parlait à voix basse à Indiana, il la tutoyait" (149) becomes "shortly after he noticed that, when Sir Ralph spoke to Indiana in an undertone, he used the more familiar form of address" in Ives (115) and "he noticed that when Ralph spoke quietly to Indiana, he said 'tu'" in Raphael (102). Hochman explicitates: "He noticed that her cousin used the familiar 'tu' when he spoke to her privately" (114), whereas Richards simply removes the reference to "tu" (97). Ives, Hochman, and Raphael all clarify the second "he," but only Raphael assumes that the readers will know what "tu" refers to. The clarification of the pronoun does not seem consistent with Raphael's overall approach of bringing the author to the reader, but considering the intended audience of her translation (students), it certainly makes sense.

As the above discussion has suggested, instructors teaching *Indiana* in English can take advantage of the existence of several translations and choose the one that best corresponds to the purpose of their course. They would do well, however, to discuss their choice of the translation and the reasoning behind it, thus laying the groundwork for the focus of the course. Those choices and the discussion about them will inevitably challenge students' assumptions that newer necessarily means better. The translations of *Indiana*, like that of any other text, embody different readings and different interpretations, no matter how aware the translators were of those interpretations. In short, by reflecting on the reasons for their choice of a particular translation; using several translations, or at least excerpts from several translations; and discussing the similarities and differences among the translations, instructors will "encourage students to read with translation in mind" (Maier 18).[12]

NOTES

[1] There seems to be only one copy left of this translation, and it is held by the Lilly Library at the University of Indiana, Bloomington. The text reads extremely awkwardly and is unlikely to have found many readers. A publisher's notice in the inside back cover states, "In Justice to the Translator of 'Indiana' we should state that his last proofs were not received at our office at the hour we were compelled to go to press." This may explain some of the errors. In a long footnote to Sand's preface, the translator defends Sand as "one of the first geniuses of the age" who "is unquestionably female . . . a lady in the proper sense of the term, of high social respectability and refinement" (1). This defense is surprisingly aggressive. He announces, "I have taken the liberty of changing the gender of the personal pronouns referring to the author. . . . In the present case, concealment of the author is not desirable, were it any longer practicable; on the contrary, *not* to conceal may be useful as well as proper. In this country, the author of Indiana [sic] is in general known only through the caricaturing of the miserable bigots of the *London Quarterly*, and other Reviews, and of some echoing blockheads of the press, who always propagate such calumnies with an avidity proportionate to their ignorance of the subject" (1). Because the translation is unavailable (the only existing copy is in very bad shape and unavailable electronically) and of poor quality, it will not be of use to instructors presenting *Indiana* in English.

[2] Nabu Press publishes public domain reprints and sells them on *Amazon*. The Nabu *Indiana* reprint is a reproduction of a 1923 edition.

[3] The 1870 edition of the Richards translation has been digitalized and can be accessed through *Hathi Trust* (http://catalog.hathitrust.org/api/volumes/oclc/22702505.html). The Ives translation is available in the University of Adelaide's e-book repository (http://ebooks.adelaide.edu.au/s/sand/george/indiana/); the text is very clearly formatted and includes illustrations.

[4] "Personnage" is often used in French with negative connotations.

[5] Tilby ignores Thompson's opening paragraph: "Of all French writers, George Sand made the most impression in England in the 1830s and 1840s. More than Hugo, much more than Balzac, she stood for English readers as a symbol of the post-revolutionary writing of France" (11). That Thompson is not exaggerating is demonstrated by the quotation that appears on the title page of the 1870 edition of Richards's translation: "George Sand is probably the most influential writer of our day. Her genius has been felt as a power in every country of the world where people read any manner of books. She is, beyond comparison, the greatest living novelist in France. The prose of George Sand stands out conspicuous for its wonderful expressiveness and force, its almost perfect beauty."

[6] According to *WorldCat*, Richards was born in 1820, which means that the translation was published when he was thirty.

[7] Sand's foreword and prefaces are not included in Richards's translation of *Indiana*.

[8] He is so prolific that the *Oxford Encyclopedia* entry on Sand intimates that one person could not do this work alone, an interesting comment, considering that Sand herself wrote over ninety novels, four volumes of plays, three volumes of short stories, an autobiography, and twenty-five volumes of correspondence (Tilby 1226).

[9] This standard work is still in print.

10. Since the introduction by John Isbell to Raphael's translation of *Corinne* documents that her husband finished the notes for that novel because of her untimely death, one can safely assume that Raphael also did the notes for *Indiana*.

11. Literally, "enforcée sous le manteau de cette vaste cheminée" is "deep under the mantel of this large fireplace."

12. For a list of recommendations in choosing a translation, see Maier.

Character Study: The Art of the Literary Portrait in *Indiana*

Christopher Bains

In *Indiana*, George Sand concerns herself with both the complexity of individual morality and the shifting psychological patterns of her characters. Indeed, what makes her novel so compelling is the use of repeated encounters with specific literary characters — considered from distinct narrative perspectives as well as from varying temporal and spatial dimensions. She paints a dynamic portrait in which characters, political ideas, ideals, and aspirations evolve when subjected to outside forces. For this reason, Sand's portraits reference both neo-classic and Romantic traditions in portrait painting, the first with emphasis on the individual in her social setting and the second with exploration of the mood of its subject (Martin-Dehaye 157). Since the broad themes of marriage and the role of women are predominant in the novel, students tend to pay less attention to Sand's in-depth textual portraits. Yet these approaches do not have to be mutually exclusive. Given the centrality and proliferation of portraits in *Indiana*, I propose to students that an analysis of the formal complexity of Sand's textual portraiture might serve as a point of departure for a better understanding of the novel as a whole.

The learning objectives for teaching character portraits are the following: First, students will acquire a better understanding of how characters are presented, evolve, and stand out across the novel. Second, students will attempt close readings of character portraits, which acknowledge a plurality of interpretations. Areas of particular attention include the presentation of characters in the opening scenes, the dynamics of their interaction, and the difficulty of discerning motivation and intent. Third, students will discuss how issues of race, class, gender, and marriage inform these portraits. These objectives can be dealt with separately or simultaneously, depending on the teacher, the students, and the passage being discussed.

We discuss some of the following questions: What do we know about the narrator? What perspective does he bring to the portraiture process? While the narrator often recounts the story in an omniscient voice, the characters also speak for themselves through direct discourse and epistolary form—how do we come to terms with characters who provide conflicting views on one another? Does this dissonance disrupt our reading experience? At times the narrator's omniscience joins the words and the thoughts of the characters—how does this process take place, and what is the explanation provided in the text? These are just a few of the points that students might consider.

Indiana: *A Novel of Shifting Character Portraits*

Sand's voice as a novelist heralds a new system of characterization, whereby portraiture is not a fixed description of state but a complex network of relationships that evolve as the characters confront new circumstances, beliefs, and environments. Sand accords a great deal of weight to the choice of subject and background of each character, as well as to details, development, precision, and perspective. Through this process, she seemingly transgresses the narrative codes of many novels: character portraits in *Indiana* are not a foundation for action; rather, action is a gateway to further portraits and a profound encounter with characters. I distinguish character portrait in *Indiana* from those in other novels in which the characters are introduced early to make way for action. Honoré de Balzac's *Le père Goriot* (1835) fits this latter model. The many characters of Balzac's novel are presented to make room for suspense, intrigue, and action; they are also very much a product of their Parisian reality. Sand, on the other hand, is more concerned with the complex portrayal of a few characters, as she varies perspective and situation to reveal nuance and change. I usually assign both novels over the course of the semester so that students can compare their narrative technique and perspective.

The opening scene of *Indiana* is already fraught with tension when it comes to character portrayal; something is amiss in the relationship of the three characters:

> Par une soirée d'automne pluvieuse et fraîche, trois personnes rêveuses étaient gravement occupées, au fond d'un petit castel de la Brie, à regarder brûler les tisons du foyer et cheminer lentement l'aiguille de la pendule. Deux de ces hôtes silencieux semblaient s'abandonner en toute soumission au vague ennui qui pesait sur eux; mais le troisième donnait des marques de rébellion ouverte. . . .

> Ce personnage, beaucoup plus âgé que les deux autres, était le maître
> de la maison, le colonel Delmare.   (49 [19])

> On a chilly wet autumn evening, in a little manor house in Brie, three
> people, lost in thought, were solemnly watching the embers burn in the
> fireplace and the hands make their way slowly round the clock. Two of these
> silent individuals seemed submissively resigned to the vague boredom
> that oppressed them. But the third showed signs of open rebellion. . . .
> This person, who was much older than the other two, was the master of
> the house, Colonel Delmare.   (15)

Despite the novel's title, the first character the narrator names is not Indiana
but Colonel Delmare: we learn that he is agitated and older than the two others,
beautiful Indiana and dreary Sir Ralph. Sand provides only one small paragraph
of introduction for her eponymous heroine in the opening sequence. Significantly, nineteen-year-old Indiana is presented to us as being out of place with
her old husband, who, conversely, is represented and signified by each old and
worn-out piece of furniture in the house. In the same paragraph, the narrator
mentions that she is "toute fluette, toute pale, toute triste," 'slender, pale, and
sad' (50 [20]; 16), which marks her differences with the old masculine world
surrounding her. The development of Indiana's physical portrait is intermittent
and becomes increasingly detailed as the novel progresses.

Sir Ralph Brown is introduced third by the narrator, pointing to his identity
as an outsider and to his third-wheel status. At first, it would seem that he is
a less interesting subject for a portrait than Colonel Delmare: "mais le moins
artiste des hommes eût encore préféré l'expression rude et austère de Delmare
aux traits régulièrement fades du jeune homme" 'But the least artistic of men
would nevertheless have preferred Delmare's harsh, austere look to the young
man's regular insipid features' (51 [20]; 16). Students might be able to detect a
slight contradiction in the portrait of Sir Ralph: the narrator acknowledges that
Ralph, despite his overall insipid expressions, has certain strikingly handsome
physical attributes. This tension reveals itself to be capital to the dynamic of
the novel, where characters are often not as they seem. Once again, I find a
comparison with Balzac to be helpful. In a text such as *L'auberge rouge* (1831),
students can find similar details that raise red flags as to the true identity of
characters, often linked to their mysterious past. In *Indiana*, however, these
same suspicions make us aware of the inscrutability of motivation and the possibility of mistaken perceptions. To complicate an objective appreciation of Sir
Ralph, the narrator concedes that, "mais peut-être la jeune et timide femme de
M. Delmare n'avait-elle jamais encore examiné un homme avec les yeux" 'but
perhaps M. Delmare's shy, young wife had never yet looked closely at a man'
(51 [21]; 16). This remark says as much about Indiana and her relationship with
Ralph as it does about Ralph. At this early juncture, the narrator insists on Indiana's inability to look closely at a man, while hinting that there might be more

there than just appearances. Indeed, Ralph's interest as a character in the novel lies in his *apparent* lack of interest.

A discussion of Sand's technique of literary portraiture in this opening sequence is strengthened by comparisons with portraiture in painting. Sand herself draws this parallel through her use of a vocabulary of painting and her comparison of the opening series of portraits with a shadowy painting by Rembrandt. She is preparing her tableau for the eruption of an outside element, Raymon de Ramière, who will change the focal point. This character upends the "immobilité de la scène" 'the stillness of the scene' (53 [22]; 18), when he arrives half-dead and bloodied after being shot by the colonel. Students might discuss the theatrical effect of his entrance on the portraiture process, a conversation that could illuminate how and why violence affects Indiana, Ralph, and Noun differently.

The narrator and characters formulate hypotheses with respect to Raymon, creating a climate of mystery surrounding motivation and intent. Indiana suggests that Raymon might be a thief, whereas Delmare suspects him of being Indiana's lover: "Madame Delmare prend bien de l'intérêt à ce godelureau qui pénètre chez moi par-dessus les murs !" 'Madame Delmare takes a great interest in this womanizer who steals into my grounds by climbing over the wall!' (65 [33]; 29). These different suppositions prove to be false, though prophetic of Raymon's later actions, and humanize the different characters by placing them in the position of the reader-student, who is also engaged in interpreting character motivation.

Students discover that Raymon is "de la plus noble figure, et vêtu avec recherche" 'a very aristocratic-looking young man, elegantly dressed' (63 [31]; 27), qualities that Ralph woefully lacks. Corresponding to his physical grace and style, his mastery of language is in striking contrast to the expressionless and wooden Ralph. Raymon's elegance with words can extricate him from most quandaries, such as explaining what he was doing at night on the Delmares' estate or in Indiana's room. Although Raymon easily dupes the domestic help with his words, Sir Ralph and Delmare remain skeptical of the intruder's story. Indiana, for her part, is open to considering Raymon's story, as implausible as it might be. Sand seems to suggest throughout the novel that outward form—external signs of charm, refinement, education, and class—are to be distrusted. This is particularly true of Raymon's use of language. To the contrary, Ralph, who seems almost invisible to Indiana, demonstrates narrator-like omniscience and remains a master character interpreter as he mysteriously seems to know the motivations and actions of others.

Indiana's creole domestic, Noun, is linked to Indiana: both were nourished from the same wet nurse (Noun's mother), a relationship that confers milk-sibling status on them. This breastfeeding kinship would seemingly overcome questions of race and class. Yet, on the narrative level, Noun is both conflated with Indiana and contrasted sharply with her. On one hand, Noun represents the ghost-like presence of her past and the double of Indiana herself; on the other, she remains well differentiated. The narrator states that Noun is "pleine de sang créole ardent et passionné" 'overflowing with the full-blooded ardour and passion of a Creole' (60 [29]; 25), a portrait consistent with nineteenth-century ideas about female creole sexuality, which emphasize its irrepressible and mysterious qualities. But this is not just a male perspective; Françoise Ghillebaert points out that the clothes worn by Noun, "saturated with the maid's sensuality, now arouse Indiana" and "connote an unbearable sensuality that Indiana strives to resist" (82). I might ask students if they can identify other instances of female-to-female bonding, such as between Madame de Ramière and Indiana in chapter 21. How do the students characterize these expressions of love or solidarity?

From these opening passages of the novel, students should be able to take away the general shape and form of Sand's narrative strategy, which involves varying the points of view to leave one guessing as to whose version corresponds most closely with reality. As Robert Godwin-Jones indicates, "the characters themselves seem almost aware of being subjects in a painting or a *tableau vivant*" (15). Through the careful analysis of these portraits, students should engage the subtle play and shifting alliances between characters and the narrator: he tends to echo or adopt the opinion of a particular character, convincing the reader of a position that he may later abandon.

Breaking the Linearity of Character Portraits

In Balzac's *Le père Goriot*, character description is part of an introductory exposition that occurs before actions take center stage. Portraiture in *Indiana* is a recurrent process that starts, stops, and resumes at various moments of the story. Thus portraits in *Indiana* are neither linear nor continuous; rather, individuals reveal themselves differently under different circumstances. Character portraits are reactive to situation and reflect the shifting nature of human psychology and experience. To illustrate, I might ask students how they read a particular character, such as Colonel Delmare, at the beginning, middle, or end of the novel. How does his portrait reflect his changing economic fortunes and escalating marital strife?

Examples of character transformations can focus student discussion on various techniques that Sand uses to break the linearity of character portraits. One way that she does this is by returning to an earlier portrait and providing additional information. While we see a similar form of supplementation in Stendhal and Balzac—whereby dialogue and behavior transform characters across the novel—Sand's portraits are more dynamic: details are filled in slowly. In chapter 14, Sand gives depth to the three male characters: the reactionary (Delmare), the opportunist (Raymon), and the idealist (Ralph). In the introduction to the Gallimard edition of the novel, Béatrice Didier affirms that the characters take on a mythic dimension and represent "des forces antagonistes" 'antagonistic forces' (16). Sand is doing more than just reinforcing the realism of the passage when Delmare, Raymon, and Ralph defend their respective political ideals: Napoléon's empire, the constitutional monarchy, the republican values of the French Revolution. As Isabelle Naginski puts it, "The confrontation of ideologies is at the same time a confrontation of antithetical rhetorics" (*George Sand: Writing* 62). Thus we can encourage students to explore several hidden oppositions under the surface of the portrait—old /new, rhetoric/content, said/ unsaid—that add to the unspoken truths of Sand's textual representations. Indiana's ideas on society are noticeably not part of this debate, nor are they taken seriously when voiced in the subsequent chapter. Yet Indiana has already been the object of a substantial moral portrait, one that underscored her opposition to an unjust and patriarchal system. This solitary portrait reveals a fundamental unwillingness to tolerate Delmare's cruel and unforgiving vision of a woman's place in society:

> Mais, en voyant le continuel tableau des maux de la servitude, en supportant les ennuis de l'isolement et de la dépendance, elle avait acquis une patience extérieure à toute épreuve, une indulgence et une bonté adorables avec ses inférieurs, mais aussi une volonté de fer, une force de résistance incalculable contre tout ce qui tendait à l'opprimer.   (88 [56])

> But, through continually seeing the ills of slavery and enduring the vexations of solitude and dependence, she had acquired an unshakeable external patience and an adorable forbearance and kindness to her inferiors; but she had also acquired a will of iron and an incalculable strength of resistance to everything which tended to oppress her.   (51)

Here, the description of her moral fortitude is presented as an objective and previously acquired state, thanks to the narrator's use of the pluperfect tense ("avait acquis"). Students might discuss how this nonlinear supplement introduces the idea of her future defiance and the autonomy of her belief system. This slow and deliberate development deepens the reader's (and the student's) relationship with the characters.

A second component is Sand's transformation or reversal of the original portrait of a character. The narrative's first few tableaux paint Sir Ralph as tedious and uninspiring. It is telling that in one of these early portraits the narrator adduces that Ralph is even more boring than the genre painting of him in Indiana's room. Sand overwrites this reinforced or supplemented image with a final portrait in direct discourse. The narrator, who stepped aside during this time, intervenes on the side of Ralph and the "truth": "Si le récit de la vie intérieure de Ralph n'a produit aucun effet sur vous . . . , c'est que j'ai été l'inhabile interprète de ses souvenirs, c'est que je n'ai pas pu exercer non plus sur vous la puissance que possède la voix d'un homme profondément vrai dans sa passion" 'If the tale of Ralph's inner life has had no effect on you . . . it's because I've been an incompetent interpreter of his memories; it's because I haven't been able to exert over you the power contained in the voice of a man whose passion is deep and genuine' (329 [263]; 260; trans. modified). Although the narrator might be accused of being a negligent scribe of Sir Ralph's monologue, he can hardly be criticized for understating Ralph feelings for Indiana, as Ralph's lyric monologue comes to us in direct discourse and has not been mediated. A more likely scenario involves a greater rhetorical device that confers finished status to this transformed portrait of Ralph after his being seemingly relegated, over several hundred pages, to the role of the benevolent voyeur (as his portrait in Indiana's bedroom suggests). This final transformed portrait overwrites previous textual images of Ralph as the emasculated interloper between Indiana and Raymon. Nevertheless, Sand carefully prepares us for the transformation of Ralph when he saves her from suicide in the Seine. These scenes and those that follow contribute to an overall portrait of Ralph that is decidedly complex and nuanced, one that reveals him to be a worthy life partner for Indiana.

By this point in the discussion, students might understand that Sand's use of detail can contradict their previous impressions of characters. They might remember that Raymon prevents his archrival Ralph from committing suicide and that the colonel's final words belie tenderness toward Indiana. For students, these recollections complicate the reading of the characters as completely monolithic entities. If students see characters as representing complex value systems (which give rise to tension, contradictions, and a whole host of potential outcomes), Indiana's decision to leave Delmare for Raymon becomes more far reaching in its implications. As does, inversely, Laure de Nangy's decision to marry Raymon:

> Calme et philosophe, elle en avait pris son parti, et ne trouvait point Raymon coupable; elle ne le haïssait point d'être calculateur et positif comme son siècle; seulement, elle le connaissait trop pour l'aimer . . . elle faisait, en un mot, consister son héroïsme à échapper à l'amour, comme madame Delmare mettait le sien à s'y livrer.   (290 [231–32])

> Calmly and philosophically, she had accepted the situation and did not blame Raymon. She did not dislike him for being calculating and materialistic like the age he lived in, only she knew him too well to love him. . . . In a word, she made her heroism consist in avoiding love as Madame Delmare placed hers in yielding to it.   (226)

The narrator's explanations in this passage allow students to develop more nuanced positions on the characters; Raymon and Laure de Nangy are not necessarily evil but schooled in the way of the world and perfect exemplars of nineteenth-century materialist values. Here, I might emphasize to students the degree to which these character portraits reflect and critique nineteenth-century social reality.

Sand's third nonlinear method is the stacking of portraits, which blurs the lines between disparate characters. Students are often able to give several examples of this phenomenon, since echoes of previous descriptions of characters and situations resonate throughout the novel. Through Raymon's eyes, Noun morphs into Indiana, and Indiana into Noun. Indiana is tempted to suicide by water as Noun was. The temporary blurring of identity between the two characters foregrounds their creole heritage, and they represent reverse reflections of a shared colonial past. Students often point to the link between the two women in symbolic terms as well. Noun's continuing appearance in the novel through fantastic visions, despite her suicide at the end of part 1, signifies a stain of culpability that follows both Raymon and Indiana and is pursued through metonymy: Indiana wears Noun's ring and presents strands of Noun's hair, whereas Raymon imagines seeing her footsteps. It is not until the conclusion of the novel in Île Bourbon that Noun's presence effectively wanes. Students might also mention Sir Ralph as the double of Raymon. Often arriving in Raymon's wake, Sir Ralph remains throughout most of the novel physically just slightly offset from Raymon, as if they complete each other on both narrative and affective levels. Discussion questions might include the following: What effect does this blurring of boundaries have? Does it suggest a loss of individual autonomy? How does the stacking of portraits call attention to or enhance our literary experience?

Who Owns the Portrait?

When it comes to the portraits of characters throughout the novel—by the narrator, by the major characters, by others—the issue of perspective is capital. I point out to students that the linguistic system of a novel challenges us on two fronts: first, the narrator can be differentiated from the author and be seen as a fictional entity whose status and authority might be questioned,[1] and, second, the characters' opinions about one another multiply viewpoints, thus resisting a unifying vision of each character.

In *Indiana*, students notice early on that the unidentified male narrator is both intervening and opinionated. Brigitte Diaz considers the brutality of the narrator as a technique that establishes the realism and impartiality of perspective ("'Ni romantique'" 48). In fact, one defining characteristic of the narrator is his misogynous discourse: he calls women naturally foolish, for instance. On this point, he allies himself with Sir Ralph, who has been shown to have negative judgments on women (ch. 2). This convergence of perspectives gives credence to the statements of the narrator in the conclusion, when he states that Ralph recounted his story ("mon histoire" 'my story' [338 (271); 267]) to him, which we (the readers) have just read. But how did the omniscient narrator of the novel access information to which Sir Ralph was not privy? Furthermore, Indiana gives a final portrait of the others that would seemingly have to be divergent from his in many respects if she had told it in her own words, but she recedes from the conclusion while Ralph recounts his version of events to the narrator. Students might argue that the male storytellers' biases against women lead us to treat their perspective with skepticism, yet Ralph and the narrator remain the source for most of what we know. This is tricky for many reasons, as "Indiana's erasure" contributes to her victimization (Massardier-Kenney, *Gender* 18). Yet Indiana remains committed to "her dream of being freed from patriarchal bondage" (Schor, *George Sand* 53), and her withdrawal from the novel can be seen as Sand's way of maintaining the ideals and integrity of her portrait in a male-dominated narrative.

What about the characters who redo and analyze one another's portraits? In *Indiana*, characters offer competing impressions of one another, either through the narrator's omniscient exposition or through direct dialogue. The following passage opposes Raymon and Indiana in their portraits of Sir Ralph:

> Sa figure (pardon si je vous blesse) annonce un homme complètement nul; cependant il y a du bon sens et de l'instruction dans ses discours quand il daigne parler; mais il s'en acquitte si péniblement, si froidement, que personne ne profite de ses connaissances, tant son débit vous glace et vous fatigue. . . .
>
> Il y a du vrai dans ce portrait, répondit Indiana, mais il y a aussi de la prévention. Vous tranchez hardiment des doutes que je n'oserais pas résoudre. . . .   (156 [115])

> "Forgive me if I'm hurting you, but his face suggests a complete nonentity. Yet there's good sense and sound information in what he says when he deigns to speak. But he does so with such difficulty and lack of emotion that nobody profits from his knowledge, his manner of speaking puts you off so much and is so tedious. . . ."
>
> "There is some truth in that portrait, replied Indiana, but there's also prejudice. You boldly hit on doubts that I wouldn't dare acknowledge. . . ."   (108)

Whereas Raymon's portrait of Ralph is overwhelmingly negative, Indiana allows for a certain play of opposing forces: she remains decidedly more charitable than Raymon while acknowledging the possibility that he might not be completely misguided in his judgment. Indiana takes on here the role of Sand, allowing for a plurality of interpretations as unique or biased as the actors of the novel themselves. Indiana's credulity makes her more susceptible to errors in judging character and, as a consequence, more prone to having her impressions discussed and modified subsequently.

The perspective that students might have on a particular character depends on how they relate to the many evolving and opposing portraits: Is Indiana to be lauded as an ultimate risk taker in love or condemned as a reckless social dissident? Is the colonel the embodiment of the constraints of nineteenth-century marriage or a hapless character who makes Indiana's quest for freedom possible? Do Laure de Nangy and Raymon represent shameless opportunism or unapologetic realism? Is Ralph an altruistic presence who benevolently watches over Indiana or a cynical manipulator who, over most of novel, misleads others about his intentions? Students can debate these questions and many others in the quest for a deep understanding of the stakes of Sand's novel.

Sand makes more than one reading possible through her use of seemingly endless chains of character description. These character portraits resist simplistic interpretations since the characters often articulate divergent points of view. Sand's technique of portraiture does not imply that characters do not have a narrative existence of their own but rather that they become defined through their interactions with plot and character. Indeed, the components of the characterizations, and the changes therein, draw their source, and thus their meaning, from the actions that cause, inform, and modify the characters. Still, students might find that the conclusion of the novel resists the ultimate unmasking of the characters. Ultimately, they must discern who is seeing or telling the novel's truth most honestly and judiciously.

NOTE

[1] On the distinction between author and narrator, see Cohn; Genette.

The Melodramatic World of *Indiana*

John T. Booker

From our perspective today, *Indiana*, like *Le rouge et le noir* or *Le père Goriot*—all three published within the brief span of five years—stands at a remarkably fertile juncture for the French novel. In certain respects, as students quickly recognize, George Sand's novel, like Stendhal's and Honoré de Balzac's, reflects the Romantic period in which it was written. At the same time, with its opening description of a somber evening in the "petit castel de la Brie" 'little manor house in Brie' (49 [19]; 15) or the more general reflection of shifting political currents and the mores of contemporary society in the closing years of the Bourbon restoration, *Indiana* can appear as realistic as the works of Stendhal and Balzac. In 1993, Naomi Schor took a different approach, mounting a vigorous defense of Sand's work in general, starting with her first novel, by promoting its idealism (*George Sand*). Several years later, in an effort to define more precisely Sand's contribution to the nineteenth-century novel, Margaret Cohen argued that *Indiana* exemplifies the "sentimental social novel" that would become "realism's principal competition across the 1830s and 1840s" (9).

But it is also important to look back and recognize the extent to which *Indiana*—like the novels of Balzac, as both Peter Brooks and Christopher Prendergast have shown—is clearly informed by melodrama, which flourished from the turn of the century in France and continued to evolve, in conjunction with the English Gothic novel and then the French *roman noir*, right through the Romantic period. To be sure, *Indiana* is not simply what one might call a melodramatic novel—were that the case, it would be much less interesting than it is. But an awareness of the basic features of melodrama—notably, the range of character types and the fundamental structure and particular rhythm of its plot—can throw interesting light on certain aspects of Sand's first novel, including its controversial conclusion.

Students may need a bit of prompting to make them realize that the spirit of melodrama is alive and well even now, in any number of popular novels, films, television programs, or computer games. For as Brooks has asserted, "The melodramatic mode, broadly understood, is a central fact of the Romantic and modern sensibility" (608). The world of melodrama stages a Manichaean conflict between the forces of good and evil, in which the former are destined to prevail. At the heart of the stereotypical melodramatic intrigue are three character types: an innocent heroine, a villain who persecutes her, and a hero who comes to her defense. Chance encounters and surprising turns of fortune can be common, and the inevitable outcome, the triumph of right over wrong, may seem ultimately to owe more to the agency of a benevolent providence than to the logic of a realistic plot. Part of the enduring appeal of melodrama, in fact, as Prendergast has suggested, is that "it allows the mind to shift ambivalently to and fro between the longing for order and the excitements of disorder, to slip back and forth from the soothing caress of moral safety to the seductive attractions of danger and violence" (8–9).

In its original context of early-nineteenth-century theater, French melodrama, for all of its formulaic qualities, was not monolithic. Jean-Marie Thomasseau distinguishes two basic stages: classical melodrama (1800–23), defined and dominated by the work of the prolific René-Charles Guilbert de Pixérécourt, and romantic melodrama (1823–48), associated especially with the plays of Victor Ducange, whose *L'auberge des Adrets*, staged in 1823, is seen as a turning point. In the typical scenario of classical melodrama, an initial state of harmony is disrupted by the intrusion of a villain (*traître* or *tyran* in French) who persecutes an innocent and virtuous heroine for motives that may include vengeance, ambition, or money but rarely love (Thomasseau 28). Two other character roles of interest figure prominently: the heroine's father, who represents authority and justice more than paternal affection, and a protector in the service of the heroine (32).[1] Thomasseau stresses, too, the importance of a moment or scene of *reconnaissance* ("recognition") that serves to clear up the misunderstandings or undo the villain's machinations that have allowed the plot to develop, thus setting the stage for the eventual transition back to a new state of equilibrium (28–29).

Under Napoléon's regime, as one might expect, classical melodrama reflected—and thereby helped foster and maintain—an essentially conservative outlook, emphasizing respect for civic, patriotic, and military values. With the fall of the empire, and especially under the influence of a developing Romantic aesthetic, melodrama began to give more play to the depiction of unhappy love or on occasion even adulterous passions (31, 35). Thomasseau notes as well the presence (more frequent again as we move into the Romantic period) of a "personnage mystérieux sachant tout, voyant tout, jouissant d'une manière d'ubiquité et arrivant toujours à point nommé pour sauver l'innocent" 'mysterious character knowing everything, seeing everything, enjoying a kind of ubiquity and always arriving just at the right moment to save the innocent' (39; my trans.). And as Marie-Pierre Le Hir points out, in the theater of Ducange, the villain—easily enough identified as such in classical melodrama—may actually be "bien intégré à la société; souvent il fait partie de l'élite" 'well integrated into society; often he is part of the elite' (*Romantisme* 24; my trans.). More generally, she notes, "Ducange replace les notions de bien et de mal dans un contexte social, moral et politique bien précis, celui du monde contemporain" 'Ducange resituates the notions of good and evil in a very precise social, moral, and political context, that of the contemporary world' ("Représentation" 19; my trans.).

Such an overview, however simplistic, will enable students to begin to sense what *Indiana* owes to melodrama, starting with the roles of the principal characters, as they take shape in the first few sequences of the novel. In the opening scene, a dull autumn evening at the Delmare property, Indiana—clearly designated as the heroine of the novel that bears her name—appears worthy of sympathy, if not an outright victim. Her cousin Ralph, depicted at the outset as an essentially passive figure, expresses concern for her "état purement maladif" 'state of ill-health' (58 [27]; 23), which he diagnoses as depression, and the narrator refers to her as "cette femme rêveuse et triste" 'this pensive, sad woman' (59 [28]; 24). For the moment, it is her husband, Delmare, who appears to be her oppressor. Presented emphatically in the initial paragraphs as "le maître de la maison" 'the master of the house' (49 [19]; 15), he is the only one able to move (albeit only to pace back and forth), while Indiana and Ralph sit immobile, as if fixed in place by his very presence and his riveting gaze. Throughout the novel, the term "maître" 'master' is associated regularly with Delmare, whether by Indiana or by the narrator, and the latter refers to him later as her "tyran" 'tyrant' (272 [215]; 210). Interestingly enough, however, the narrator characterizes Delmare's tone of voice, when he speaks to Indiana, as "moitié père, moitié mari" 'partly a father's and partly a husband's' (54 [23]; 19)—Delmare is, it turns out, some forty years older than his young wife. When we get a more complete version of Indiana's background, we learn that she was raised by "un père bizarre et violent" 'an eccentric, violent father' (88 [56]; 51) and that, in marrying, "elle ne fit que changer de maître" 'she had only changed masters' (88 [56]; 51). By his very age, then, but especially by his attitude and actions with respect to Indiana, Delmare would also seem to embody something of the stern paternal presence one finds in the theater of Pixérécourt.

Although Indiana may appear to be cast initially in the role of passive victim, we soon get a glimpse of the underlying strength of her character when she takes the initiative in tending to a wounded intruder on Delmare's property (Raymon de Ramière, come for a clandestine rendezvous with Noun) with "un sang-froid et une force morale dont personne ne l'eût crue capable" 'a sang-froid and moral strength of which no one would have thought her capable' (64 [32]; 28). The narrator fills out the description of her character in the following sequence, set in Paris during the winter months. While he continues to suggest that she is a victim by referring to her in quick succession as "pauvre enfant," "pauvre jeune femme," and then "pauvre captive" 'poor girl,' 'poor young woman,' and 'poor captive,' (87, 88, 89 [55, 55, 57]; 50, 50, 52), he also mentions her "volonté de fer, une force de résistance incalculable contre tout ce qui tendait à l'opprimer" 'will of iron and an incalculable strength of resistance to everything which tended to oppress her' (88 [56]; 51). It is in the same context that we learn of Indiana's long-standing and stereotypically romantic dream, which provides further insight into her outlook:

> Un jour viendra où tout sera changé dans ma vie, où je ferai du bien aux autres; un jour où l'on m'aimera, où je donnerai tout mon cœur à celui qui me donnera le sien; en attendant, souffrons; taisons-nous, et gardons notre amour pour récompense à qui me délivrera.   (89 [56])

> A day will come when my life will be completely changed, when I shall do good to others; it will be a day when I shall be loved and I shall give my

whole heart to the man who gives me his. Meanwhile I must suffer, say
nothing, and keep my love as a reward for my deliverer.   (51)

The phrasing here, fairy-tale-like in certain respects, suggests a willingness—or
perhaps even an underlying desire?—to suffer, accepting (or embracing) the
role of victim, while waiting for that someone who will, she wants to believe,
eventually come to her rescue.[2]

It is in that Paris sequence as well that we get a real sense of Raymon's character, as he comes to play an integral role in Indiana's life and assumes—in a more
active manner than Delmare, now—the apparent mantle of villain. Rhetori-
cally gifted but easily swept away by his own words, as the narrator makes clear
(83 [51]; 46), Raymon impulsively sets his sights on seducing Indiana and seems
to the naive and inexperienced young woman to personify that long-awaited
man of her dreams. From the start of their relationship, ironically, she fears for
his safety should he come into conflict (as she assumes he inevitably must) with
her "tyran" 'tyrant' (90 [58]; 53)—that is, Delmare. In a key scene where Raymon succeeds in catching Indiana alone, he overwhelms her by the virtuosity
and sheer volume of his lyrical flights of romantic rhetoric. Vowing by turns to
keep and protect her "en maître jaloux" 'like a jealous master' (95 [61]; 56) and
to serve her "en esclave" 'as a slave' (95 [61]; 56),[3] he brushes aside her periodic,
brief interjections of token resistance. When he manages eventually to kiss her,
Indiana faints, but rather than press his advantage, as one might expect a true
villain to do in a fictional world not governed by the laws of melodrama—as Val-
mont does, for example, in *Les liaisons dangereuses*, when he has the présidente
de Tourvel at his mercy—Raymon panics, rings for the servants, and then finds
himself in an embarrassing position when Noun appears. As it turns out, this
is just the first in a series of critical moments when Indiana, like the heroine-
victim of classical melodrama, finds herself in peril of one sort or another but
invariably is spared serious harm.

One of the significant aspects of this Paris sequence, although it will not be
apparent to students at a first reading, is the fact that Ralph is not present, having
withdrawn to his own property when Delmare and Indiana went to the capital
for the winter. It is during the following sequence (back at the Delmare estate,
where Raymon has asked Noun to meet him) that the importance of Ralph's
role begins to emerge, if only at first in a figurative or symbolic manner. The
morning after Raymon has slept with Noun in Indiana's room, he berates himself, with characteristic rhetorical flourish, for having defiled the "lin virginal"
'virginal sheets' of her bed and put to flight the "ange" 'angel' who guarded it
(106 [72]; 65; trans. modified). The irony of this last assertion becomes evident
later, when Indiana escapes or is rescued in effect from a series of perilous situations by what at times can only seem to be a supernatural providence. When
Raymon then discovers a man's portrait overlooking Indiana's bed and learns it
is that of her cousin Sir Ralph, he is immediately jealous: "Il la surveille, il la
garde, il suit tous ses mouvements, il la possède à toute heure!" 'He watches

over her, he protects her, he follows all her movements, she is his at any time!' (109 [75]; 68). It is in this oblique fashion that Ralph's role as Indiana's ubiquitous and dedicated guardian is announced.

We see the various facets of that role begin to manifest themselves during the three days of hunting that Ralph hosts (pt. 2, chs. 12–14). As Raymon takes advantage of the occasion to pursue a renewed degree of intimacy with Indiana, assuring her that he loves her, not just for her beauty, but for her "âme pure et divine" 'pure, divine soul' (148 [108]; 101), and swearing to devote himself to her, "corps et âme" 'body and soul' (149 [109]; 101), she silences him abruptly when Ralph approaches. Over the following days, the latter is invariably close by, always watching, intercepting the slightest glances between the other two, and thoroughly frustrating the impatient Raymon, who becomes increasingly irritated by the presence of this persistent "chaperon" 'chaperon' (152 [111]; 104). Jealous as well of the degree of easy familiarity that Ralph displays with Indiana, Raymon finally asks her to "explain" her cousin, for "qui pourrait pénétrer sous son masque de pierre?" 'who could see through his stony mask?' (156 [115]; 108). In her ensuing account (only a first, partial version of Ralph's story, as it turns out), she relates how Ralph came to ask Delmare for permission to live with them, assuring the elderly husband that he looked on Indiana "comme ma sœur, et plus encore comme ma fille" 'as my sister and even more as my daughter' (159 [117]; 111). That last remark suggests in effect the paternal—or paternalistic—aspect of Ralph's role that increasingly manifests itself in his relationship with Indiana. And she adds, with some measure of bitterness to her tone, that Ralph's "protection, autrefois si courageuse devant le despotisme de mon père, est devenue tiède et prudente devant celui de mon mari" 'protection, formerly so brave against my father's tyranny, has become lukewarm and prudent against my husband's' (160 [118]; 111–12).

Once Ralph finally begins to take an active part in the fictional events (just over halfway through part 2, now), the basic distribution of roles is established, though none of the principal characters in Sand's novel turns out to play as simple a role as one would expect to find in classical melodrama. Of the three men in Indiana's life, Delmare certainly is the least complex and most constant; his essential temperament and manner—those of a would-be villain, one might say—are in evidence from the opening paragraphs. Although master of his modest domain, and of his wife, at least under the law, the fact that he is old enough to be her father (if not her grandfather) makes him understandably insecure. While he projects at times something of the bluster that one might associate with a melodramatic villain and is referred to as a *tyran* on more than one occasion, he also calls to mind the stereotypical image, familiar in French literature from the Middle Ages on, of the older husband mortally afraid of becoming a cuckold. Even when he does eventually explode into violence against Indiana, throwing her down and with the heel of his boot leaving on her forehead the "marque sanglante de sa brutalité" 'blood-stained mark of his brutality'

(269 [212]; 207), she makes it clear to him that she remains morally independent and unbroken.

Raymon, for his part, certainly appears to assume the role of villain in a more active and consistent manner than Delmare. And he is the sort of villain found in romantic melodrama, well integrated into the social world of his time, whereas Delmare remains a vestige of the Napoleonic era. It is Raymon's pursuit of Indiana as an amorous conquest—encouraged, ironically, by her own persistent desire to see in him the man of her romantic dreams—that drives the plot through most of the novel (chs. 5–28). In contrast to Indiana's naïveté, Raymon's attitude is fundamentally realistic. The narrator's periodic accounts of his cool calculations, whether with respect to Indiana or to his prospects in life more generally, leave no doubt as to his ultimate intentions and so shape the reader's inevitable perception of him as a despicable character. When a critical change in government ministries, followed in short order by a bout of "rhumatisme aigu" 'acute rheumatism' (261 [206]; 200) and then the death of his doting mother, prompts Raymon to take serious stock of his present situation and future options, he decides to seek a socially and financially advantageous marriage. That does not stop him, however, from sending to Indiana a carefully crafted letter that he knows will entice her to return to France, where she will, he feels confident, make a "maîtresse soumise et dévouée" 'submissive, devoted mistress' (266 [210]; 204). One might add that, to the extent that Raymon is a villain in this fictional world, he gets the reward he deserves in marrying Laure de Nangy, a young woman with her own keenly realistic sense of the mores of contemporary society and who is more than his match when it comes to cynicism and calculation. When we get a brief glimpse of their interactions, later in the novel (297–98 [238]; 232–33), it is clear not just that she dominates Raymon but that she takes great satisfaction in doing so.

As for Ralph, who turns out unexpectedly to be the most important of the three men in Indiana's life (and certainly the most complex), much of his strength as a character, even before his role becomes fully apparent, lies in his perspicacity. In the opening sequence, he is the only one to read the situation correctly and realize (much to the relief of the wary Delmare) that the unidentified intruder is interested in Noun, not Indiana (69–70 [37]; 33). It is Ralph as well who later notices Raymon's fright on revisiting the spot where Noun's body was found (138–39 [100–01]; 92–93) and surmises that Raymon was largely responsible for her suicide. By the time the narrator tells us that Ralph is "plus observateur que ses réflexions ne l'annonçaient" 'more observant than you would think from the thoughts he expressed' (124–25 [87]; 80), that should be clear to any attentive reader.

It is in large measure Ralph's perspicacity that enables him to play so well his chosen role as Indiana's protector. From the hunting sequence on, he is almost always near her. When Delmare has to travel to Antwerp, for example, to deal with the bankruptcy of a firm on which his own financial affairs depend, Ralph "semblait déterminé à remplacer M. Delmare pour la surveillance" 'seemed determined to replace [him] as far as surveillance was concerned" (178 [135]; 128). Once Delmare has been forced to sell his property, Ralph follows them diligently to Paris, where he later appears just in time to prevent Indiana from drowning herself in the Seine. Eventually, as the Delmares are boarding a ship in Bordeaux, he shows up unexpectedly at the last moment and accompanies them back to Île Bourbon, where, "comme une mystérieuse providence, il veillait sur elle" 'like a mysterious providence, he watched over her' (258 [203]; 197). When Delmare threatens periodically to become physically abusive, the sound of stirring in Ralph's room signals the presence of "la discrète et patiente sollicitude du protecteur" 'Indiana's discreet, patient, solicitous protector' (259 [204]; 198). And when Indiana decides to return to France to be with Raymon, she finds it very difficult to thwart Ralph's "clairvoyance" 'perspicacity' and slip away (274 [217]; 212). In short, Indiana's cousin would seem to be the epitome of the melodramatic protector, as described by Thomasseau. That Ralph's role has been established in an obvious manner is acknowledged in effect by the narrator (and by Sand herself, no doubt) when Indiana comes to her senses in the hotel room in Paris, after she has surprised Raymon at Lagny only to find that he is married; clearly anticipating the reader's reaction, the narrator doesn't even identify the person before her eyes when she opens them: "Je n'ai pas besoin de vous dire son nom" 'I don't need to tell you his name' (301 [240]; 236).

Yet there are instances—all the more striking because they run counter to the established pattern—where Ralph, although nearby and presumably on guard, does *not* manage to protect Indiana. Standing in for Delmare when the latter is in Antwerp, for example, Ralph is unable to prevent Indiana's late-night rendezvous with Raymon in her room (although he succeeds at least in interrupting it by slipping under the door a note that her husband has returned). When Delmare does end up brutalizing his young wife on Île Bourbon, Ralph, though nearby as usual, somehow hears nothing. He subsequently dissuades Delmare from apologizing to Indiana for fear that it might undermine the husband's authority. And the night that Indiana succeeds in slipping off to board a ship for France, Ralph is unable to prevent her from doing so because he has fallen asleep while watching over *Delmare*, who is ill. These last instances might seem to suggest, symbolically at least, that part of Ralph's role is to double that of Delmare, to watch over Indiana not so much to pursue his own interest in her but to see that she remains the wife—or possession, in effect—of her husband. Viewed in that perspective, the paternalistic image that Ralph projects so forcefully in the conclusion—clearly taking it upon himself to shelter Indiana from any contact with the world that he deems harmful and effectively speaking for her—is not entirely surprising.

If the principal character roles in *Indiana* resemble those that one might find in romantic melodrama, it is clear that the plot of Sand's first novel remains true to the basic dynamics of classical melodrama. It is easy enough to frame this point for students by posing a very basic question, one that has to come up in any serious consideration of the novel: how best to explain what happens to Indiana, at critical points in the story?

Even the most superficial reading of *Indiana* has to leave the distinct impression that the heroine of Sand's novel lives the proverbial charmed life when it comes to escaping from dangerous situations. Like the heroine of classical melodrama, she seems predestined to be spared serious harm, even before Ralph emerges as her devoted protector or, later, on those infrequent occasions when he is simply not there for her. Indiana herself acknowledges as much early on, the morning after discovering Raymon hiding in her room (although she misinterprets his reason for being there), when she reflects on the events of the previous day: "C'est Dieu qui l'a voulu ainsi . . . ; sa providence m'a rudement éclairée, mais c'est un bonheur pour moi" 'It's God who willed it so. . . . His providence has given me a rude awakening, but it's a good fortune for me' (118 [83]; 76). When she goes to Raymon's apartment in Paris and effectively offers herself to him, the narrator suggests that, had he taken his time, "elle était à lui peut-être" 'she might have been his' (221 [171]; 166), but he becomes too impatient: "Indiana eut peur. Un bon ange étendit ses ailes sur cette âme chancelante et troublée; elle se réveilla et repoussa les attaques du vice égoïste et froid" 'Indiana took fright. A good angel spread its wings over that wavering, troubled soul. She recovered herself and repulsed the cold selfish attacks of vice' (221 [171]; 166). Janet Hiddleston, in her concise and useful study of the novel, repeatedly refers to Ralph as Indiana's "guardian angel" (17, 28, 32, 33), but clearly the sort of supernatural protection from which Indiana appears to benefit in this fictional world goes beyond the agency of her dedicated protector. Ralph has the final word on the matter in explaining to his young friend in the conclusion why he and Indiana did not in fact end up leaping together to their deaths, as they were poised to do: "l'ange d'Abraham et de Tobie . . . descendit sur un rayon de la lune, et . . . il étendit ses ailes argentées sur ma douce compagne" 'the angel of Abraham and Tobias . . . came down on a moonbeam and . . . spread his silvery wings over my sweet companion' (340 [272]; 268).

For the reader attuned to the underlying dynamics of melodrama that run through *Indiana*—or, put more simply, whose expectations have been shaped by them, if only subconsciously—even the novel's conclusion, however implausible and problematic it may appear in certain respects,[4] can hardly come as a complete surprise. On the contrary, given the way events have repeatedly unfolded at key junctures and once Ralph has finally revealed himself fully to Indiana, it would have been quite surprising if the two of them had *not* ended up being able to enjoy the rest of their life together, whatever the particular circumstances. For in the melodramatic imagination (to allude again to Brooks), it is a given that truth must ultimately triumph over deception, right over wrong. And although Indiana's final situation, in the eyes of many readers, may hardly constitute an unconditional happy ending, there is no doubt that it is presented as a positive outcome. In the original preface to *Indiana* (1832), Sand anticipates and responds preemptively to a range of possible criticism from potential readers; to those who might complain that she has not shown "la vertu récompensée d'une façon assez éclatante" 'virtue rewarded in a striking enough way' (41; 8; trans. modified), she answers, tongue in cheek, that "le triomphe de la vertu ne se voit plus qu'aux théâtres du boulevard" 'the triumph of virtue is only to be seen nowadays at the boulevard theatres' (41; 8–9), the principal venues for melodrama. But her novel, faithful to the fundamental laws of melodrama, does deliver in the end that essential triumph of good over evil that the twists and turns of the plot have effectively led us to anticipate.

NOTES

[1] Thomasseau also notes the frequent presence, in classical melodrama, of a character whose role is simply to provide moments of comic relief from the emotionally charged conflict between villain and heroine that is at the center of the drama (32, 37–38).

[2] Both Bordas (*Éric Bordas* 68) and Didier ("Ophélie" 91) have suggested that Indiana may to some extent *enjoy* playing the role of victim.

[3] For a thorough and perceptive treatment of the play of master-slave imagery in *Indiana*, see Christiansen.

[4] For a sampling of the extensive body of criticism that has been devoted to the conclusion, see Dayan; Godwin-Jones; Harkness, "Writing"; Ippolito; and Petrey, *In the Court*.

Performing Sand's Pedagogical Project in *Indiana*

Shira Malkin

This essay identifies the theatrical aspects of George Sand's 1832 novel and suggests how these aspects can be brought to the fore through in-class performance. Indeed, *Indiana* reads like a four-act drama (followed by an epilogue) featuring vividly developed characters and carefully composed tableaux that alternate with scenes of passionate dialogic exchanges and monologues (spoken or epistolary). These tableaux and scenes are accompanied by voice and stage directions and are punctuated by authorial commentary. As scholars have established, Sand eliminated most of these reader-directed addresses and digressions in subsequent editions (Didier, Notes 382–83n1). Yet the remaining metanarrative intrusions, as well as each edition's preface, indicate that, while wishing to entertain, Sand also hoped to create the opportunity for readers to maintain a certain distance from the story. Such a critical distance would allow them to actively engage with the issues she intended to raise.

In her 1842 preface, Sand ostensibly refutes taking on the role of "pédagogue" 'schoolmaster' (43; 11), a criticism that she reports was leveled against her to ridicule her project. She clearly states, however, that as a novelist writing tales that may offer "une apparence frivole" '[a] frivolous appearance' (44; 11), she intends to fulfill the serious task of denouncing the plight of women and to advocate their fairer treatment: "Ceux qui m'ont lu sans prévention comprennent que j'ai écrit *Indiana* avec le sentiment . . . de l'injustice et de la barbarie des lois qui régissent encore l'existence des femmes dans le mariage, dans la famille et la société" 'Those who have read me without prejudice understand that I wrote *Indiana* influenced by a feeling . . . of the injustice and barbarity of the laws which still govern the existence of women in marriage, in the family, and in society' (46–47; 13). In her 1832 preface, Sand had already spelled out her pedagogical project: she meant to bear witness to the personal and social tragedies created by these inequalities (37; 5) and to make a decisive impact on her readership: "Avec le caractère de triste franchise qui l'enveloppe, [l'auteur] pense que son récit pourra faire impression sur des cerveaux ardents et jeunes" '[The author] thinks that, with its quality of sad truthfulness, his tale will be able to make an impression on young, eager minds' (40–41; 8; trans. modified).

To gauge whether Sand's efforts to convince her audience can be made relevant in today's literature courses, I invite students to do a performative reading of key scenes that highlight the heroine's plight. After providing them with an overview of the genre of melodrama and of romantic dramatization, I have students enact some of the verbal and nonverbal exchanges Sand created for her characters. I also encourage them to use their imagination to embody the narrator's comments or to supplement his silences. These guided activities can help enhance students' grasp of the text's inner dynamics and of the author's plea for social reform.

In her 1832 preface, Sand squarely situates her narrative in the context of melodrama, a genre that dominated contemporary literature and stage productions, by predicting that readers expecting a grandiose resolution to Indiana's story would be disappointed. In her novel, she insists, virtue is not rewarded as strikingly as is customary in boulevard theaters (41; 8–9). Although Sand does not set out to adhere to the extravagant dramatizations of such popular entertainment, she is nonetheless fully aware that her novel features stock characters and situations typical of melodrama. They include Indiana, a young, innocent female protagonist from the colonies, and her husband, Delmare, a coarse, jealous, older colonel who served under Napoléon. Indiana falls in love with a dashing womanizer, Raymon de Ramière, who pursues her daringly then humiliates and abandons her. A victim of both her husband and her undeserving lover, she is repeatedly saved from dishonor and death by her chivalrous cousin Ralph Brown. Despite all the odds and after she returns to Réunion (then Île Bourbon), Indiana ends up finding happiness with Ralph, who has been in love with her since childhood.

Sand explains in the 1832 preface that each major character represents a type. Indiana is Woman. She embodies "les *passions* comprimées, . . . supprimées par *les lois*" 'passions, repressed, . . . suppressed by *the law*' (40; 7). Ralph, for his part, is "l'homme de bien," the good man ready to sacrifice his happiness to avoid disrupting social order (41; 8). Delmare stands for the law, whereas Raymon represents society and the false morality that governs it—namely, a charade, a theatrical illusion (41; 8). We see that Raymon uses his mastery of language and of the art of seduction to function efficiently in this elegant and ruthless world (83 [51]; 46). Indeed, unlike timid Indiana, inarticulate Delmare, and taciturn Ralph, Raymon is described as a powerful writer and speaker or performer who, in his public and his private life,

> connaît bien toutes les finesses de la langue. C'est une reine prostituée qui descend et s'élève à tous les rôles, qui se déguise, se pare, se dissimule et s'efface; c'est une plaideuse qui a réponse à tout, qui a toujours tout prévu, et qui prend mille formes pour avoir raison.   (130 [93])

> is familiar with all the subtleties of language. It is like a queen turned into a prostitute who, demeaning and raising herself, plays all parts, who disguises herself and decks herself in finery, dissembles and conceals herself; it is like a litigant who has an answer to everything, who has always foreseen everything, and has a thousand ways of being right.   (85)

One of the most potent dramatic aspects of *Indiana*, then, is the tension between silence and eloquence, the conflict between those who cannot (or will not) express themselves and those who can. Another dramatic issue centers on the question of discernment: when faced with someone's irresistible "puissance de conviction" 'power of conviction' (83 [51]; 46), how can the disenfranchised (learn to) distinguish between truth and deceit?

Sand's novel demonstrates that language is the weapon of the upper class. Only Raymon; Indiana's aunt, the marquise of Carvajal; and Laure de Nangy know how to use it to their advantage. At the Spanish embassy ball, and later in the marquise's salon, where he officially launches his seduction of Indiana, Raymon displays his brilliant wit to her while sparring with Carvajal on the subject of love. His passionate declaration, one among many, amounts to "une attaque si vive et si habile" 'such a sharp and skilful attack' on poor, defenseless Indiana that she confesses she does not know how to play the game (87–88 [55]; 50). Far from weakening her appeal, however, Indiana's inability to respond in kind to this "entretien épineux" 'dangerous conversation' (88 [55]; 50) is matched by her obvious physical response to it, much to Raymon's delight: "Elle avoua en rougissant qu'elle ne savait rien de tout cela, et Raymon, ivre de joie en voyant ses joues se colorer et son sein se gonfler, jura qu'il le lui apprendrait" 'She blushingly admitted that she knew nothing about all that and Raymon, overjoyed at seeing her face change colour and her breast heave, swore that he would teach her' (88 [55]; 50).

Indiana therefore reads like a cautionary tale about the rhetoric of love that gullible, inexperienced female readers find in tragic novels (90 [58]; 53) or in real-life encounters with manipulative men and mistake for sincerity (83 [51]; 46). While Sand in 1832 did not provide a viable resolution for Indiana's restricted, unhappy life as a married woman—other than personal or social suicide—she builds a strong case about the consequences of her heroine's legal and linguistic powerlessness. On one hand, Sand shows compassion for Indiana, an enslaved woman (90 [57]; 52) who has been taught to blindly obey her father and husband (88–89 [56]; 51) and who yearns for love, salvation, and ultimately respect (250 [196]; 191). On the other, through her narrator's repeated and timely ironic intrusions, Sand judges harshly Indiana's misguided choices (like her desire to believe her lover at all costs), and she invites us to do the same.

The scenes I have selected represent key points in Indiana's relationship with Raymon and feature the narrator's explicit or implicit commentary. They include the events in Indiana's bedroom in Lagny leading to Noun's suicide (ch. 8) and the scene where Indiana waits for Raymon in his Paris bedroom to seek his help, three days before Delmare will take her back to Réunion (ch. 20).

To prepare for our theatrical study of the scenes, I give students take-home tasks. They are to read the passage out loud several times and observe its overall tone and rhythm—and any possible shifts therein. Next, they fill out assigned rubrics to account for the scene's details and to imagine it as if it were unfolding on a stage or as part of a film sequence. Students first identify the main action and its context, the setting, and the characters. And, since the narrator in *Indiana* also expresses his opinions at times, I challenge the students to treat him as a character in this exercise. Second, students look for the significance of light, sound or silence, objects, and costumes. Third, they pay attention to composition and character grouping. (In the Powell edition, Tony Johannot's etchings can be quite useful.) Finally, students examine what motivates the characters' dialogic and nonverbal interaction and whether their purpose evolves or remains static.

Next I have students synthesize these results with a partner or in groups of three to capture the essence of the passage(s). This activity requires the students to get up and perform their findings in front of the class. The following prompts may help facilitate how best to gauge the tone, mood, and idea of a passage: Can we give the scene a title? What core moments, words, or movements best summarize the scene? Each group is then asked to come up with two or three distinct manners of showing one key word or moment. Often this may simply mean striking a pose and making sure that the individual or group blocking clearly conveys the main message. The class has to decide which choice is the most powerful, visually and emotionally, and explain why. In this type of interactive work, which borrows from Augusto Boal's *Games for Actors and Non-actors* and Viola Spolin's *Improvisation for the Theater*, there is no set answer since the goal is exploration. Although standing up in front of the class and experimenting with the narrative may seem daunting at first, this activity does not require students to be actors (or directors). It is not about showing off one's acting skills but about being willing to play with the text, by doing, by using one's body, in a creative manner.

Once the visuals are shared with the class, I ask students to go back to the text and write a shortened version of the passage(s), to be acted out at our next meeting. Prompts for paring down the narrative focus on using whatever physical image worked best in the previous exercise to symbolize the point of the scene, keeping the dialogic exchanges intact, and transforming the narrator into a full-fledged character whenever possible.

Sand depicts the way her characters speak and move as if she were composing a score, catching every nuance of intonation and feeling. Those numerous acting tags and stage indications can be eliminated from the rewritten piece. Instead, they become part of how students use their voices and embody their characters. But when Sand's narrator behaves like a bona fide character who gives texture and meaning to a scene, students should be free to experiment with how best to incorporate his voice in the dialogue they create. They should also decide whether he is addressing his remarks to the audience (251–52 [197]; 192), to the other characters, or to both. Some may opt to follow the text and have the narrator deliver his words in a straightforward manner. Others may choose to split what he says and to assign it to two or more students to achieve a choral effect, especially if the message conveyed seems important. If several groups work on the same scene at the same time, they can perform different ways of showcasing the narrator. As in the earlier exercise, the class discusses the various choices and justifies which version best represents the essence of the scene.

Let us now examine two specific examples. The first scene takes place the evening after Noun has disguised herself as Indiana to win back Raymon. It starts with "quand tout à coup le roulement d'une voiture se fit entendre" 'when suddenly they heard the sound of a carriage' (111–12 [77]; 70) and concludes with Noun's suicide at the end of chapter 8 (119 [83]; 76). This passage is composed of two sections. The first, which takes place in Indiana's bedroom up until Raymon leaves, is pure formulaic melodrama. The other, occurring the following morning on the castle grounds, by the river, is more lyrical in tone. Each will need to be handled differently.

The first section could be entitled "Virtue Deceived." This "scène étrange" 'strange scene' (114 [79]; 72), in which each character is at cross-purpose with the others, is saturated with high-intensity expressions like "épouvantée" 'terrified' (113 [79]; 71), "l'air égaré" 'distraught' (115 [80]; 73), "sa fierté de femme outragée" 'her pride as a woman insulted' (116 [80]; 73), "sa tremblante et misérable complice" 'his trembling, wretched accomplice' (117 [81]; 74). To show how the accumulation of such terms emphasizes the melodramatic quality of the dialogue and of the action, students can write a metacommentary for the narrator to be delivered as an aside to the audience, thus punctuating the dialogic exchange of the three characters. These interventions could cause the action to freeze periodically into snapshots or living tableaux. The challenge in creating a series of tableaux here is to determine the most striking moments in a scene where one finds repeated *coups de théâtre* (Indiana's unexpected arrival, her discovery of Raymon hiding in her alcove); on-going pathos (her grief and indignation at Noun's and Raymon's betrayals, Noun and Raymon kneeling to beg for her forgiveness, Noun's hatred of her lover); much frenetic stage business to keep the bedroom door closed to save Indiana's reputation; and secrets kept hidden (Noun's love for Raymon as well as her pregnancy) or shockingly revealed (Noun's discovery that Raymon has been courting Indiana). The powerful characters here are the two women caught in the web of Raymon's deceit, as shown by their body language. Their respective moments of discovery, however divergent, are given equal dramatic weight, both verbally and nonverbally, as when Noun grips Indiana's arm with anger to demand the truth (115 [80]; 73) or when Indiana regains her self-control (by wrapping a shawl around herself) and manages to dismiss Raymon and Noun with cool dignity (116–17 [81]; 74).

The second section concludes the novel's first act. Starting with Noun's silence and her odd disappearance, it describes Indiana's early morning walk, which prompts her resigned interior monologue about her fate (118–19 [83]; 76) and then stages her shock at finding Noun's body. It is important to note that, in contrast to the high emotional pitch of the previous section, Noun's death is treated with remarkable restraint. The novel's original edition had the narrator address the audience to justify why, as a storyteller, he refrained from exploiting the easy sensationalism that a detailed description of the horrific state of Noun's corpse would have yielded (Didier, Notes 382–83n1). Sand here does not aim to achieve an expected, transparent melodramatic effect. Rather, she chooses to underplay the scene to mobilize the readers' sympathy and to expose the tragic injustice of this human loss.

Through her narrator, Sand intends the scene to be a "teachable moment": not only do women (regardless of their class and race) lack agency, but they may also be painfully unaware of the causes of their demise. On one hand, Indiana experiences a rude awakening regarding Raymon's passionate tirades: "maintenant je sais ce qu'il faut croire de cette éloquence menteuse que les hommes savent dépenser avec nous" 'for now I know what to make of the lying eloquence that men know how to lavish on us' (119 [83]; 76). On the other, however, Indiana has no idea why Noun has died. Indeed, when Ralph finally tells her why a year later (182–84 [139–40]; 131–33), it is too late. Because she is in love with Raymon, she cannot hear the truth. Therefore Indiana's walk along the river in this section (119 [83]; 76) is an opportunity for students to stage Indiana's moment of discovery of Noun's death and her initial response to it. Keeping the focus on Indiana, students can supplement the text's deliberate restraint. They can elaborate on it in performance, either through words or pantomime, using props (the fabric of Noun's dress) and soundscapes (the ripples on the water, Indiana's piercing shriek, which could be voiced or silent and could even be shared by several actors). For further didactic effect, students can refer to Indiana's actual lament for Noun, which occurs two months later (126 [88–89]; 81–82). Reflecting on why it takes Indiana so long to verbalize her grief, the class could rewrite that eulogy and have Indiana say it at the very end of this scene. It would be worthwhile to ask students to pay attention to the dramatic value of shifting the timing of Indiana's lament. Some may find that this placement does not fit the narrative flow. This, in turn, could yield a fruitful discussion about why Sand chose to postpone it until the following chapter.

Our second scene takes place a year later, at a time when Indiana, though conflicted about Raymon, is still under his spell (215–23 [167–72]; 162–68). By now, however, he has become Delmare's friend and has tired of her. Indiana confronts Raymon in his bedroom, at night, in a reversal of the first scene, when he had been the one violating her privacy. In performance, students notice that the struggle between the characters hinges on the language they use to frame and influence their experience. By going to Raymon's house to escape Delmare's decree that she must follow him back to Île Bourbon, Indiana is literally fighting for her life (219 [170]; 165). She thinks it took courage to flee and to come to him. Raymon, for his part, thinks it was only "une imprudence incroyable" 'unbelievably imprudent' (216 [167]; 162) and calls her move "une étourderie" 'a blunder' (219 [169]; 164). The discrepancy between their goals (she seeks his help; he wants her to leave him alone) creates a crisis (217 [168]; 163), which Sand uses as another teachable moment, especially since the narrator's voice is deeply embedded in the scene.

The complex character of the omniscient narrator is clearly delineated here, and students can therefore easily flesh him out. He intervenes to provide a subtext to what the characters say or pretend to mean, as in the three instances when he enables the audience to hear what cynical Raymon thinks about Indiana's plan to involve him. Similarly, the narrator reveals that while at first Indiana presents a cool, self-contained front, her body is betraying her feelings of dread (217 [168]; 163). Yet the narrator also allows himself to express his own ambivalence toward Indiana. At first, the narrator feels pity (215 [167]; 161), since Indiana has trusted Raymon's promise that he would protect her from her husband. But this is the scene where she will be stripped of her illusions. Raymon realizes he has been caught in the trap of his own eloquence (217 [168]; 163). Unprepared to justify his lies, he fights back. Calling her insane and naive, he brutally discredits the very rhetoric he has skillfully deployed for several months to woo her, reducing it to the language and values found in cheap romance novels aimed at the lower classes (217 [168]; 163).

The narrator's role of cautioning women, whether French or creole, about what is truth or fiction is rehearsed several times in the novel, in particular at the end of chapter 12 (150–51 [110]; 103). But in this scene, the narrator shifts our attention from Raymon's caddish behavior to Indiana's responsibility in what happens to her. And he is outraged by the persistence of her gullibility. Unlike the first scene, Indiana is no longer naive, as she now demonstrates when she proudly pleads her case for his help. But Raymon is not interested in being her savior. Instead, he wants to conquer her pride and decides the moment has come to seduce her before sending her home (220 [170]; 165). As he launches once more into one of those passionate declarations of love he has just criticized, both he and Indiana become entranced yet again by the power of his performance. While the narrator can tolerate Raymon's deceiving himself about the sincerity of his emotions, he becomes incensed when, against her better judgment, Indiana is so swayed by Raymon's speech that she is ready to give in to his advances: "Honte à cette femme imbécile!" 'Shame on that foolish woman!' (220–21 [171]; 166). The student playing the narrator should address both the audience and Indiana when he admonishes her sternly for still wanting to believe Raymon's flowery, hollow eloquence.

Students note that the climax of this scene is tied almost comically to two objects, a clock and a glass of water. Whereas in the first section of the first scene, the bedroom door was the melodramatic prop whose degrees of aperture symbolized Indiana's reputation, here it is the clock that functions as an ironic counterpoint to Raymon's haste to conquer his prey before day break: "Pendant un quart d'heure il aima passionnément Madame Delmare" 'For a quarter of an hour he loved Madame Delmare passionately' (220 [170]; 166). Students can experiment with staging how the passage of time dictates Raymon's actions (turning him into an automaton) and show how time works in Indiana's favor. As Raymon tries hurriedly to force himself on her, she resists. After a struggle, he pushes her back, drinks a large glass of water, and thus breaks the spell. Because his time is up, Raymon drops his mask of passion and reveals his indifference toward her by coolly asking her to leave. That is when Indiana finally loses all her illusions about Raymon. The narrator's comment on (and to) Indiana is a slightly exasperated "at last!" Students enacting Indiana need to show what specific gesture or expression causes her to finally acknowledge the ray of light that "lui montr[a] à nu l'âme de Raymon" 'laid Raymon's heart bare before her' (222 [171]; 167).

The denouement finds both characters drained by their respective ordeals. Raymon has been found out, and Indiana has been enlightened (for now) about his real nature. But Indiana's new understanding is of no help to her, Sand suggests, since the heroine does not have the personal capability nor the social options that would allow her to resolve her impasse with Delmare. Echoing Noun's withdrawal before her suicide in the first scene, Indiana gradually turns catatonic. For fear she will commit suicide like the other woman (222 [172]; 168), Raymon locks her up and goes to seek his mother's help. As a final exercise, I would challenge the class to imagine what happens to Indiana during his absence. Given what has just occurred, can students create and perform a short interior monologue to articulate what she may be thinking at the end of this scene compared with her train of thought at the beginning (this monologue can be verbal or mimed)? And, based on their interpretation of Indiana's state of mind, can the class predict what will happen next?

I have tried to show that one of Sand's pedagogical goals with *Indiana* is to use the tropes of melodrama to dramatize the plight of the women of her day. By putting virtuous, if not misguided, heroines in physically or morally perilous situations, Sand wishes to create a sense of empathy in her public and to convince them change must occur. I have singled out two scenes from among many with much potential for theatrical reading. I have suggested that by working collaboratively in small groups and performing the text and their creative rewrites in front of one another, students can engage with the novel's issues from within. Learning to tease out and embody the voice of Sand's active, opinionated narrator enables students to appreciate how he enriches the story. His presence offers guidance and criticism, in the hope that both the heroine and the audience will be moved by the consequences of the actions of the enslaved woman and will endeavor to break her chain.

NOTE

I wish to thank Gloria Baxter, professor of theater emerita at the University of Memphis and award-winning director and playwright at the Voices of the South theater company, for her insights on narrative theater, which she has practiced in the United States and abroad for over forty years.

Romantic Realism in *Indiana*

Allan H. Pasco

George Sand's *Indiana* (1832) provides an opportunity to review the salient themes of Romanticism: frustrated love, passion, melancholy, egotism, imagination, suicide, incest, and nature. Undergraduate and graduate student discussions that probe this long but significant list, supplemented with brief, in-class papers for third- and fourth-year undergraduate students, help draw the class's work on the Romantics together. In the process, it is also possible to highlight other important but less emphasized preoccupations like youth, the present, narrative devices, and the realism that preoccupied writers throughout much of the eighteenth and early nineteenth centuries. While Sand's works are generally categorized as Romantic, they were in fact early transitional works bridging Romanticism and realism at mid-century.[1] Although Romantics did not emphasize traits such as scientific objectivity, materialism, and money that mark mid-century realism, they had long been anxious to portray a true reality. Sand insisted in her letter to Emile Regnault of 27 February 1832 that the subject of her book "n'est ni romantique . . . ni frénétique. C'est de la vie ordinaire, c'est de la vraisemblance bourgeoise" 'is neither romantic . . . nor frenzied. It is ordinary life, bourgeois verisimilitude' (*Correspondance* 2: 46; my trans.). Indiana's trajectory fits the Romantic mode until it arrives at the conclusion, when Indiana and Ralph leave fantasy behind and create a relatively mundane, everyday sort of life, notwithstanding the solitude and exoticism of their Île Bourbon retreat. The conclusion weighs heavily on the significance of the Romantic text that precedes it, compelling a review of the rest of the novel. The dreams that Indiana pursued through earlier portions of the book are revealed as foolish, and she and Ralph commit themselves to each other in a seemingly permanent relationship.

From Romanticism to Ordinary Life

Although *Indiana* can be used in a class as the sole example of Romanticism, it teaches best when the class already has a grasp of the major characteristics of the movement. Once students have read *René*, *Adolphe*, *Ourika*, and *Le rouge et le noir*, they can read Sand's novel closely, to learn to go beyond the common definitions, focusing on the characters' self-centered natures, and recognize the way Romantics used images like hair, hunting, and water or intertextual allusions to Ophelia and *Paul et Virginie*. Such images join with major themes to prepare the radical break between the subjective passion of the novel's fourth part and the banal reality of the conclusion. Student readers accompany Indiana and Sir Ralph to the precipice, when the failure and frustration typical of Romanticism bring the heroine and her longtime guardian to the point of suicide. Following *Werther*, *Atala*, and scores of other novels, they declare that their desires will be gratified in heaven and prepare to leap to a new life.[2] On turning the page, however, we are surprised to see that Indiana and Sir Ralph are not only alive and well but indeed enjoying love in a tropical paradise.

This last portion of the novel has long been a problem for critics. Why are the heroes still alive? How can one explain this new life? In class, I briefly summarize the insights of other readers. Recent critics have either attempted to relate the early narrator with the one incarnated in the conclusion or separated them, identifying the first with Sir Ralph Brown.[3] There is, of course, nothing that definitively identifies the narrator of the first four parts, though that of the conclusion has been given flesh and blood.

Véronique Machelidon is particularly struck by Indiana's concluding melancholia ("Female Melancholy"), despite the fact that Sand has integrated this emotion into the heroine's reality of everyday life with memories of the past. And indeed, Indiana does seem melancholic: it is stated that Indiana has "manières [qui] ont gardé quelque chose de lente et de triste qui est naturel aux créoles, mais qui, chez elle, me parut avoir un charme plus profond . . . ; et, quand sa bouche sourit, il y a encore de la mélancolie dans son regard" 'something of the languid melancholy which is natural to Creoles but which, in her, seemed to contain a more fundamental charm . . . and when her mouth smiles, there is still melancholy in her eyes' (337 [270]; 266). This melancholic sentiment detected by Machelidon is further elaborated in the conclusion:

> [Indiana] aussi dut avoir des retours de tristesse . . . car l'âme se fait au malheur, elle y prend racine [dans l'habitude du malheur] et ne s'en détache qu'avec effort. . . . Enfin, comme il arrive dans les affections profondes et vraies, le temps, au lieu d'affaiblir notre amour, l'établit et le scella.   (341 [273])

> She too must have had recurrent attacks of melancholy . . . for it takes root in the soul, which becomes used to unhappiness, and is detached from it only with difficulty. . . . At last, as happens with deep, genuine attachments, time, instead of weakening our love, confirmed and sealed it.   (269)

James M. Vest, who has pointed to the fantastic qualities that fill Indiana's dreams and color her reality, insists on the appropriateness of the conclusion, for here the narrator, a dreamer, has come to enjoy a world of fantasy and romance ("Dreams"). Although the conclusion is indeed an integral part of the novel, and certainly not breaking the tone of the whole, it seems to me important to recognize that a furious storm brings the narrator to abandon the meditation in which he has lost himself and his "puérile prétention" 'childish pretention' to make sense of the surrounding violent landscape (333 [266]; 262). Unable for the moment to return to civilization, it takes him several, dangerous days to make his way through the flooding and fog and stumble across the hut where he seeks refuge.

A storm, a hut, and the exotic landscape of Île Bourbon are redolent of Jacques-Henri Bernardin de Saint-Pierre's *Paul et Virginie* (1787). Bernardin and his friend Jean-Jacques Rousseau, like Sand, were convinced that only the powerful virtue of a child of nature like Virginie could resist the influence of civilization while she was at her aunt's in metropolitan France.[4] Sand declares in her 1832 preface, "le triomphe de la vertu ne se voit plus qu'aux théâtres du boulevard . . . dans ces jours de décadence morale" 'we only see virtue triumphing in light comedies . . . in these days of moral decadence' (41; my trans.). Finally, but not until the conclusion, Sir Ralph and Indiana have escaped society and submitted to nature. Only then can they enjoy a simple life of virtue. Welcomed by Ralph, the narrator of the conclusion eventually hears the couple's story, which we have just read in the preceding four parts and which leaves no doubt of the book's lesson: since a life of peace is impossible in society, Ralph and Indiana have withdrawn to a tropical paradise surrounded by nature.

Indiana's understanding of reality was regrettably inadequate. In a bad marriage, under the delusion that her unrealistic (Romantic) fantasies could be realized with someone like Raymon, Indiana was as unsophisticated as her servant and foster sister, Noun, and thus unable to understand Ralph's value: "[E]lle ne rêva plus que de fuite, de solitude et d'indépendance; elle roula dans son cerveau meurtri et douloureux mille projets d'établissement Romanesque dans les terres désertes de l'Inde ou de l'Afrique" 'Indiana dreamt only of flight, solitude, and independence. In her wounded, grief-stricken mind, she turned over a thousand plans for settling romantically in the desert lands of India or Africa' (273 [215]; 210). Her inadequate grasp of real life is epitomized when she runs away from her churlish husband to sail back to France in the hopes of resuscitating her affair with Raymon.

On reading *Indiana*, critics like John T. Booker think of the naive, self-destructive Romanticism of Emma Bovary. Only with great difficulty and not until the book's conclusion do the capriciousness of Raymon, the brutishness of the sailors rowing her Indiana to the boat, and Sir Ralph's contrary reliability break through Indiana's stubborn fantasies. While she dreams of running away from Île Bourbon, she is taken by "un étrange vertige" 'a strange giddiness' and offers "tous les symptômes de la folie" 'all the symptoms of madness' (254 [199–200]; 194). There is no doubt about the power of her "désir dans toute son intensité dévorante" 'desire in all its consuming intensity' (254 [200]; 195). Unfortunately for her, the force of her longing does not make the object of her love reciprocate: "Elle vécut ainsi des semaines et des mois sous le ciel des tropiques, n'aimant, ne connaissant, ne caressant qu'une ombre, ne creusant qu'une chimère" 'She lived thus for weeks and months beneath the tropical sky, loving, knowing, cherishing only a shadow, going only more deeply into a dream' (254 [200]; 195). Her dreams are romantic fantasies devoid of substance.

Although Sand (like Stendhal and Balzac) made outrageous claims of free and unfettered novelistic creation in her 1832 preface—"J'ai écrit *Indiana* . . . sans aucun plan, sans aucune théorie d'art ou de philosophie dans l'esprit" 'I wrote *Indiana* . . . without any plan, without any aesthetic or philosophical theory in mind' (35; 3)—on close examination of *Indiana*, it proves to be a highly structured work of art in the Romantic literary tradition. The conclusion, and the structural anacoluthon that separates it from the preceding chapter, arrests the story of suicide and establishes a story of married peace and joy. It has long been a point of contention, and Charles Augustin Sainte-Beuve, who criticized its strange implausibility and lack of continuity, is frequently cited in this regard.[5] While it is common for critics to conclude that Sand and other artists are in error, I have found it particularly helpful to assume that authors made authentic choices in their creations. Such an a priori position helps lead students to an a posteriori recognition of suggestive innovations. It is then at least possible in most cases to help students tease out what the author was attempting, after which valid judgment of the novel as a work of art becomes possible.

The break between the two final chapters and the conclusion is rendered even more acute by the overt introduction of another dreamer, the conclusion's scribe, who is forced into confrontation not with fantasy but with material reality in the jungle paradise. What Béatrice Didier calls "une rupture du ton romanesque" 'a rupture in the novel's tone' (Notes 395n9; my trans.), thus separating the conclusion from the rest of *Indiana*, encourages students to reconnect the disjointed elements by dealing with the novel's undergirding metaphoric chains and Romantic topoi. The narrator is allowed to go beyond the malicious rumors of the world into the intimacy of Indiana and Ralph's life. Nothing indicates that the visitor continues to dream; rather, he appreciates the couple's companionate bliss in the reality of their making.

I ask students to plumb the text to ferret out a satisfactory explanation for the fact that the couple does not end up dead like Noun. The text suggests briefly that perhaps Ralph strayed off in the wrong direction or an angel spread his protective wings over them (339–40 [272]; 268). The break in the text emphasizes the importance of the change in their lives. Indiana is no longer enslaved to unrealistic fantasies; rather, she has recognized the value of Ralph and a simple life of virtue in the midst of nature. She has joined Ralph in a life of true love that would be impossible in society. Earlier, she had dreamed of this solution: "[E]lle construisait son ajoupa solitaire sous l'abri d'une forêt vierge . . . ; elle se réfugiait sous la protection de ces peuplades que n'a point flétries le joug de nos lois et de nos préjugés" 'She was already building her solitary hut in the shelter of a virgin forest . . . ; she was seeking refuge in the protection of those peoples who have not been debased by the yoke of our laws and prejudices' (273 [216]; 211).

Stylistic Innovation and Major Themes

In my class, we explore how *Indiana* contains many common Romantic themes, such as youthful illusions and the youthful desire for immediacy. At the same time we also delve into technical innovations that are associated with realist writings and that are already present in Romantic texts like *Indiana*. What Nigel Harkness calls the "structural and narrative gap" that occurs between the fourth part and the conclusion constitutes an innovation ("Writing" 116). It separates *Indiana* from typical, Romantic formula fiction. I remind students that great Romantics used apparent infelicities of style, voice, and structure to emphasize patterns and depth of feeling and sincerity. We wonder how Sand's young people could have turned away from suicide to live together in a wilderness far from civilization. Students should have little trouble with Sand's anacoluthon, however, for the break symbolizes death to society, followed by heaven in nature. Leaving behind the "grande et terrible lutte de la nature contre la civilization" 'nature's terrible, great struggle against civilization' (272 [215]; 210), Indiana and Ralph instead embrace nature and civilization together.

I remind students that Indiana is nineteen, and, though ten years older, Sir Ralph is "dans toute la force et dans toute la fleur de la jeunesse" 'in the full strength and flow of youth' (51 [20]; 16). Rebellious in the face of society's standards, unwilling to bow to the attitudes reflected in shifting opinion, wrapped up in self-centered egotism, Romantic heroes like Indiana insisted on their own dreams. Instead of coming to terms with her marriage, Indiana passed her life dreaming: "Un jour viendra où tout sera changé dans ma vie, où je ferai du bien aux autres; un jour où l'on m'aimera, où je donnerai tout mon cœur à celui qui me donnera le sien" 'A day will come when I will be completely changed, when I shall do good to others; it will be a day when I shall be loved and I shall give my whole heart to the man who gives me his' (89 [56]; 51). Romantics almost always wished for a fulfilling love, but not just any love—they wanted an impossible love that transcended ordinary affection. Engaging in an incestuous or adulterous love, for example, was forbidden, since both were deemed sinful perversions by the church and traditional morals. The challenge to the author was to emphasize the impossibility of bringing love to fruition without diminishing the passion. The conflict was a much-exploited theme for Romantics.[6]

Almost inevitably, Romantics fell in love with people they could not have, and they were fascinated by the terrible, personal frustration that came from translating the dreams of future joy into the agony of present reality, where love could not be consummated. As the final impossibility, only purity and virtue could elicit the absolute love they envisioned. Romantic heroines who submitted to their lovers sullied their characters and thus rendered their love unworthy. Students will have noticed that like other Romantic lovers Indiana and Ralph are related by their common history and by blood. At this point it is useful to discuss the problems that arise from this relationship, what it meant in their society and what it means in ours. She was raised with him, and he served as her teacher and protector. He was, she says, her only companion. She refers to him as her brother, and he to her as his daughter. In fact, they were cousins. Perhaps their decision to make a life outside society in the tropical jungle was motivated by the church's disapproval, since it would condemn their union as incestuous.[7]

Indiana emphasizes immediacy, another common trait of Romanticism, though a Romantic's present is almost always filled with frustration and misery—and unreasonable dreams of the future. Incapable both of learning from the past and of making realistic plans for what was to come, Romantics gave primacy to their most current dreams. They remained optimistic that they could actualize their fantasies, however much they were doomed to frustration. In the conclusion of the novel, however, Sand finds a way for Indiana to live isolated from destructive outside influences in an unimpeded enjoyment of a different, though real, present. Sir Ralph says, "Nous parlons rarement du passé, rarement aussi de l'avenir" 'We rarely speak of the past, rarely too of the future' (342 [274]; 270). They are happy in the present.

For Romantics, the villain was frequently the contemporary patriarchal society that oppressed women like Indiana. She nonetheless displays startling energy repeatedly, on the hunt, in standing up in full revolt to Delmare, and on her way from Île Bourbon to France. Despite her frail body and apparent timidity, she possesses "un courage plus que masculin" 'a more than masculine courage' (162 [120]; 113). Still, her inability to succeed indicates that she is lacking something. As Peter Dayan recognizes, she needs a man, a liberator, with whom as a woman of her day in a patriarchal society she "would be able to realize herself fully" (157). Neither her husband nor Raymon can fulfill this role, and even with Ralph she must leave civilization and turn to nature for the strength of purpose and freedom from social opinion that will allow her to be a fully functional human being. The world and the person she dreams of growing into, as Harkness and Dayan agree, cannot be realized within the framework of society.

From Romanticism to Realism

Already in 1831 and 1832, when *Indiana* was composed, despite Romanticism's startling success with *Hernani*, the movement was making subtle shifts into realism. Novels, melodramas, and *physiologies* fed the desire of the public for clear descriptions of people and situations in the new postrevolutionary society. Subjective dreams and imaginings were losing place to objective depictions of concrete reality. The Romantics consistently felt that their outrageous dreams were within the realm of possibility, and, instead of giving in to cynicism, they posited an afterlife that made a joyous conclusion possible. Indiana says, "Sois mon époux dans le ciel et sur la terre . . . et que ce baiser me fiance à toi pour l'éternité!" 'Be my husband in heaven and on earth . . . and let this kiss pledge me to you for all eternity' (330 [264]; 260).

Sand's love of a happy ending went a step further than the common eighteenth-century hope for a "better life by far," though Didier calls the concluding episode the weakest of the novel ("Ophélie" 89). The conclusion nevertheless explains virtually everything except the actual words and thoughts that moved the couple from the precipice to the garden of their future delight. Given that society has refused Indiana and Sir Ralph the happiness they wish, the author continues the basic realism of her plot. Far removed from society's corrupt wiles and gossip, they find the peace of true love and virtue. By no means ready to trust in a happy ending in life after death, Sand recognized that Indiana's boat does not have to sink like Virginie's. Her characters can simply descend the hill and commit their lives to perfect love outside society. Here the water will be neither as still as that where Noun drowned herself nor as well regulated as the Seine that attracted Indiana. Its raging tumult recognizes true passion, in the midst of a nature that encourages and guards over it.

In my course, students will have read *René*, and sometimes *Adolphe* and *Ourika*, so having them outline the transition from an unhappy life that remains incomplete to a new life where characters can enjoy their love removed from civilization will allow at once for a thorough familiarity with Sand's novel and a deeper understanding of Romanticism. *Indiana* vividly shows students the importance that Romantics accorded youth, and it further emphasizes the artistic freedom that had come through the all too overt rebellion against the art of the classics. Authors were no longer imprisoned in stultified alexandrines. They begin to display surprising innovations that they wield with varying expertise. But perhaps more interesting than the innovative narrative anacoluthon in *Indiana* is the fact that it leads to a complete reversal of preceding themes. The dreams and frustration of the first parts of the novel are recast, highlighting the peace and tranquility that Indiana and Ralph achieve when they are able to escape society.

NOTES

[1] As Georges May makes clear throughout his *Dilemme du roman au XVIIIe siècle*, the attitudes, customs, and details of everyday life are not just verisimilar but true in most eighteenth-century novels. It is clear from the novel of the day that the public had little patience with the improbable. Nineteenth-century realism was also a well-prepared outgrowth of Romanticism. People looked to the novel for insight into their society. A plethora of eighteenth- and early-nineteenth-century novels claim to tell nothing but the truth. Simon Nicolas Henri Linguet actually rebukes Crébillon *fils* for having "corrected" reality in his novels (239).

[2] For a discussion of suicide, see Pasco, *Sick Heroes* 134–56.

[3] See, e.g., Dayan, who sees Ralph as the narrator of third and fourth parts and the dominant voice of the conclusion (160), and Godwin-Jones, who separates the narrators (26–28, 303–04).

[4] Didier also discerns the strong flavor of *La nouvelle Héloïse* and the *Etudes de la nature*, in addition to the explicit allusion to *Paul et Virginie* (Notice 368–69; Sand mentions Bernardin's novel [101, 318 (67, 254); 61, 250–51]). See also Prasad, "Espace colonial"; Bonin, although I do not believe that the text of *Indiana* will permit the ironic reading Bonin suggests (on distinguishing irony from allusion, see Pasco, *Allusion* 22–38).

[5] Sainte-Beuve's review of *Indiana* first appeared in *Le national* on 5 October 1832 and has been republished in Brix's *Portraits contemporains*; Harkness provides an excellent bibliography and summary of this controversy ("Writing"). Didier, whose disapproval is explicit in "Ophélie dans les chaînes," says in the introduction to her 1984 edition of *Indiana* that "le dénouement a désappointé certains lecteurs" 'the conclusion disappointed some readers' (25; my trans.). She believes that Sand situated it outside time and "en quelque sorte hors du roman" 'in a way outside the novel' (25; my trans.) and is thus, as Sainte-Beuve argued, unrealistic.

[6] For a discussion of incest in the Romantic novel, see Pasco, *Sick Heroes* 109–32.

[7] In the Charte de 1830, marriage was prohibited between brother and sister, but no mention is made of cousins (*Quarante codes*, titre V, "Du marriage" 29–31).

Ending with *Indiana*:
Romance, Romanticism, the Novel

Margaret Waller

It is safe to assume that George Sand's 1832 novel *Indiana* would guarantee a galvanizing first reading assignment or a mid-semester wake-up in a variety of courses. But in my course The Romantic Other, I save *Indiana* as the perfect big bang for the end.[1] Doing so in this French literature seminar on romance and the excluded other in the Romantic novel has three advantages. First, with no knowledge of the novel's romantic predecessors and cultural context, students might well be mystified by *Indiana*'s melodramatic plot, grandiose rhetoric, and heavy-handed moralizing. But after reading Sophie Cottin's *Claire d'Albe* (1799), François-René de Chateaubriand's *René* (1802), Germaine de Staël's *Corinne, ou l'Italie* (1806), and Claire de Duras's *Ourika* (1824), they see *Indiana* as a strikingly modern and audacious revision of its predecessors' themes, characters, worldview, and tragic dilemmas. The comparison throws into relief Sand's representation of the other side of romantic love—a social and political problem for which it is imperative that we imagine solutions.

My second reason for ending with *Indiana* is practical. Late in the semester, everyone's energy, including my own, starts flagging. Though *Indiana* is long and dense, the students at the highly selective liberal arts college where I teach usually find it easier reading than its Romantic precursors in part because Sand's writing meets the criteria for intelligibility that modern fiction, films, and television shows have led them to expect. In any case, the novel's psychosexual fetishism, its skewering of personal and political hypocrisy, and its unexpected plot twists mean that assigning *Indiana* in manageable amounts over the course of the last weeks guarantees that class discussion remains lively.

Third, The Romantic Other offers a fresh approach to the French Romantic novel, as well as a fifteen-week genealogy of modern notions of romance through the lens of social difference. Despite the "hook-up" generation's supposedly cynical view of romance, many of my students look to love and marriage as the single most important personal solution to their problems and even a political cure-all, as in the current struggle for marriage equality. Given its iconoclasm and wider view, *Indiana* ends The Romantic Other with fireworks.

Charting the Course

The prerequisites for The Romantic Other are minimal (four semesters of college-level French or the equivalent) and do not include a gender and women's studies course. This means that students' linguistic, analytic, and literary skills and their background, interests, and majors vary widely. Nevertheless, since individual student progress and the seminar's success depend on their active participation, I get all the students talking to one another and to me in the first five minutes of the first day of class.

After briefly introducing the three main subjects of the course (romance, Romanticism, and the novel), I ask students to take a few minutes to brainstorm in pairs all the verbs, nouns, adjectives, images, and books or movies that come to mind when they think of love and romance. Any and all associations, including contemporary references from the United States, are acceptable as long as students are speaking French. The class then shouts out ideas to me, which I scribble all over the board. Doing so creates a basic shared vocabulary and usually a few inside jokes to the latest variations on this theme, such as vampires, to which we return often during the semester. This mind map of the romantic commonplaces of this sampling of twenty-first-century college students in the United States is the course's first cultural text, which we examine for underlying assumptions and exclusions. Who or what is the romantic other today? To give students some historical and cultural perspective on marriage, part of their homework is to read and discuss with at least two friends who are not in the class Stephanie Coontz's eye-opening, one-page article, "A Pop Quiz on Marriage."

I spend the rest of that first day demystifying the seminar, revealing it as a process that reflects recent developments in studies of the Romantic novel and feminist criticism as well as shifting cultural priorities and personal blind spots. I briefly describe how and when each of the primary texts they will read has fallen in or out of scholarly and popular favor over the past century: the canonical (*René*), the underread (*Claire d'Albe* and *Corinne*), and the newly overread (*Ourika* and *Indiana*).

I explain, too, one of the course goals: learning how to write a persuasive critical research paper developing an argument about gender and power relations in one or more of our novels by integrating close reading with a great deal of secondary research. I find that modeling critical thinking throughout the course with secondary reading makes students more knowledgeable, interesting, and motivated writers. After we finish reading a novel, each student must come to class prepared to summarize, evaluate, and debate one or two of the articles he or she has chosen from the large selection on electronic reserve. Such exercises help students learn to identify the various schools and trends in modern literary criticism and understand themselves as part of a community and a continuing conversation. Since critics rarely compare several works by different authors as I ask students to do in their papers, this practice also gives them the opportunity to do more original work.

To give the course its intellectual foundation, I assign for the second class excerpts from three critical works in English with study questions in French. The first is Leslie Rabine's two-page preface to her book *Reading the Romantic Heroine: Text, History, Ideology*. In this pioneering study of romance narratives in Western literature, Rabine provides a succinct if debatable definition of the myth of romantic love: "As a heterosexual, private, total, exalted love, it is supposed to give meaning to an otherwise drab existence, and allow us to transcend daily life to a higher plane. Whether fatal passion or happily-ever-after fantasy, it has always been a total love, combining sexuality, emotional intimacy, and self-reflecting intellect" (vii). The preface also offers feminist tools for understanding the contradictory power of romantic love narrative: "it provides one of the few accepted outlets through which women can express their anger and revolt against their situation in a patriarchal order" even as "it idealizes and eroticizes women's powerlessness and lack of freedom" (viii).

Second, I assign several sections of the introduction to Tony Tanner's *Adultery in the Novel: Contract and Transgression*. Though adultery per se is a temptation only in *Claire d'Albe*, *Corinne*, and *Indiana*, there is much in Tanner that is useful: Rousseau's idea of voluntary submission to a social contract, Bataille's insight about voluntarism as violence in another guise, and the way the word *adultery* and its practice represent "an inassimilable conflation of what society insists should be separate categories and functions" because it reveals social rules "to be arbitrary rather than absolute" (12–13). Discussion includes when, how, and for what purposes "unadulterated" love, marriage, and the nuclear family are romanticized and have come to seem natural in Western society, with frequent reference to Coontz's pop quiz on marriage.

The third reading assignment is from Margaret Cohen's introduction to *The Sentimental Education of the Novel*. No work has done more to resuscitate nineteenth-century sentimental novels for the twenty-first century. Cohen argues that most scholars of French literary history are biased toward realism's detailed descriptions of a specific historic setting and its suspense-driven plot featuring "a parade of unprincipled characters motivated by self-interest and desire" (32). Focusing exclusive attention on "masterpieces" (by men), they have made writers such as Honoré de Balzac and Stendhal modern heroes while ignoring and belittling the best-selling works of the realists' biggest competitors: sentimental novels by women. Though their "concentrated and abstract plot, ethically driven characters, absence of material details, and [an] ineluctable narrative movement towards a dénouement evident from the beginning" make them hard to read today, Cohen shows them as "answers to questions we can no longer hear" (32, 29). Particularly useful is the notion of the sentimental "double bind"—two equally valid but contradictory moral imperatives—that characterizes such novels.

Since most students know very little about French history, I usually spend the last half of the second class soliciting their responses to images of late-eighteenth- and early-nineteenth-century French culture. I correct their assumptions about social class, women's roles, and rights from the ancien régime to the July Monarchy and draw up a basic time line of the literary field and the dizzying number of regime changes during that period. Frequent references to these points in the first two thirds of the course pay off when students read *Indiana* and need to understand the conflicting political positions represented by the three male characters, not to mention the novel's depiction of the revolution of 1830.

Tying in Indiana

One obvious way to introduce *Indiana* is to face head-on the problem of the novelist who remains more famous for her love life than for her life's work. I often assign Naomi Schor's introduction to *George Sand and Idealism*—in which Schor recounts the myths and facts about Sand as stages of her (mis)identification with the author and draws a parallel to the blind spots in twentieth-century literary criticism about Sand's work—as well as excerpts from Cohen. Whereas Schor locates *Indiana* under the sign of literary idealism, Cohen makes the case for seeing the text as a sentimental social novel, the preferred genre for female writers of the 1830s and 1840s. The two critics share a common question: given that England abounded in women realist writers during this period, "[w]hy were there no French women realists?" (Cohen 8).

However I frame *Indiana*, the previous weeks of The Romantic Other have given students most of the literary and historical context they need. Sand's novel begins, for example, with Indiana; her embittered and tyrannical older husband, Colonel Delmare; and Indiana's taciturn English cousin, Sir Ralph Brown, gloomily gathered by the fireside in a château outside Paris on a rainy autumn evening. Students instantly note the proliferation of mundane but telling details of setting that were absent in most of the preceding novels, and they recognize Indiana and Ralph as characters who, like René and Ourika, are presented as so withdrawn and alienated that they must be coaxed out of their silence. Indeed, the scene looks ideal for a lengthy soul baring as in Chateaubriand and Duras and as in many pages of *Corinne*. But until Ralph abruptly commands his dog, Ophelia, to sit, about five pages into the text, no one but the chatty, unidentified narrator speaks. As in Chateaubriand and Staël, Sand's narrator increases suspense by withholding information while hinting at a mystery. The beginning contrasts most sharply with *Claire d'Albe*, which is almost entirely told through Claire's intimate letters to her cousin Elise. On the basis of these and other formal differences among the novels, students are able to discuss how and when various choices make representations of melancholy, alienation, or ill-fated love more or less palpable or palatable to readers.

The chatty style, ironic tone, opinionated attitude, and clear gender identification of the narrator in *Indiana* distinguish the novel from all its Romantic precursors. A comparison with the loquacious but more respectful and formal narrator in *Corinne* and *Ourika* underscores how Sand, who first published *Indiana* under the name G. Sand, uses a specific and male rather than a generic gender-neutral narrator both to secure and undermine the male authority that playing this persona allows her to enjoy. Meanwhile, in her three prefaces Sand uses still other versions of the authorial voice. Comparing the prefaces' form and content to those in *Claire d'Albe* and *René* throws into relief Sand's relatively plainspoken yet rabble-rousing style. It also demonstrates that Sand, like her precursors, uses the preface to claim yet disavow her work, making the novel itself an other for the author.

One advantage of *Indiana* as the last work in The Romantic Other is that un-like any of the preceding texts, it thematizes romance and the romance novel as both cause and effect of social inequalities of opportunity and aspiration. The text links Indiana's *romanesque* (romantic) imagination to the profound naïveté and ignorance of this young white woman from the French colony Île Bourbon (now Réunion) and her loveless marriage to the considerably older Delmare but also to the romance novel itself. Raymon de Ramière unscrupulously par-rots the eloquent passion typical of the genre but also excoriates it as the kind of cheap fiction a ladies' maid would read (205, 217 [158, 168]; 152, 163). Later, Indiana adds her own damning assertion that it is as if she had learned about life from those "riantes et puériles fictions où l'on intéresse le cœur au succès de folles entreprises et d'impossibles félicités" 'optimistic, childish fictions in which the heart becomes interested in the success of crazy enterprises and im-possible joys' (247 [193]; 189).

Key to students' understanding of the text and its contradictions is getting them to debate to what extent *Indiana*, like the other Romantic novels they have read, is an attack on such fiction, an example of it, or something else altogether. Indeed, far from abjuring the Romantic trope of love as subjugation, Sand's novel raises it to a fever pitch for political purposes. For example, Delmare baldly states his right to reign over his wife as her tyrannical master, making him a clear example of the injustices that can be committed in marriage's name. Meanwhile Indiana pleads for her right to love Raymon as the most abject slave but later cries out, as Sand's 1842 preface does, against a patriarchal order in which half of the human race is the subjugated other whose "malheur . . . entraîne celui de l'homme, comme celui de l'esclave entraîne celui du maître" 'distress . . . entails that of men, as the distress of the slave entails that of the master' (46; 13).

As for what Sand's novel does with the differences that race and culture make, Duras's *Ourika* is an obvious and useful point of comparison. Bought out of slavery in Africa at the age of two and raised in France, Ourika, by the time she is of marrying age, has the education, values, and even wealth that almost entirely the same as those of the white aristocrats around her. She is considered unmarriageable solely on the basis of her black skin. The situation dramatically exposes the absurdity of racial prejudice, but it also means that the crucial difference in the novel begins as something skin deep before it be-comes internalized. By contrast, *Indiana* presents social and cultural as well as racial and emotional otherness. The heroine and her foster sister, Noun, both grew up in the French colonies, which makes them "créoles." But Indiana is an upper-class white woman, whereas Noun, who acts as her servant in France, is probably "créole" in another sense as well: of mixed race. Though Indiana has an undeniable race and class advantage in France, both women find themselves easy prey for civilization's corruption, which takes the form of the romantic but predatory Raymon.

For Ourika, her internalization of prejudice becomes an illness that kills her softly, but the consequences of the mismatch between Indiana and Noun's romantic ideals and the mistreatment they suffer are graphic, dramatic, and brutal. Indiana gives up her body and soul and goes temporarily mad; Noun commits suicide by drowning. Indeed, the level of explicit violence in *Indiana* is practically unheard of in the novel's predecessors. In class, we consider to what extent this extreme dramatization of victimhood justifies or undercuts the protests against the social order by Indiana in her letters and by Sand in her prefaces. So, too, the class debates the role of passing references to real slavery in almost all the novels, including *Indiana*. To what extent does this common Romantic comparison of unhappy love, social isolation, and second-class citizenship with slavery erase the brutal material and mental conditions of it as historical fact?

As a romantic hero, Ralph is a clear descendent of Frédéric, René, and Oswald, and these intertextual comparisons help students appreciate the gamut of Romantic masculinity as both social critique and idealizing fantasy of what a heroine might want. But unlike Frédéric or René, Ralph is a romantic hero trapped in a realist world of cynical self-interest. In this sense his situation, which he reveals in his long, grandiloquent confession of his feelings to Indiana in part 4, is not unlike that of Oswald's experience of unprecedented violence and deception in revolutionary France. Indeed, comparing *Indiana* with *Corinne*, published twenty-five years earlier, students see that the Napoleonic empire, the Bourbon restoration, and the July Monarchy seem to have only exacerbated the nation's worst character defects. In *Corinne*, for example, Staël's narrator subjects the comte d'Erfeuil, Oswald's friend and traveling companion, to some good-natured mockery for his typically French egotism. Nevertheless his character flaws seem inconsequential next to the excoriating representation of Raymon's ego in *Indiana*; nor does Erfeuil have anything like Raymon's political connections or knowingly wield his social power to do grave personal harm. Raymon's persuasive eloquence appears as a vile perversion of Corinne's spellbinding and uplifting oratory and rhetoric. Students see that the Romantic novel has come a long cynical way from the sentimental novel's more benevolent assumptions about human nature and society.

Even so, *Indiana* is the only work in the course that allows for anything resembling a happy (albeit implausible) end. Claire d'Albe, René, Corinne, and Ourika all die by the end of the novels, leaving a few loved ones and presumably the reader to mourn their tragic fate. There is nothing to be done, no imaginable future. By contrast, having narrowly avoided a double suicide, Indiana and Ralph, in the conclusion, seem to have made the great escape to a simple and isolated but idyllic life devoted to honest commerce and good works in the lush natural setting of Indiana's home, Île Bourbon. Schor explains this implausible ending as consonant with Sand's version of idealism: a "refusal to reproduce mimetically and hence to legitimate . . . a man-made system of laws that enables the enslavement of both women and blacks" (*George Sand* 54). Indeed, in their new life, Ralph and Indiana buy the freedom of infirm slaves whom they hire as servants. Even so, the freed slaves operate like shades in the novel, with no story, no voice of their own. In that sense, Indiana resembles them, beings who do not count and have withdrawn into silence—an eerie recall of the novel's unhappy beginning. To what extent has Indiana simply changed masters?

Ending with *Indiana* does not necessarily mean that the novel has the last word. Two works I have used help bring our debates into the present, making The Romantic Other less "other." The chapter on *Indiana* in Sandy Petrey's *In the Court of the Pear King* locates the text quite specifically in its July Monarchy cultural and political context (70–94). Focusing on the period's essential oxymoron (the attempt to establish a bourgeois monarchy), Petrey also ties the questions of state legitimacy and Sand's play with gender identity to modern-day debates about essentialism versus constructionism in ways that spark classroom discussion.

Assigning the 1992 French film *Un cœur en hiver* (1992), directed by Claude Sautet, also works well. Although Sautet's film is an update of Mikhail Lermontov's Russian novel *A Hero of Our Time* (1839), the film can also be viewed as a contemporary rewriting of *Indiana* with several important twists. In the film's love triangle, Daniel Auteuil, who is like the mild-mannered Ralph and the melancholic René, nevertheless plays the fatal man, a Raymon figure. Meanwhile his boss, a confident and gregarious Raymon type, takes the role of the infinitely patient and long-suffering protector Ralph, who is married not to a painfully naive Indiana but to a Corinne figure, a fantasy worthy of Staël of a modern heroine as female genius. An acclaimed violin virtuoso, the beautiful Camille (Emmanuelle Béart) is neither an outsider nor, since she is married to the Ralph figure, an innocent. Even so, Camille falls for the taciturn, melancholy, and withdrawn Romantic hero. In the film, modern French society offers the freedoms—social mobility, ubiquitous adultery, easy divorce—that presumably dissolve the usual social obstacles to romantic love. Even so, the "hero of our time" has a familiar flaw: he cannot love Camille as she dreams she could and should be loved. Why this is impossible is a matter for classroom debate. So is the question, What makes the hero's refusal of romantic love so discomfiting to a twenty-first-century audience?

Whether or not I finish the course with a modern coda, The Romantic Other reveals that romantic love, even though it is often denigrated as feminine, is a powerful myth for men and women alike and for society as a whole that is inextricably bound up with questions of social difference, identity, and exclusion. Though the course will undergo many variations over the years to come, I know it will always include *Indiana*. Given the timeliness of its questions, the power of its prose, and the ambitious reach of Sand's vision of a more equitable world, I cannot imagine teaching The Romantic Other without it.

NOTE

[1] Thanks to Janet Beizer, who let me borrow her course title.

NOTES ON CONTRIBUTORS

James Smith Allen is professor of history and associate provost for academic affairs at Southern Illinois University, Carbondale. He is the author of *Poignant Relations: Three Modern French Women, In the Public Eye: A History of Reading in Modern France, 1800–1940* and *Popular French Romanticism: Authors, Readers, and Books in the Nineteenth Century* and the editor of *"In the Solitude of My Soul": The Diary of Geneviève Bréton, 1867–1871* (trans. James Palmes). He is working on a book-length monograph, "Sisters of Another Sort: Women and Freemasonry in Modern French Civic Life, 1737–1940."

Christopher Bains is associate professor of French at Texas Tech University. He is the author of *De l'esthétisme au modernisme: Théophile Gautier, Ezra Pound* and of articles on Gautier, Pound, and the early years of the *Paris Review* in such journals and books as *Etudes Littéraires, Revues modernistes anlgo-américaines: Lieux d'échange, lieux d'exil,* and *The Oxford Critical and Cultural History of Modernist Magazines.*

Carolyn Vellenga Berman is associate professor of literature at the New School. She is the author of *Creole Crossings: Domestic Fiction and the Reform of Colonial Slavery,* of essays in *Just below South: Intercultural Performances in the Caribbean and the Southern United States* and *Bernardin de Saint-Pierre et l'océan Indien,* and of recent articles in *Novel* and *Victorian Literature and Culture.* She is working on a book provisionally entitled "Representing the People: Dickens, Parliament, and the Popular Press."

Kathrine Bonin is assistant professor of French language and culture at Arcadia University. She is the author of articles in *Nineteenth-Century French Studies, George Sand Studies, Women in French Studies,* and *French Review* and is working on a book on late-eighteenth-century and early-nineteenth-century European exoticism. Her research and teaching interests include teaching all levels of French language, eighteenth- and nineteenth-century French literature, French and francophone film, and French for the professions.

John T. Booker is associate professor at the University of Kansas. With Allan Pasco, he edited *The Play of Terror in Nineteenth-Century France* and has published articles on Constant, Stendhal, Balzac, Sand, Flaubert, Gide, and Mauriac and contributed to the MLA volume on Balzac's *Old Goriot.* He teaches graduate courses on the French novel from *La Princesse de Clèves* to the Romantic period to the twentieth century, the first-person novel and narration, and narrative explorations from Balzac to the New Novel and has received several awards for excellence in teaching.

Aimée Boutin is professor of French at Florida State University. She is the author of *City of Noise: Sound and Nineteenth-Century Paris,* as well as of *Maternal Echoes: The Poetry of Marceline Desbordes-Valmore and Alphonse de Lamartine.* She has published on Sand, Balzac, Baudelaire, and Romantic women poets in scholarly journals such as *Nineteenth-Century French Studies, Romance Studies, Romanic Review, French Forum,* and *L'Esprit Créateur.* She is a contributor to the forthcoming MLA volume on teaching Baudelaire's prose poems.

Patrick M. Bray is associate professor of French at Ohio State University. He is the author of *The Novel Map: Space and Subjectivity in Nineteenth-Century French Fiction*, of book articles on Sand and the theater, and of articles in journals such as *Yale French Studies* and *French Forum*; with Phillip John Usher, he is the editor of *Building the Louvre: Architectures of Art and Politics*. His research focuses on nineteenth- and twentieth-century French literature, critical theory, and text and image.

Peter Dayan is professor of word and music studies at the University of Edinburgh. He is the author of *Mallarmé's Divine Transposition, Nerval et ses pères, Lautréamont et Sand, Music Writing Literature, from Sand via Debussy to Derrida*, and *Art as Music, Music as Poetry, Poetry as Art, from Whistler to Stravinsky and Beyond*. His work focuses on word and music studies and relationships between the arts, 1850–1960, and his teaching interests include nineteenth-century French literature; poetry, music, and translation; comparative literature.

Molly Krueger Enz is associate professor of French at South Dakota State University. She has published scholarly articles in a variety of journals, including the *French Review, Nineteenth-Century French Studies, Journal of the African Literature Association*, and *African Studies Quarterly*. Her current research examines the diverse identities of mixed-race characters in nineteenth-century French and contemporary francophone fiction set in the Caribbean and sub-Saharan Africa.

Nigel Harkness is professor of French at Newcastle University. A specialist of nineteenth-century literature, particularly questions of gender, he is the author of *Men of Their Words: The Poetics of Masculinity in George Sand's Fiction*. He is currently preparing an edition of *Elle et lui* for the Honoré Champion edition of Sand's complete works and working on a monograph provisionally entitled "Written in Stone: Literature and Sculpture in Nineteenth-Century French Culture."

Doris Kadish is Distinguished Research Professor Emerita of French and Women's Studies of the University of Georgia. She is the author of *Fathers, Daughters, and Slaves: Women Writers and French Colonial Slavery, Politicizing Gender: Narrative Strategies in the Aftermath of the French Revolution*, and *The Literature of Images: Narrative Landscape from* Julie *to* Jane Eyre and editor of several volumes, including *Translating Slavery* (with Françoise Massardier-Kenney), *Sarah* (with Deborah Jenson), *The Saint Domingue Plantation, La chaumière africaine, La famille noire*, and *Slavery in the Caribbean Francophone World*.

Véronique Machelidon is associate professor of foreign languages and literatures at Meredith College. She has published articles in *George Sand Studies* and an English translation of Boudjedra's *Mines de rien, Underground Unknown Unseen: Immigrant Coal-Crackers in France*. She specializes in nineteenth-century French, English, and German narrative with a theoretical focus on feminism, gender, psychoanalysis and narrative technique. She is coediting an anthology of essays on immigration in Maghrebi-French literature for Manchester University Press.

Shira Malkin is associate professor of French at Rhodes College. A specialist of drama and nineteenth-century French literature, she is trained as an actor and a director. She was the guest editor of a special issue of *George Sand Studies* on Sand and the theater and is the author of articles on the commedia dell'arte, Sand's output as a playwright, and

Jacques Copeau. She is currently preparing critical editions of the plays *Françoise* and *Mademoiselle La Quintinie* for the Honoré Champion edition of Sand's complete works.

Françoise Massardier-Kenney is professor of French and director of the Institute for Applied Linguistics at Kent State University. She is the editor of the American Translators Association Scholarly Series and coeditor of *George Sand Studies*. Her publications include *Gender in the Fiction of George Sand*, *Translating Slavery* (vols. 1 and 2, edited with Doris Kadish), and translations of Sand's *Valvèdre* and Antoine Berman's *Toward a Translation Criticism: John Donne*. Her work has appeared in *Translation Studies* and *Nineteenth-Century French Studies*, and her research focuses on cognition and literature and on retranslation.

Margaret E. McColley is the author of several essays on francophone women's travel in global colonial contexts. She has taught courses in French and francophone studies at the College of William and Mary and Rhodes College. In the summer of 2013 she traveled around the periphery and through the interior of Réunion (Île Bourbon), gaining insight into the island's social, historical, and geographic landscape.

Isabelle Hoog Naginski is professor of French and director of the International Literature and Visual Studies program at Tufts University. She is the author of *George Sand: Writing for Her Life*, which was also published in French (*George Sand: L'écriture ou la vie*), and *George Sand Mythographe*; the editor of *George Sand: Pratiques et imaginaires de l'écriture*, *Actes du Colloque international de Cerisy-la-Salle* (with B. Diaz), a special issue of *Revue des sciences humaines* on Sand, and critical editions of *Spiridion* and *Lélia*; and coeditor in chief of *George Sand Studies*.

Allan H. Pasco is Hall Distinguished Professor of Nineteenth-Century Literature at the University of Kansas. He is the author of *Inner Workings of the Novel*, *Revolutionary Love in Eighteenth- and Early-Nineteenth-Century France*, *Balzacian Montage*, *Sick Heroes: French Society and Literature in the Romantic Age*, *Allusion*, *Novel Configurations*, and *The Color-Keys to* A la recherche du temps perdu and the editor of *Nouvelles françaises du dix-neuvième siècle* (the second edition of which recently appeared) and *The Play of Terror in Nineteenth-Century France* (with John T. Booker). His teaching focuses on eighteenth-, nineteenth- and twentieth-century French literature.

Lynn Penrod is professor of French in the Department of Modern Languages and Cultural Studies and lecturer in the Faculty of Law at the University of Alberta. She is the author of *Hélène Cixous* and of articles on Sand, Beauvoir, LeClézio, Cixous, Tournier, Rochefort, and Colette, as well as various literary translations. Her research interests include women's writing in French, French children's literature, and translation theory and literary translation, and she is working on several translation projects.

Lauren Pinzka is senior lecturer at Yale University. The author of essays on the French Enlightenment and nineteenth-century French literature, her work has appeared in several collections and in journals such as *Nineteenth-Century French Studies*, *George Sand Studies*, *George Sand Aujourd'hui*, and *Iris*. Her research interests include nineteenth-century French literature, gender studies, myth and memory in modern France, the representation of Paris in French and American literature, and psychoanalytic criticism.

David A. Powell is professor of French in the Department of Romance Languages and Literatures at Hofstra University. He is the author of *While the Music Lasts: The*

Representation of Music in the Works of George Sand and has published critical editions of *Jacques* and *Indiana*. His articles on Sand have appeared in *Études littéraires, Romantic Review*, and *George Sand Studies*; he has also published chapters in *George Sand: Intertextualité et polyphonie, George Sand: Une écriture expérimentale, George Sand: Pratiques et imaginaires de l'écriture, Novel Stages, George Sand: Écritures et représentations, Présences de l'Italie dans l'œuvre de George Sand*, and *L'empire des signes*. He has also published on nineteenth-century French literature, nineteenth- and twentieth-century Québécois literature, representations of music in literature, and queer theory, as well as on musical resonances in Verlaine's and Mallarmé's poetry. His current project is on queer narrative strategies in early-nineteenth-century novels.

Pratima Prasad is associate professor of French at the University of Massachusetts, Boston. She is the author of *Colonialism, Race, and the French Romantic Imagination* and the editor, with Susan McCready, of *Novel Stages: Drama and the Novel in Nineteenth-Century France*. Selected articles and essays include "Intimate Strangers: Interracial Encounters in Romantic Narratives of Slavery" (in *L'Esprit Créateur*); "L'insularité, 'l'indigénisme' et l'inceste dans *Paul et Virginie*" (in *L'autre en mémoire* [ed. Laporte]); "Contesting Realism: Mimesis and Performance in George Sand's Novels" (in *XIX: Journal of the Society of Dix-Neuviémistes*); "Espace colonial et vérité historique dans *Indiana*" (in *Études littéraires*); "Uncovering Narrative Convention in Sand's *Lélia*" (in *George Sand Studies*); "Displaced Performances: The Erotics of George Sand's Theatrical Space" (in *Romance Notes*); and "Deceiving Disclosures: Androgyny and George Sand's *Gabriel*" (in *French Forum*).

Charles J. Stivale is Distinguished Professor of French at Wayne State University. He is the author of *Œuvre de sentiment, œuvre de combat: La trilogie de Jules Vallès, La temporalité romanesque chez Stendhal: "L'echafaudage de la Bâtisse," The Art of Rupture: Narrative Desire and Duplicity in the Tales of Guy de Maupassant, The Two-Fold Thought of Deleuze and Guattari: Intersections and Animations, Disenchanting les Bons Temps: Identity and Authenticity in Cajun Music and Dance*, and *Gilles Deleuze's ABCs: The Folds of Friendship*. His research focuses on the nineteenth-century French novel and on Deleuze and Guattari.

Margaret Waller is professor of French at Pomona College. She is the author of *The Male Malady: Fictions of Impotence in the French Romantic Novel* and the translator of Kristeva's *Revolution in Poetic Language*. She wrote the introduction to the French edition and English translation of Duras's *Ourika* for the MLA Texts and Translations series and is also the author of numerous essays, which have appeared in books on early Romantic fiction and painting, the French Romantic novel, Balzac and realism, and French and francophone masculinity.

WORKS CITED

Allen, James Smith. *Popular French Romanticism: Authors, Readers, and Books in the Nineteenth Century*. Syracuse: Syracuse UP, 1981. Print.

Les amours romantiques: Laure et Adriani. Dir. Josée Dayan. 1984. Television. Antenne 2.

Anderson, Benedict. *Imagined Communities: Reflections on the Origin and Spread of Nationalism*. London: Verso, 1983. Print.

Augé, Marc. *Non-lieux: Introduction à une anthropologie de la surmodernité*. Paris: Seuil, 1992. Print.

Au pays de George Sand. Dir. Jean Epstein. Films Jean Epstein, 1926. Film.

Balzac, Honoré de. *Physiologie du mariage*. Paris: Gallimard, 1971. Print.

Barry, Joseph. *Infamous Woman: The Life of George Sand*. Garden City: Doubleday, 1977. Print.

Barthes, Roland. *Mythologies*. Paris: Seuil, 1957. Print.

———. "Sémiologie et urbanisme." *Œuvres complètes*. Vol. 2. Paris: Seuil, 2002. 1277–86. Print.

Baudelaire, Charles. *Œuvres complètes*. Paris: Laffont, 1980. Print.

Berman, Antoine. *Toward a Translation Criticism*. Trans. Françoise Massardier-Kenney. Kent: Kent State UP, 2009. Print.

Berman, Carolyn Vellenga. *Creole Crossings: Domestic Fiction and the Reform of Colonial Slavery*. Ithaca: Cornell UP, 2006. Print.

Bernard-Griffiths, Simone. "*Indiana*, roman de l'étrangère." *Le chantier de George Sand / George Sand et l'étranger: Actes du Xe colloque international*. Ed. Tivadar Gorilovics and Anna Szabó. Debrecen: Kossuth Lajos Tudományegyetem, 1993. 211–23. Print.

Bernardin de Saint-Pierre, Jacques-Henri. *Paul et Virginie*. 1788. Paris: Bookking Intl., 1993. Print.

Bertier de Sauvigny, Guillaume de. *La restauration*. Paris: Flammarion, 1955. Print.

Béteille, Arlette. "Où finit *Indiana*? Problématique d'un dénouement." *George Sand: Recherches nouvelles*. Ed. Françoise van Rossum-Guyon. Groningen: Groupe de Recherches sur George Sand de l'Université d'Amsterdam, 1983. 62–73. Print. CRIN 6–7.

"Bilieux." *Grand dictionnaire universel du XIXe siècle*. By Pierre Larousse. Paris: Larousse, 1866–90. Print.

Blackburn, Robin. *The Overthrow of Colonial Slavery, 1776–1848*. London: Verso, 1988. Print.

Blum, Hester. "The Prospect of Oceanic Studies." *PMLA* 125.3 (2010): 670–70. Print.

Boal, Augusto. *Games for Actors and Non-actors*. Trans. Adrian Jackson. 2nd ed. New York: Routledge, 2002. Print.

Bonin, Kate. "The Edifying Spectacle of a Drowned Woman: Sympathy and Irony in *Indiana*." *George Sand Studies* 28 (2009): 1–13. Print.

Booker, John T. "*Indiana* and *Madame Bovary*: Intertextual Echoes." *Nineteenth-Century French Studies* 31 (2002–03): 226–36. Print.

Bordas, Éric. *Éric Bordas commente* Indiana *de George Sand*. Paris: Gallimard, 2004. Print.

———, ed. *George Sand: Écritures et représentations*. Paris: EurEdit, 2004. Print.

Boutin, Aimée. "*Indiana* au pays des hommes: Narration et sociabilité masculine dans le roman de George Sand." Bordas, *George Sand* 123–33.

Bowman, Frank Paul. *Le Christ romantique, 1789: Le sans-culotte de Nazareth*. Geneva: Droz, 1973. Print.

Brody, Jennifer DeVere. *Impossible Purities: Blackness, Femininity, and Victorian Culture*. Durham: Duke UP, 1998. Print.

Brooks, Peter. "The Melodramatic Imagination." Hollier 602–08.

Brown, Sterling. "A Century of Negro Portraiture in American Literature." *Black and White in American Culture*. Ed. Jules Chametzky and Sidney Kaplan. Amherst: U of Massachusetts P, 1969. 333–59. Print.

———. "Negro Character as Seen by White Authors." *Journal of Negro Education* 2 (1933): 179–203. Print.

Buchet-Rogers, Nathalie. "*Indiana* et *Ferragus*: Fondements de l'autorité narrative et esthétique chez Sand et Balzac." *George Sand Studies* 18 (1999): 47–64. Print.

Caplan, Jay. *Framed Narratives: Diderot's Genealogy of the Beholder*. Minneapolis: U of Minnesota P, 1985. Print.

Cate, Curtis. *George Sand: A Biography*. New York: Avon, 1976. Print.

Certeau, Michel de. *Arts de faire*. 1980. Paris: Gallimard, 1990. Print. Vol. 1 of *L'invention du quotidien*.

Charlie, Victor. Rev. of *Indiana*, by George Sand. *Journal des débats* 21 July 1832. Print.

Chateaubriand, François-Auguste-René de. *Atala [and] René*. Paris: Pocket, 1999. Print.

Christiansen, Hope. "Masters and Slaves in *Le rouge et le noir* and *Indiana*." *The Play of Terror in Nineteenth-Century France*. Ed. John T. Booker and Allan H. Pasco. Newark: U of Delaware P, 1997. 197–208. Print.

Code civil des Français: Édition originale et seule officielle. A Paris, d'Imprimerie de la République, An XII 1804. *Assemblée nationale*. Assemblée Nationale; Bibliothèque Nationale de France; Jouve, n.d. Web. 1 Apr. 2015. <http://www.assemblee-nationale.fr/evenements/code-civil-1804–1.asp>.

Code Napoleon; or, The French Civil Code. Trans. a barrister of the Inner Temple. Washington: Beard, 1999. Print.

Le code noir ou Edit du roi. *Assemblée nationale*. Assemblée Nationale, n.d. Web. 1 Apr. 2015. <http://www.assemblee-nationale.fr/histoire/esclavage/code-noir.pdf>.

Un cœur en hiver. Dir. Claude Sautet. AFMD, 1992. Film.

Cohen, Margaret. *The Sentimental Education of the Novel*. Princeton: Princeton UP, 1999. Print.

Cohn, Dorrit. *Transparent Minds: Narrating Modes for Presenting Consciousness in Fiction*. Princeton: Princeton UP, 1978. Print.

Combeau, Yvan, et al. *Histoire de La Réunion de la colonie à la région*. Paris: Nathan-VUEF, 2000. Print.

Coontz, Stephanie. "A Pop Quiz on Marriage." *Stephanie Coontz*. Evergreen State Coll.; Coontz, 19 Feb. 2006. Web. 28 Apr. 2015. <http://www.stephaniecoontz.com/articles/article24.htm>.

Corbin, Alain. *Historien du sensible. Entretiens avec Gilles Heuré*. Paris: La Découverte, 2000. Print.

———. *Le temps, le désir et l'horreur. Essais sur le dix-neuvième siècle*. Paris: Aubier, 1991. Print.

Cottin, Sophie. *Claire d'Albe*. Ed. Margaret Cohen. New York: MLA, 2002. Print. Text vol.

Crecelius, Kathryn J. *Family Romances: George Sand's Early Novels*. Bloomington: Indiana UP, 1987. Print.

"Créole." *Grand dictionnaire universel du XIXᵉ siècle*. Ed. Pierre Larousse. Vol. 5. 1869. Genève: Slatkine, 1982. Print.

Darnton, Robert. "Readers Respond to Rousseau: The Fabrication of Romantic Sensitivity." *The Great Cat Massacre and Other Episodes in French Cultural History*. New York: Vintage, 1985. 214–56. Print.

Daut, Marlene L. "'Sons of White Fathers': Mulatto Vengeance and the Haitian Revolution in Victor Séjour's 'The Mulatto.'" *Nineteenth-Century Literature* 65.1 (2010): 1–37. Print.

Davis, David Brion. *The Problem of Slavery in the Age of Revolution, 1770–1823*. Oxford: Oxford UP, 1999. Print.

Dayan, Peter. "Who Is the Narrator in *Indiana*?" *French Studies* 52 (1998): 152–61. Print.

d'Eichtal, Gustave, and Ismaël Urbain. *Lettres sur la race noire et la race blanche*. Paris: Paulin, 1839. Print.

Desai, Guarav. "Oceans Connect: The Indian Ocean and African Identities." *PMLA* 125.3 (2010): 713–20. Print.

Desport, Jean-Marie. *De la servitude à la liberté: Bourbon des origines à 1848*. Région Réunion: Océan; Comité de la Culture, de l'Education et de l'Environnement, 1988. Print.

Deutellbaum, Wendy, and Cynthia Huff. "Class, Gender, and Family System: The Case of George Sand." *The (M)Other Tongue: Essays in Feminist Psychoanalytic Interpretation*. Ed. Shirley Nelson Garner et al. Ithaca: Cornell UP, 1985. 260–79. Print.

Diaz, Brigitte. "*Indiana*, un roman moderne." *La modernité de George Sand: Actes du colloque Tunis*. Ed. Amina Ben Damir. Tunis: Centre d'Études et de Recherches Économiques et Sociales, 2007. 73–88. Print.

———. "'Ni romantique, ni mosaïque, ni frénétique': *Indiana*, un roman expérimental." *George Sand, une écriture expérimentale*. Ed. Nathalie Buchet-Ritchey, Sylvaine Egron-Sparrow, Catherine Masson, and Marie-Paule Tranvouez. New Orleans: PU du Nouveau Monde, 2006. 45–66. Print.

Dickenson, Donna. *George Sand: A Brave Man, the Most Womanly Woman*. New York: St. Martin's, 1988. Print.

Didier, Béatrice. "La fiction exotique dans Indiana." *Sulla via delle Indie Orientali: Aspetti della francofonia nell'oceano Indiano / Sur la route des Indes Orientales: Aspects de la francophonie dans l'océan Indien.* Ed. Paolo Carile. Paris: Nizet, 1995. 283–92. Print.

———. Introduction. Sand, *Indiana* [ed. Didier] 7–34.

———. Notes. Sand, *Indiana* [ed. Didier] 373–95.

———. Notice. Sand, *Indiana* [ed. Didier] 356–72.

———. "Ophélie dans les chaînes: Étude de quelques thèmes d'*Indiana.*" *Hommage à George Sand.* Ed. L. Cellier. Paris: PU de France, 1969. 89–92. Print. Publications de la Faculté des Lettres et Sciences Humaines de l'Université de Grenoble 46.

Doin, Sophie. *La famille noire suivie de trois nouvelles blanches et noires.* Paris: L'Harmattan, 2002. *Francophone Slavery.* By Doris Kadish. Web. 20 Feb. 2015.

Dubois, Laurent. *The Avengers of the New World: The Story of the Haitian Revolution.* Cambridge: Harvard UP, 2005. Print.

Duras, Claire de. *Ourika.* Ed. Joan DeJean and Margaret Waller. New York: MLA, 1994. Print. Text vol.

Eisler, Benita. *Naked in the Marketplace: The Lives of George Sand.* Berkeley: Counterpoint, 2007. Print.

Les enfants du siècle. Dir. Diane Kurys. Studio Canal, 1999. Film.

"Esclave." *Dictionnaire de français Littré.* Reverso-Softissimo, n.d. Web. 1 Feb. 2012.

Flaubert, Gustave. *Trois contes.* 1877. Introd. and ed. Pierre-Marc de Biasi. Paris: Flammarion, 2007. Print.

France, Peter, ed. *The Oxford Guide to Literature in English Translation.* Oxford: Oxford UP, 2000. Print.

Francophone Slavery. By Doris Kadish. U of Georgia, n.d. Web. 29 Jan. 2015. <http://slavery.uga.edu/index.html>.

Frappier-Mazur, Lucienne. "George Sand et généalogie: Adultère, adoption et légitimation dans *Confession d'une jeune fille,* 1864." *George Sand Studies* 17 (1998): 3–16. Print.

Genette, Gérard. *Narrative Discourse.* Oxford: Blackwell, 1980. Print.

George Sand, 1804–1876. Ministère de la Culture et de la Communication, n.d. 29 Jan. 2015. <www.georgesand.culture.fr/fr/index.htm>.

Gerson, Noel Bertram. *George Sand: A Biography of the First Modern Liberated Woman.* New York: McKay, 1972. Print.

Ghillebaert, Françoise. *Disguise in George Sand's Novels.* New York: Lang, 2009. Print. Currents in Comparative Romance Langs. and Lits. 94.

Gilbert, Sandra M., and Susan Gubar. *The Madwoman in the Attic: The Woman Writer and the Nineteenth-Century Literary Imagination.* New Haven: Yale UP, 1979. Print.

Girard, René. *Deceit, Desire, and the Novel: Self and Other in Literary Structure.* Trans. Yvonne Freccero. Baltimore: Johns Hopkins UP, 1965. Print.

Godwin-Jones, Robert. *Romantic Vision: The Novels of George Sand.* Birmingham: Summa, 1995. Print.

Grégoire, Henri. *Considérations sur le mariage et sur le divorce adressées aux citoyens d'Haïti*. Paris: Baudouin frères, 1823. *Francophone Slavery*. By Doris Kadish. Web. 20 Feb. 2015.

Grossman, Kathryn. "How to Be Popular: Intertextuality in *Indiana, Notre-Dame de Paris*, and *Thérèse Raquin*." 2012. TS.

Harkness, Nigel. *Men of Their Words: The Poetics of Masculinity in George Sand's Fiction*. London: Legenda, 2007. Print.

———. "Writing under the Sign of Difference: The Conclusion of *Indiana*." *Forum of Modern Language Studies* 33 (1997): 115–28. Print.

Harlan, Elizabeth. *George Sand*. New Haven: Yale UP, 2004. Print.

Hause, Steven C., and Anne R. Kenney. *Women's Suffrage and Social Politics in the French Third Republic*. Princeton: Princeton UP, 1984. Print.

Hecquet, Michèle. "*Indiana*: Accents stendhaliens." *George Sand Studies* 18 (1999): 27–33. Print.

Hiddleston, Janet. *George Sand, Indiana, Mauprat*. Glasgow: U of Glasgow French and German, 2000. Print.

Hirsch, Michèle. "Questions à *Indiana*." *Revue des sciences humaines* 165 (1977): 117–29. Print.

Hobsbawm, E. J. *The Age of Revolution: Europe, 1789–1848*. New York: New Amer. Lib., 1962. Print.

Hoffmann, Léon-François. *Le nègre romantique: Personnage littéraire et obsession collective*. Paris: Payot, 1973. Print.

Hofmeyr, Isabel. "Universalizing the Indian Ocean." *PMLA* 125.3 (2010): 721–29. Print.

Hollier, Denis, ed. *A New History of French Literature*. Cambridge: Harvard UP, 1989. Print.

Holmberg, Tom. *The Civil Code: An Overview*. Napoleon Series, n.d. Web. 22 Mar. 2013.

Hovey, Tamara. *A Mind of Her Own: A Life of the Writer George Sand*. New York: Harper, 1977. Print. HarperCollins Children's Books.

Hunt, Lynn. *The Family Romance of the French Revolution*. Berkeley: U of California P, 1992. Print.

———. *Politics, Culture, and Class in the French Revolution*. Berkeley: U of California P, 1984. Print.

Impromptu. Dir. James Lapine. MGM, 1991. Film.

Indiana. Dir. Edmond Tiborovsky. ORTF, 1966. Television. Première chaîne.

Ippolito, Christophe. "La conclusion d'*Indiana*." *Revue d'histoire de la littérature française* 109 (2009): 555–72. Print.

Irigaray, Luce. *This Sex Which Is Not One*. Trans. Catherine Porter and Carolyn Burke. Ithaca: Cornell UP, 1985. Print.

Jack, Belinda. *George Sand: A Woman's Life Writ Large*. New York: Knopf, 2000. Print.

James, C. L. R. [Cyril Lionel]. *The Black Jacobins*. 1989. New York: Penguin, 2001. Print.

James, Henry. "George Sand." *Henry James: Literary Criticism*. Vol. 2. Ed. Leon Edel. Cambridge: Lib. of Amer., 1984. 696–788. Print.

———. "George Sand." *Notes on Novelists*. New York: Scribner's, 1914. 160–244. Print.

Jennings, Lawrence. *French Anti-slavery: The Movement for the Abolition of Slavery in France, 1802–1848*. Cambridge: Cambridge UP, 2000. Print.

Jenson, Deborah. *Trauma and Its Representations: The Social Life of Mimesis in Post-revolutionary France*. Baltimore: Johns Hopkins UP, 2001. Print.

Jordan, Ruth. *George Sand: A Biographical Portrait*. New York: Taplinger, 1976. Print.

Jordan, Winthrop D. *White over Black: American Attitudes toward the Negro, 1550–1812*. New York: Norton, 1968. Print.

Jutrzenka. Dir. Jaime Camino. Estela; Tibidabo, 1969. Film.

Kadish, Doris. "George Sand, Napoleon, and Slavery." *George Sand et l'empire des lettres*. Ed. Anne E. McCall Saint-Saëns. New Orleans: PU de France, 2004. 3–24. Print.

———. "Representing Race in *Indiana*." *George Sand Studies* 11.1–2 (1992): 22–30. Print.

Kudlick, Catherine J. *Cholera in Post-revolutionary Paris: A Cultural History*. Berkeley: U of California P, 1996. Print.

Laforgue, Pierre. "*Indiana*, ou le féminin et le romanesque entre politique et social." *Romantisme* 28.99 (1998): 27–37. Print.

Lanser, Susan. *Fictions of Authority*. Ithaca: Cornell UP, 1992. Print.

Lanson, Gustave. *Histoire de la littérature française*. U of Toronto Libs, n.d. *Internet Archive*. Web. 22 Dec. 2014.

Lefèvre, Théodore. "Planisphère avec les cartes séparées de toutes les colonies françaises." *Gallica*. Bibliothèque Nationale de France, n.d. Web. 17 May 2015. <http://gallica.bnf.fr/ark:/12148/btv1b53093484n/f1.zoom.r=colonies%20 francaises.langEN>.

Le Hir, Marie-Pierre. "La représentation de la famille dans le mélodrame du début du dix-neuvième siècle: De Pixérécourt à Ducange." *Nineteenth-Century French Studies* 18 (1989–90): 15–24. Print.

———. *Le romantisme aux enchères: Ducange, Pixerécourt, Hugo*. Amsterdam: Benjamins, 1992. Print.

Linguet, Simon Nicolas Henri. *Mélanges de politique et de littérature extraits des annales de M. Linguet, pour server à l'histoire du XVIIIe siècle*. Bouillon: n.p., 1778. Print.

Little, Roger. "Coloring Noun: More Black Funk." *George Sand Studies* 21 (2002): 22–27. Print.

Louis Antoine Roussin. Département de La Réunion. Musée Léon Dier, n.d. Web. 24 Feb. 2015. <http://www.cg974.fr/images/pdf/culture/roussin-dossier -documentaire.pdf>.

Loxley, Diana. *Problematic Shores: The Literature of Islands*. New York: St. Martin's, 1990. Print.

Machelidon, Véronique. "Female Melancholy and the Politics of Authori(ali)ty in George Sand's *Indiana*." *George Sand Studies* 27 (2005): 24–47. Print.

———. "George Sand's Praise of Creoleness: Race, Slavery and (In)Visibility in *Indiana.*" *George Sand Studies* 28 (2009): 27–45. Print.

Maestri, Edmond, ed. *Esclavage et abolitions dans l'océan Indien.* Paris: L'Harmattan; U of Réunion, 2002. Print.

Maier, Carol. "Choosing and Introducing a Translation." *Literature in Translation: Teaching Issues and Reading Practices.* Ed. Maier and Françoise Massardier-Kenney. Kent: Kent State UP, 2010. 11–21. Print.

Martin-Dehaye, Sophie. *George Sand et la peinture.* Paris: Royer, 2006. Print.

Massardier-Kenney, Françoise. *Gender in the Fiction of George Sand.* Amsterdam: Rodopi, 2000. Print.

———. "*Indiana,* lieux et personnages féminins." *Nineteenth-Century French Studies* 19 (1990–91): 65–71. Print.

Maturin, Charles. *Melmoth the Wanderer.* 1820. Ed. Douglas Grant. Introd. Chris Baldick. Oxford: Oxford UP, 1998. Print.

Maurois, André. *Lélia: The Life of George Sand.* Trans. Gerard Hopkins. London: Cape, 1953. Print. Trans. of *Lélia ou la vie de George Sand.*

May, Georges. *Le dilemme du roman au XVIIIᵉ siècle. Étude sur les rapports du roman et de la critique (1715–1761).* Paris: PU de France, 1963. Print.

McClintock, Anne. *Imperial Leather: Race, Gender, and Sexuality in the Colonial Conquest.* New York: Routledge, 1995. Print.

McPhee, Peter. *The French Revolution, 1789–1799.* Oxford: Oxford UP, 2002. Print.

"Meredith to Launch PRISM Experience in Fall 2010." *Meredith College.* Meredith Coll., 28 Jan. 2010. Web. 20 May 2015. <http://www.meredith.edu/news/meredith-to-launch-prism-experience-in-fall-2010>.

Miller, Christopher L. *Blank Darkness: Africanist Discourse in French.* Chicago: U of Chicago P, 1985. Print.

———. *The French Atlantic Triangle: Literature and Culture of the Slave Trade.* Raleigh: Duke UP, 2008. Print. Trans. as *Le triangle atlantique français: Littérature et culture de la traite négrière.* Trans. Thomas Van Ruymbeke. Rennes: Perséides, 2011.

Miller, Nancy K. *Subject to Change: Reading Feminist Writing.* New York: Columbia UP, 1988. Print.

———. "Writing (from) the Feminine: George Sand and the Novel of the Female Pastoral." *The Representation of Women in Fiction.* Ed. Carolyn Heilbrun and Margaret Higonnet. Baltimore: Johns Hopkins UP, 1983. 124–51. Print.

Moscovici, Claudia. *Gender and Citizenship: The Dialectics of Subject-Citizenship in Nineteenth-Century French Literature and Culture.* Lanham: Rowman, 2000. Print.

Moses, Claire Goldberg. *French Feminism in the Nineteenth Century.* Albany: State U of New York P, 1984. Print.

Moses, Claire Goldberg, and Leslie Wahl Rabine, eds. *Feminism, Socialism, and French Romanticism.* Bloomington: Indiana UP, 1993. Print.

Mozet, Nicole. *George Sand: Écrivain de romans.* Paris: Pirot, 1997. Print.

Musset, Alfred de. *Confessions d'un enfant du siècle.* Paris: Gallimard, 1973. Print.

Naginski, Isabelle Hoog. "George Sand et le réalisme prophétique." Bordas, *George Sand* 45–66.

———. *George Sand: L'écriture ou la vie*. Trans. Nadine Dormoy and Naginski. Paris: Champion, 1999. Print. Trans. of *George Sand: Writing for Her Life*.

———. *George Sand: Writing for Her Life*. New Brunswick: Rutgers UP, 1991. Print.

Nesci, Catherine. *Le flâneur et les flâneuses. Les femmes et la ville à l'époque romantique*. Grenoble: ELLUG, 2007. Print.

Nora, Pierre. "Entre mémoire et histoire." *Les lieux de mémoire*. Ed. Nora. Paris: Gallimard, 1997. 23–43. Print.

Nord, Philip. *The Republican Moment: Struggles for Democracy in Nineteenth-Century France*. Cambridge: Harvard UP, 1995. Print.

Notorious Woman. Dir. Warris Hussein. Perf. Rosemary Harris. BBC, 1974. Television.

Nye, Robert A. *Masculinity and Male Codes of Honor in Modern France*. Berkeley: U of California P, 1993. Print.

Offen, Karen. *European Feminisms, 1700–1950: A Political History*. Stanford: Stanford UP, 2000. Print.

Pasco, Allan H. *Allusion: A Literary Graft*. Charlottesville: Rookwood, 2002. Print.

———. *Sick Heroes: French Society and Literature in the Romantic Age, 1750–1850*. Exeter: U of Exeter P, 1997. Print.

Peabody, Sue. *"There Are No Slaves in France": The Political Culture of Race and Slavery in the Ancien Régime*. Oxford: Oxford UP, 1996. Print.

Petrey, Sandy. "George and Georgina Sand: Realist Gender in *Indiana*." *Textuality and Sexuality: Reading Theories and Practices*. Ed. Judith Still and Michael Worton. Manchester: Manchester UP, 1993. 133–47. Print.

———. *In the Court of the Pear King: French Culture and the Rise of Realism*. Ithaca: Cornell UP, 2005. Print.

———. "Men in Love, Saint-Simonism, *Indiana*." *George Sand Studies* 14 (1995): 35–44. Print.

Peyre, Henri. *Qu'est-ce que le romantisme?* Paris: PU de France, 1971. Print.

Pinkney, David. *The French Revolution of 1830*. Princeton: Princeton UP, 1972. Print.

Pitons, Cirques, and Remparts of Reunion Island. UNESCO World Heritage Centre, n.d. Web. 22 Mar. 2013.

Planté, Christine. *La petite sœur de Balzac: Essai sur la femme auteur*. Paris: Seuil, 1989. Print.

Plott, Michèle. "Divorce and Women in France." *Encyclopedia of 1848 Revolutions*. Ed. James Chastain. Chastain, n.d. Web. 22 Mar. 2013.

Poli, Annarosa. *George Sand et les années terribles*. Bologna: Patron, 1975. Print.

Powell, David A. *George Sand*. Boston: Twayne, 1990. Print. Twayne World Authors.

———. "George Sand." *Dictionary of Literary Biography: Nineteenth-Century French Fiction Writers: Romanticism and Realism, 1800–1860*. Ed. Catherine Savage Brosman. Detroit: Bruccoli Clark Layman, 1992. 238–54. Print.

————. "George Sand." *Encyclopedia of Lifewriting*. Ed. Margarette Jolly. Vol. 2. London: Fitzroy Dearborn, 2001. 776–78. Print.

————. Introduction. Sand, *Indiana* [ed. Powell] 7–17.

Prasad, Pratima. "(De)Masking the 'Other' Woman in George Sand's *Indiana*." *Romance Language Annual* 8 (1997): 104–09. Print.

————. "Espace colonial et vérité historique dans *Indiana*." *Études littéraires* 35.2–3 (2003): 71–86. Print.

————. "Intimate Strangers: Interracial Encounters in Romantic Narratives of Slavery." *L'Esprit Créateur* 47.4 (2007): 1–15. Print.

Prendergast, Christopher. *Balzac: Fiction and Melodrama*. London: Arnold, 1978. Print.

Pyatt, Félix. Rev. of *Indiana*, by George Sand. *L'artiste* 27 May 1832. Print.

Les quarante codes des Français. Limoges: Barbou Frères, 1845. Print.

Rabine, Leslie. "George Sand and the Myth of Femininity." *Women and Literature* 4 (1976): 2–17. Print.

————. *Reading the Romantic Heroine: Text, History, Ideology*. Ann Arbor: U of Michigan P, 1985. Print.

Racault, Jean-Michel. *Mémoires du Grand Océan: Des relations de voyage aux littératures francophone de l'océan Indien*. Paris: PU de la Sorbonne, 2007. Print.

Raimon, Eve Allegra. *The "Tragic Mulatta" Revisited: Race and Nationalism in Nineteenth-Century Antislavery Fiction*. New Brunswick: Rutgers UP, 2004. Print.

Reddy, William M. *The Invisible Code: Honor and Sentiment in Postrevolutionary France, 1814–1848*. Berkeley: U of California P, 1997. Print.

Régent, Frédéric. *La France et ses esclaves: De la colonisation aux abolitions, 1620–1848*. Paris: Grasset, 2007. Print.

Reid, Roddey. *Families in Jeopardy: Regulating the Social Body in France, 1750–1910*. Stanford: Stanford UP, 1993. Print.

"Reunion (Ile Bourbon), Mauritius (Ile de France)." *Archives nationales d'outre-mer*. Archives Nationales d'Outre-Mer, n.d. Web. 17 May 2015. <http://www.archivesnationales.culture.gouv.fr/anom/en/Presentation/Empires-coloniaux-francais-09.html>.

Revinin, Régis, ed. *Hommes et masculinités de 1789 à nos jours*. Paris: Autrement, 2007. Print.

Rogers, Nancy E. "Slavery as Metaphor in the Writings of George Sand." *French Review* 53.1 (1979): 29–35. Print.

Ronsin, Francis. *Le contrat sentimental: Débats sur le mariage, l'amour, le divorce, de l'Ancien Régime à la Restauration*. Paris: Aubier, 1990. Print.

Rouquette, Dominique. *Les Meschacébéenes*. Paris: Librairie de Sauvignat, 1839. Print.

Rousseau, Jean-Jacques. *Émile ou de l'éducation*. 1763. *Œuvres complètes*. Vol. 4. Ed. Bernard Gagnebin and Marcel Raymond. Paris: Gallimard, 1969. 245–877. Print.

Rumsey, David. *Ile Bourbon, Ile de France: Afrique 57. David Rumsey Map Collection*. Cartography Assocs., n.d. Web. 22 Mar. 2013.

Ruston, Sharon. *Shelley and Vitality*. London: Palgrave, 2005. Print.

Sainte-Beuve, Charles Augustin. Rev. of *Indiana*, by George Sand. *Le national* 5 Oct. 1832. Print.

———. Rev. of *Indiana*, by George Sand. *Portraits contemporains*. Ed. Michel Brix. Paris: PU de Paris-Sorbonne, 2008. 385–92. Print.

Sala-Molins, Louis. *Le code noir ou le calvaire de Canaan*. Paris: PU de France, 1987. Print.

Salomon, Pierre. Introduction. *Indiana*. By George Sand. Ed. Salomon. Paris: Garnier, 1983. i–lii. Print.

———. *Née romancière: Biographie de George Sand*. 1953. Grenoble: Glénat, 1993. Print.

Sand, George. "Aux membres du comité central." Sand, *Correspondance* 8: 400–08.

———. *Correspondance de George Sand*. Ed. Georges Lubin. 25 vols. Paris: Garnier, 1964–91. Print.

———. "H. de Latouche." *Autour de la table*. Paris: Michel Lévy frères, 1875. 229–60. Print.

———. *Indiana*. New York: Dillon and Hooper, 1845. Print.

———. *Indiana*. Ed. Béatrice Didier. 1984. Paris: Flammarion Folio, 1987. Print.

———. *Indiana*. Trans. Eleanor Hochman. Introd. Marilyn Yalom. New York: Signet, 1993. Print.

———. *Indiana*. Trans. George Burnham Ives. Whitefish: Kessinger, 2011. Print.

———. *Indiana*. Ed. David A. Powell. Newark: U of Delaware P, 2008. Print. European Masterpieces.

———. *Indiana*. Trans. Sylvia Raphael. Introd. Naomi Schor. Oxford: Oxford UP, 2008. Print.

———. *Indiana: A Love Story with a Life of Madame Dudevant*. Trans. George W. Richards. 1850. Philadelphia: T. B. Peterson and Brothers, 1888. Print.

———. *Œuvres autobiographiques*. Ed. Georges Lubin. 2 vols. Paris: Gallimard, 1971. Print. Originally *Histoire de ma vie*. 1855.

———. *Œuvres complètes, 1932*. Paris: Champion, 2008. Print.

———. "IV: A Jules Néraud." *Lettres d'un voyageur*. *Gallica*. Bibliothèque Nationale de France, 15 Oct. 2007. Web. 17 May 2015. <http://gallica.bnf.fr/ark:/12148/bpt6k1061085/f111.image>.

———. *Story of My Life: The Autobiography of George Sand: A Group Translation*. Ed. Thelma Jurgrau. Albany: State U of New York P, 1991. Print.

Satellite View and Map of Réunion. One World—Nations Online, n.d. Web. 22 Mar. 2013.

Schleiermacher, Friedrich. "On the Different Methods of Translation." Trans. Waltraud Bartscht. *Theories of Translation*. Ed. Rainer Schulte and John Biguenet. Chicago: U of Chicago P, 1992. 36–54. Print.

Schor, Naomi. *George Sand and Idealism*. New York: Columbia UP, 1993. Print.

———. "Idealism." Hollier 769–74.

———. "Idealism in the Novel: Recanonizing Sand." *Yale French Studies* 75 (1988): 56–73. Print.

————. Introduction. Sand, *Indiana* [trans. Raphael] vii–xxii.

————. "The Portrait of a Gentleman: Representing Men in (French) Women's Writing." *Representations* 20 (1987): 113–33. Print.

————. "This Essentialism Which Is Not One: Coming to Grips with Irigaray." *Differences* 1.2 (1989): 38–58. Print.

Sedgwick, Eve Kosofsky. *Between Men: English Literature and Male Homosocial Desire*. New York: Columbia UP, 1985. Print.

Seigworth, Gilbert R. "A Brief History of Bloodletting: Bloodletting over the Centuries." *Red Gold, Blood Basics*. PBS, 23 and 30 June 2002. Web. 4 May 2015. <http://www.pbs.org/wnet/redgold/basics/bloodlettinghistory.html>.

Sohn, Anne-Marie. *"Sois un homme!": La construction de la masculinité au XIXe siècle*. Paris: Seuil, 2009. Print.

Sollors, Werner. *Neither Black nor White yet Both: Thematic Explorations of Interracial Literature*. Cambridge: Harvard UP, 1997. Print.

A Song to Remember. Dir. Charles Vidor. Columbia Pictures, 1945. Film.

Song without End. Dir. Charles Vidor and George Cukor. Columbia Pictures, 1960. Film.

Spolin, Viola. *Improvisation for the Theater*. 3rd ed. Chicago: Northwestern UP, 1999. Print.

Staël, Germaine de. *Corinne, ou l'Italie*. Paris: Gallimard, 1999. Print.

Stendhal. *De l'amour*. Paris: Gallimard, 1980. Print.

————. *Histoire de la peinture en Italie*. Paris: Gallimard, 1996. Print.

————. *Le rouge et le noir*. Paris: Gallimard, 1972. Print.

Tanner, Tony. *Adultery in the Novel: Contract and Transgression*. Baltimore: Johns Hopkins UP, 1979. Print.

Thomasseau, Jean-Marie. *Le mélodrame*. Paris: PU de France, 1984. Print. Que sais-je?

Thompson, Patricia. *George Sand and the Victorians*. New York: Columbia UP, 1977. Print.

Tilby, Michael. "George Sand, 1804–1876: French Novelist and Dramatist." *The Encyclopedia of Literary Translation into English*. Oxford: Oxford UP, 2000. 1223–27. Print.

Tristan, Flora. *Les pérégrinations d'une paria, 1833–1834*. 1838. Paris: Hachette, 2012. Print.

Tulard, Jean. *Les révolutions de 1789 à 1851*. Paris: Fayard, 1985. Print.

Tulard, Jean, Jean-François Fayard, and Alfred Fierro. *Histoire et dictionnaire de la Révolution française 1789–1799*. Paris: Laffont, 1998. Print.

Ungvari, Tamas. "Revolution, a Textual Analysis." *Nineteenth-Century French Studies* 19.1 (1990): 1–21. Print.

Vaughan, Megan. *Creating the Creole Island: Slavery in Eighteenth-Century Mauritius*. Durham: Duke UP, 2005. Print.

Venuti, Lawrence. *The Translator's Invisibility: A History of Translation*. London: Routledge, 1995. Print.

Vergès, Françoise. *Monsters and Revolutionaries: Colonial Family Romance and Métissage*. Durham: Duke UP, 1999. Print.

Vermeylan, Pierre. *Les idées politiques et sociales de George Sand*. Brussels: U de Bruxelles, 1984. Print.

Vest, James M. "Dreams and the Romance Tradition in George Sand's *Indiana*." *French Forum* 3 (1978): 35–47. Print.

———. "Fluid Nomenclature, Imagery, and Themes in George Sand's *Indiana*." *South Atlantic Review* 46.2 (1981): 43–54. Print.

Virey, Julien Joseph. *Histoire naturelle du genre humain*. Paris: F. Dufart, 1801. Print.

Waller, Margaret. *The Male Malady: Fictions of Impotence in the French Romantic Novel*. New Brunswick: Rutgers UP, 1993. Print.

Winegarten, Renee. *The Double Life of George Sand: Woman and Writer*. New York: Basic, 1978. Print.

Zanone, Damien. "George Sand et Chateaubriand écrivains de mémoires." *Société Chateaubriand Bulletin* 47 (2005): 102–07. Print.

INDEX

Modern Language Association of America

Approaches to Teaching World Literature

To purchase MLA publications, visit www.mla.org/bookstore.

Achebe's Things Fall Apart. Ed. Bernth Lindfors. 1991.
Arthurian Tradition. Ed. Maureen Fries and Jeanie Watson. 1992.
Atwood's The Handmaid's Tale *and Other Works*. Ed. Sharon R. Wilson,
 Thomas B. Friedman, and Shannon Hengen. 1996.
Austen's Emma. Ed. Marcia McClintock Folsom. 2004.
Austen's Mansfield Park. Ed. Marcia McClintock Folsom and John Wiltshire. 2014.
Austen's Pride and Prejudice. Ed. Marcia McClintock Folsom. 1993.
Balzac's Old Goriot. Ed. Michal Peled Ginsburg. 2000.
Baudelaire's Flowers of Evil. Ed. Laurence M. Porter. 2000.
Beckett's Waiting for Godot. Ed. June Schlueter and Enoch Brater. 1991.
Behn's Oroonoko. Ed. Cynthia Richards and Mary Ann O'Donnell. 2014.
Beowulf. Ed. Jess B. Bessinger, Jr., and Robert F. Yeager. 1984.
Blake's Songs of Innocence and of Experience. Ed. Robert F. Gleckner and
 Mark L. Greenberg. 1989.
Boccaccio's Decameron. Ed. James H. McGregor. 2000.
British Women Poets of the Romantic Period. Ed. Stephen C. Behrendt and
 Harriet Kramer Linkin. 1997.
Charlotte Brontë's Jane Eyre. Ed. Diane Long Hoeveler and Beth Lau. 1993.
Emily Brontë's Wuthering Heights. Ed. Sue Lonoff and Terri A. Hasseler. 2006.
Byron's Poetry. Ed. Frederick W. Shilstone. 1991.
Works of Italo Calvino. Ed. Franco Ricci. 2013.
Camus's The Plague. Ed. Steven G. Kellman. 1985.
Cather's My Ántonia. Ed. Susan J. Rosowski. 1989.
Cervantes' Don Quixote. First edition. Ed. Richard Bjornson. 1984.
Cervantes's Don Quixote. Second edition. Ed. James A. Parr and Lisa Vollendorf.
 2015.
Chaucer's Canterbury Tales. First edition. Ed. Joseph Gibaldi. 1980.
Chaucer's Canterbury Tales. Second edition. Ed. Peter W. Travis and
 Frank Grady. 2014.
Chaucer's Troilus and Criseyde *and the Shorter Poems*. Ed. Tison Pugh and
 Angela Jane Weisl. 2006.
Chopin's The Awakening. Ed. Bernard Koloski. 1988.
Coetzee's Disgrace *and Other Works*. Ed. Laura Wright, Jane Poyner, and Elleke
 Boehmer. 2014.
Coleridge's Poetry and Prose. Ed. Richard E. Matlak. 1991.
Collodi's Pinocchio *and Its Adaptations*. Ed. Michael Sherberg. 2006.
Conrad's "Heart of Darkness" and "The Secret Sharer." Ed. Hunt Hawkins and
 Brian W. Shaffer. 2002.

Dante's Divine Comedy. Ed. Carole Slade. 1982.
Defoe's Robinson Crusoe. Ed. Maximillian E. Novak and Carl Fisher. 2005.
DeLillo's White Noise. Ed. Tim Engles and John N. Duvall. 2006.
Dickens's Bleak House. Ed. John O. Jordan and Gordon Bigelow. 2009.
Dickens's David Copperfield. Ed. Richard J. Dunn. 1984.
Dickinson's Poetry. Ed. Robin Riley Fast and Christine Mack Gordon. 1989.
Narrative of the Life of Frederick Douglass. Ed. James C. Hall. 1999.
Works of John Dryden. Ed. Jayne Lewis and Lisa Zunshine. 2013.
Duras's Ourika. Ed. Mary Ellen Birkett and Christopher Rivers. 2009.
Early Modern Spanish Drama. Ed. Laura R. Bass and Margaret R. Greer. 2006.
Eliot's Middlemarch. Ed. Kathleen Blake. 1990.
Eliot's Poetry and Plays. Ed. Jewel Spears Brooker. 1988.
Shorter Elizabethan Poetry. Ed. Patrick Cheney and Anne Lake Prescott. 2000.
Ellison's Invisible Man. Ed. Susan Resneck Parr and Pancho Savery. 1989.
English Renaissance Drama. Ed. Karen Bamford and Alexander Leggatt. 2002.
Works of Louise Erdrich. Ed. Gregg Sarris, Connie A. Jacobs, and
    James R. Giles. 2004.
Dramas of Euripides. Ed. Robin Mitchell-Boyask. 2002.
Faulkner's As I Lay Dying. Ed. Patrick O'Donnell and Lynda Zwinger. 2011.
Faulkner's The Sound and the Fury. Ed. Stephen Hahn and Arthur F. Kinney. 1996.
Novels of Henry Fielding. Ed. Jennifer Preston Wilson and Elizabeth Kraft. 2015.
Fitzgerald's The Great Gatsby. Ed. Jackson R. Bryer and Nancy P. VanArsdale. 2009.
Flaubert's Madame Bovary. Ed. Laurence M. Porter and Eugene F. Gray. 1995.
García Márquez's One Hundred Years of Solitude. Ed. María Elena de Valdés and
    Mario J. Valdés. 1990.
Gilman's "The Yellow Wall-Paper" and Herland. Ed. Denise D. Knight and
    Cynthia J. Davis. 2003.
Goethe's Faust. Ed. Douglas J. McMillan. 1987.
Gothic Fiction: The British and American Traditions. Ed. Diane Long Hoeveler
    and Tamar Heller. 2003.
Poetry of John Gower. Ed. R. F. Yeager and Brian W. Gastle. 2011.
Grass's The Tin Drum. Ed. Monika Shafi. 2008.
H.D.'s Poetry and Prose. Ed. Annette Debo and Lara Vetter. 2011.
Hebrew Bible as Literature in Translation. Ed. Barry N. Olshen and
    Yael S. Feldman. 1989.
Homer's Iliad *and* Odyssey. Ed. Kostas Myrsiades. 1987.
Hurston's Their Eyes Were Watching God *and Other Works*. Ed. John Lowe. 2009.
Ibsen's A Doll House. Ed. Yvonne Shafer. 1985.
Henry James's Daisy Miller *and* The Turn of the Screw. Ed. Kimberly C. Reed and
    Peter G. Beidler. 2005.
Works of Samuel Johnson. Ed. David R. Anderson and Gwin J. Kolb. 1993.
Joyce's Ulysses. Ed. Kathleen McCormick and Erwin R. Steinberg. 1993.

Works of Sor Juana Inés de la Cruz. Ed. Emilie L. Bergmann and Stacey Schlau. 2007.
Kafka's Short Fiction. Ed. Richard T. Gray. 1995.
Keats's Poetry. Ed. Walter H. Evert and Jack W. Rhodes. 1991.
Kingston's The Woman Warrior. Ed. Shirley Geok-lin Lim. 1991.
Lafayette's The Princess of Clèves. Ed. Faith E. Beasley and
	Katharine Ann Jensen. 1998.
Writings of Bartolomé de Las Casas. Ed. Santa Arias and Eyda M. Merediz. 2008.
Works of D. H. Lawrence. Ed. M. Elizabeth Sargent and Garry Watson. 2001.
Lazarillo de Tormes *and the Picaresque Tradition.* Ed. Anne J. Cruz. 2009.
Lessing's The Golden Notebook. Ed. Carey Kaplan and Ellen Cronan Rose. 1989.
Works of Primo Levi. Ed. Nicholas Patruno and Roberta Ricci. 2014.
Works of Jack London. Ed. Kenneth K. Brandt and Jeanne Campbell Reesman.
	2015.
Works of Naguib Mahfouz. Ed. Waïl S. Hassan and Susan Muaddi Darraj. 2011.
Mann's Death in Venice *and Other Short Fiction.* Ed. Jeffrey B. Berlin. 1992.
Marguerite de Navarre's Heptameron. Ed. Colette H. Winn. 2007.
Works of Carmen Martín Gaite. Ed. Joan L. Brown. 2013.
Medieval English Drama. Ed. Richard K. Emmerson. 1990.
Melville's Moby-Dick. Ed. Martin Bickman. 1985.
Metaphysical Poets. Ed. Sidney Gottlieb. 1990.
Miller's Death of a Salesman. Ed. Matthew C. Roudané. 1995.
Milton's Paradise Lost. First edition. Ed. Galbraith M. Crump. 1986.
Milton's Paradise Lost. Second edition. Ed. Peter C. Herman. 2012.
Milton's Shorter Poetry and Prose. Ed. Peter C. Herman. 2007.
Molière's Tartuffe *and Other Plays.* Ed. James F. Gaines and
	Michael S. Koppisch. 1995.
Momaday's The Way to Rainy Mountain. Ed. Kenneth M. Roemer. 1988.
Montaigne's Essays. Ed. Patrick Henry. 1994.
Novels of Toni Morrison. Ed. Nellie Y. McKay and Kathryn Earle. 1997.
Murasaki Shikibu's The Tale of Genji. Ed. Edward Kamens. 1993.
Nabokov's Lolita. Ed. Zoran Kuzmanovich and Galya Diment. 2008.
Works of Ngũgĩ wa Thiong'o. Ed. Oliver Lovesey. 2012.
Works of Tim O'Brien. Ed. Alex Vernon and Catherine Calloway. 2010.
Works of Ovid and the Ovidian Tradition. Ed. Barbara Weiden Boyd and
	Cora Fox. 2010.
Petrarch's Canzoniere *and the Petrarchan Tradition.* Ed. Christopher Kleinhenz
	and Andrea Dini. 2014.
Poe's Prose and Poetry. Ed. Jeffrey Andrew Weinstock and Tony Magistrale. 2008.
Pope's Poetry. Ed. Wallace Jackson and R. Paul Yoder. 1993.
Proust's Fiction and Criticism. Ed. Elyane Dezon-Jones and
	Inge Crosman Wimmers. 2003.
Puig's Kiss of the Spider Woman. Ed. Daniel Balderston and Francine Masiello. 2007.

Pynchon's The Crying of Lot 49 *and Other Works.* Ed. Thomas H. Schaub. 2008.

Works of François Rabelais. Ed. Todd W. Reeser and Floyd Gray. 2011.

Novels of Samuel Richardson. Ed. Lisa Zunshine and Jocelyn Harris. 2006.

Rousseau's Confessions *and* Reveries of the Solitary Walker. Ed. John C. O'Neal and Ourida Mostefai. 2003.

Sand's Indiana. Ed. David A. Powell and Pratima Prasad. 2016.

Scott's Waverley Novels. Ed. Evan Gottlieb and Ian Duncan. 2009.

Shakespeare's Hamlet. Ed. Bernice W. Kliman. 2001.

Shakespeare's King Lear. Ed. Robert H. Ray. 1986.

Shakespeare's Othello. Ed. Peter Erickson and Maurice Hunt. 2005.

Shakespeare's Romeo and Juliet. Ed. Maurice Hunt. 2000.

Shakespeare's The Taming of the Shrew. Ed. Margaret Dupuis and Grace Tiffany. 2013.

Shakespeare's The Tempest *and Other Late Romances.* Ed. Maurice Hunt. 1992.

Shelley's Frankenstein. Ed. Stephen C. Behrendt. 1990.

Shelley's Poetry. Ed. Spencer Hall. 1990.

Sir Gawain and the Green Knight. Ed. Miriam Youngerman Miller and Jane Chance. 1986.

Song of Roland. Ed. William W. Kibler and Leslie Zarker Morgan. 2006.

Spenser's Faerie Queene. Ed. David Lee Miller and Alexander Dunlop. 1994.

Stendhal's The Red and the Black. Ed. Dean de la Motte and Stirling Haig. 1999.

Sterne's Tristram Shandy. Ed. Melvyn New. 1989.

Works of Robert Louis Stevenson. Ed. Caroline McCracken-Flesher. 2013.

The Story of the Stone (Dream of the Red Chamber). Ed. Andrew Schonebaum and Tina Lu. 2012.

Stowe's Uncle Tom's Cabin. Ed. Elizabeth Ammons and Susan Belasco. 2000.

Swift's Gulliver's Travels. Ed. Edward J. Rielly. 1988.

Teresa of Ávila and the Spanish Mystics. Ed. Alison Weber. 2009.

Thoreau's Walden *and Other Works.* Ed. Richard J. Schneider. 1996.

Tolkien's The Lord of the Rings *and Other Works.* Ed. Leslie A. Donovan. 2015.

Tolstoy's Anna Karenina. Ed. Liza Knapp and Amy Mandelker. 2003.

Vergil's Aeneid. Ed. William S. Anderson and Lorina N. Quartarone. 2002.

Voltaire's Candide. Ed. Renée Waldinger. 1987.

Whitman's Leaves of Grass. Ed. Donald D. Kummings. 1990.

Wiesel's Night. Ed. Alan Rosen. 2007.

Works of Oscar Wilde. Ed. Philip E. Smith II. 2008.

Woolf's Mrs. Dalloway. Ed. Eileen Barrett and Ruth O. Saxton. 2009.

Woolf's To the Lighthouse. Ed. Beth Rigel Daugherty and Mary Beth Pringle. 2001.

Wordsworth's Poetry. Ed. Spencer Hall, with Jonathan Ramsey. 1986.

Wright's Native Son. Ed. James A. Miller. 1997.